EVERY AUSTRALIAN BIRD
ILLUSTRATED

EVERY AUSTRALIAN BIRD
ILLUSTRATED

LONDON:

ROBERT HALE & COMPANY

First published in Great Britain 1975
Text copyright © 1975 Rigby Limited
All photographs and paintings are copyright to
the various copyright owners
All rights reserved

ISBN 0 7091 5428 3

Robert Hale & Company
Clerkenwell House
45-47 Clerkenwell Green
London EC1R OHT

Printed in Japan

CONTENTS

INTRODUCTION

What is an Australian bird? Some experts feel the term should be wide enough to include every bird identified in mainland Australia and its dependencies; these are said to number approximately 750. Others prefer to omit the rare stragglers from other continents, reducing the total count to about 700. Yet others would include only the resident species, numbering 600. But if the list were limited to those birds which occur nowhere else in the world except as regular migrants or occasional vagrants, it would number only about 380 species.

The precise number of birds also varies because of a number of other factors. New species are still being discovered, having been overlooked previously: the last officially-recognised discovery was in 1968. As yet, expert ornithologists have failed to agree in a number of cases whether some birds are species in their own right or are merely local variations of a similar species. The last *Official Checklist of the Birds of Australia* (2nd edition) was published in 1926, with later supplements, and although work is proceeding on a new edition, publication of the first half is expected this year (1975).

The publishers of *Every Australian Bird Illustrated* have endeavoured to take a "middle-of-the-road" approach to the problems arising from the present flexible state of ornithology in Australia. Approximately 700 species are illustrated—this number includes all the resident species and omits only rare stragglers known to be residents in other lands and whose Australian sightings are infrequent and small in number. Introduced species have been included where there is evidence that they have successfully established themselves in a new environment. This volume therefore includes every bird commonly observed throughout Australia (except aviary escapees) as well as many uncommon and rare species which the average Australian may be fortunate to view only once in a lifetime.

In the light of continuing research and the absence of an up-to-date *Official Checklist*, both scientific and common names have been subject to changes reflecting the personal viewpoints of recently-published ornithologists. Scientific names are based on relationships, and changes are made as a result of research. Some species have been reclassified from one genus to another, some from one family to another, and a few have even made the round trip back to their original classification. Names also change when a bird which was previously considered a race (a variation within a species) is given species status. The scientific names in this and other recent publications may or may not be confirmed in the long-awaited new edition of the *Official Checklist*. Alternative scientific names to those used in this volume may be established from accepted reference works, a particularly helpful volume being *An Index to Australian Bird Names*, published in 1969 by the CSIRO Division of Wildlife Research, Canberra.

Common names often vary from one area to another, and in many cases these variations are mentioned in the captions to the illustrations. All alternative common names used are included in the index to this volume. Generally, the most widely-known names have been used for the major entry and other long-accepted alternatives are mentioned in the descriptive caption. Again, the CSIRO *Index* will prove a helpful further reference.

The order of illustrations conforms to the normal ornithological arrangement, based on what is often known as the World Checklist or Peters' Checklist. Some minor divergence within a genus has been necessary to maintain a pleasing design using the available illustrations.

The first serious work to illustrate every known Australian species was John Gould's limited edition of *Birds of Australia*, comprising 681 hand-coloured plates. During his personal research in Australia from 1838 to 1840, he added 300 new species to the number of Australian birds already known. Noted for their artistic merit (a set recently changed hands for $25,000), their accuracy is such that a large proportion are still considered as faithful representations of the various species. Modern printing processes are not capable of reproducing the depth of colour and texture in the originals, and a visit to a State library to inspect them would be a rewarding experience.

Gracius Broinowski, a Polish painter who settled in Australia as a young man in his twenties, published 300 colour plates in a work entitled *The Birds of Australia*, which appeared in monthly instalments from 1889 to 1891. His intention was to produce a work to replace Gould's volumes, but his effort does not appear to have gained popularity.

The next major work took twenty years to complete. *Birds of Australia* by Gregory Mathews was published in thirteen volumes in a limited edition of 225 signed copies from 1911 to 1927. Mathews also contributed to Australian ornithology by producing two journals and several other books. His knowledge and preferences had a marked effect on the 1926 *Official Checklist*.

Each of these three men—Gould, Broinowski, and Mathews—took great pains to depict the various species in their natural habitat with the correct vegetation. Other notable illustrators, such as Neville W. Cayley and more recently, Peter Slater (among others), confined much of their published work to static poses for identification purposes.

This present volume is the first work to make substantial use of full-colour photography to reproduce faithfully both bird and habitat of every Australian bird. A considerable number of Australian birds have never been photographed, and others are feared to be extinct, not having been sighted for many years. For these species, suitable artistic representations have been obtained to fulfil the aim of this work. Over eighty per cent of the illustrations are full-colour photographs and the balance is made up of illustrations from the major works listed above and also from present-day artists.

The publishers wish to acknowledge their grateful thanks to the eighty-seven photographers whose work comprises the bulk of this volume. The majority of these are amateur photographers and bird lovers, whose dedication in this most difficult field of photographic art has been amply rewarded by the outstanding photographs reproduced here. Thanks are due to the many clubs and societies—organisations involved in both ornithology and photography—which made known our requirements to their members. In addition, several of Australia's leading nature photographers have granted permission to reproduce their excellent material in this book. Acknowledgment is also gratefully given to Margo Kröyer-Pedersen and Peter Trusler, two of Australia's foremost bird artists, for permission to reproduce their work depicting some of the less common species, and to Alister Mathews for permission to reproduce illustrations from his father's work.

The publishers also wish to record their thanks for the co-operation of the following institutions in locating material for this volume and for permission to reproduce such material: The National Library of Australia, for permission to reproduce paintings by Neville H. P. Cayley (father of Neville W. Cayley) from the Mathews Collection; the Antarctic Division of the Department of Science, for permission to reproduce transparencies from their photographic library; the State Library of South Australia, for permission to copy and reproduce illustrations in their collection by John Gould, Gracius Broinowski, and Gregory Mathews; and the National Photographic Index of Australian Birds, for assistance in locating a number of photographs.

Thanks are also extended to Ted Schurmann for help in ornithological research and in preparation of the text. Special thanks are extended to the Adelaide Ornithologists' Club and its members, who provided a panel to view each transparency and as far as possible to confirm identification of the species shown. Mr Fred Lewitzka arranged this stage of the project, and in addition he took a number of photographs especially for this volume and located other photographs required.

PETER WADE
Editor

NOTE: Each caption contains the following information in the order listed:
1. Common name and scientific name.
2. Within parentheses:
    a. Average length from bill tip to tail tip;
    b. Habitat, in general terms;
    c. Status, from very common to very rare.
3. Descriptive information including some alternative common names.
4. Photographer's or artist's name in italic type in parentheses.

HABITATS OF AUSTRALIAN BIRDS

There are two outstanding factors which make the Australian continent the ideal provider of bird habitats. They are the country's vastness and its variety.

The two qualities are linked. Because of the vastness, many birds of Australia can migrate from north to south without leaving the continent. Australia has thousands of kilometres of beached or rocky coastline. It has hectare upon hectare of many types of forest, it has a huge treeless plain, a stone-strewn arid area, and vast sandy deserts. There are mountains and hill country, open areas of green grasses, and fertile farmlands. There are huge, teeming cities, and remote homesteads.

This vastness of land area also leads to a variety of climatic conditions: from the hot, tropical north, through varying temperate zones to snow-covered mountains and cold coastal waters in the extreme south. There are places of heavy rainfall and areas where rain is a rarity.

The survival of any bird species depends upon the continuance of suitable living conditions for it, conditions that offer food, shelter, protection, and individual requirements peculiar to a species. Most birds have physical adaptations to special circumstances—wings shaped for long flying, for soaring, for flitting or fluttering; strong beaks for breaking nuts; brush tongues for taking honey; waterproof feathers, webbed feet, and so on. All these things aid birds to exist in particular localities and under certain conditions. They also restrict their movement and limit their capacity to survive in unsuitable areas.

So the wide range of types of country, or, from a bird's viewpoint, of suitable habitats, leads to the rich variety of bird life with which this country is endowed. And, as often mentioned in discussions on bird species, Australia is the home of the eucalypt, a tree attractive to many kinds of birds, and the biggest single factor in determining bird presence and population.

There has been, sadly, a mass destruction of bird habitat as settlement and civilisation march on. For many species, there are fears and doubts about continued survival. It is important that all interested people should be aware of the dangers of habitat destruction.

Sometimes, in discussing the maintenance of bird habitat, financial factors are mentioned. It is important that proper value be placed on the extreme urgency of bird survival. Bird protection pays off. It is a wonderful way of retaining the true wealth of the country.

Finally, we should look at those places where the hand of man has been, or still is, at work. Advancement of civilisation does not necessarily mean dispersal of birds. Bird habitats exist in our sprawling cities, in such places where administrative bodies wisely provide and maintain parks and gardens, and where home occupants delight in doing what they can to keep birds about their property. Bird habitats exist near to busy highways, where skilled engineers and workers arrange for standing growth to "dodge the 'dozers''. Bird habitats can exist on areas where land must be cleared and swamps must be drained, if thought is given to retaining natural conditions wherever possible or to restoring the natural habitat.

Facing page:
Tropical rain forest. In this type of forest, found mainly at the "top" of the continent, growth is always luxuriant, and includes large tropical palms and native fruits. It is unique country, with its own distinctive bird life. Features of the forest are the canopy above and the thick ground covering of leaves and forest debris. *(Photograph by J. Burt)*

Top:
Temperate rain forest. This has the dampness and the denseness of its tropical counterpart, but temperatures are lower. Here, bird calls are important, as so often the birds are heard and not seen. In some areas there are reserves, with good walking tracks provided, a splendid way of opening up the forest. *(H. Frauca)*

Bottom:
Saltbush. In many places in the arid inland, the grey-green saltbush is the only growing thing to relieve the monotony of the landscape. It is said that the sea once rolled over these areas. Sometimes in saltbush country there are heavy rains, and then the countryside will come to life with a rich and varied growth and a subsequent increase in fascinating bird life. *(J. Burt)*

Top left:
Wet sclerophyll forest. These are the denser eucalyptus forests. That the gum tree is part of the Australian way of life is a maxim applying to birds as well as to man. Many bird species depend on these trees for their very existence. This country does not have the canopies of the rain forest and has its own kinds of ground growth—here, ferns. *(K. Stepnell)*

Top right:
Tall tropical woodland. The tall trees are much in demand by timber men, as they yield magnificent, multi-purpose hardwoods. The sawmiller's gain is the bird's loss. The forest carries abundant bird life, with many high nesting species, of which knowledge is still very limited. *(J. Burt)*

Bottom left:
Dry sclerophyll forest. This is fascinating country. A growing tendency is for the knapsack to carry a tree guide as well as bird book, as one goes into forest where clean-trunked gums rub limbs with heavily-barked large specimens. It is a type of timber-land found inland in the south-east, in Tas., and in the south-west corner of W.A. *(H. Frauca)*

Top left:
Semi-arid woodland. This country does not offer the variety of growth of the well-watered bush areas and, because one tree looks much like another, birds and their nests can be difficult to locate. Kangaroos and other animals are often plentiful here and it must never be thought that, because of the "sameness" of it, it is not worth exploring. *(H. Frauca)*

Top right:
Temperate woodland. Excellent bird counts may be recorded here at sun-up, with the aid of binoculars and silent walking shoes. In fact at any time of the day, a quiet entrance into an open patch can be very rewarding. In areas like this where many species of both birds and bush abound, it should be remembered, too, that there are varied places to find nests, some quite near the ground. *(J. Burt)*

Bottom right:
Arid woodland. A bird lover, in fact anybody on a nature walkabout, is sorry when it's time to leave this kind of terrain. It is full of its own significant birds, animals, and bush growth. Typically Australian, it offers some of the continent's most colourful scenery. *(J. Burt)*

Facing page top:
Tropical heathlands. The larger trees bring bigger birds and little species will flit about the lower bushes. Birds are always present where the tropical heaths grow, and both birds and bushes like these will delight camera enthusiasts, artists, and interested observer alike. Termite mounds in these areas often provide nesting sites. *(S. Berekmeri)*

Facing page bottom left:
Mangroves. There is much to see where mangroves flourish, though many people feel that there are only mangroves. As well as being home to a multitude of birds, these areas have other attractions, like colourful lilies and water plants. Occasional dead trees make ideal open perching places for birds which otherwise would stay out of sight. *(H. Frauca)*

Facing page bottom right:
Temperate heathlands. This is the country which sends the traveller home full of ideas of what to grow in his garden. He hopes, often justifiably, that the bushes will bring the same birds to his home which delighted him as he roamed through the heathland. One observer notes the time of the flowering of each bush or tree and learns when birds will be there, every year, to keep a date with the bushes they like best. *(H. Frauca)*

Top right:
Grasslands. These are the haunts of ground-dwelling birds. Not that the skies above are empty, for birds of prey are almost always in sight, wheeling slowly, often without wing movement, confirming that in the grasses there is abundant life. Some grasslands are man-made, a result of earlier land clearance. *(J. Burt)*

Centre right:
Spinifex. Spinifex country may appear dry, stony, and waterless. Yet among the spiny clusters, there is always some life, including little birds which know no other habitat. And often, as we see here, spinifex borders some exciting scenery, with bush where birds can rest or nest, making frequent forays to the grassy clumps. *(J. Burt)*

Bottom right:
Swamps. Melaleucas, the tea-tree and paperbark family, grow in these swampy places, offering food, protection, nesting nooks, and nesting material to many kinds of birds. Sometimes the water makes accessibility difficult, but a close-up view will be well worth the struggle. *(H. Frauca)*

Facing page top:
Alpine woodland. As winter's snow melts in the spring and early summer, this country comes magnificently alive with colourful carpets of wildflowers and alpine growth. Snow gums and snow grasses bring birds in an array of species. Mountain grasshoppers come in their millions, so that there is food for nectar-eaters and insect-devourers alike. *(H. Frauca)*

Facing page bottom left:
Mallee scrub. Though occupying a fairly limited proportion of the continent, the mallee country has become well known with the current new interest in nature and the establishment of a number of National Parks in this important zone. It is country unique in character, with its own scrubby growth and bird species. *(K. Stepnell)*

Facing page bottom right:
Mixed scrub. Many birds favour a particular tree variety and in country of mixed growth like this, there can be a corresponding assortment of birds. Marrying up bird and bush species is a fascinating aspect of nature observation. Ground growth in these areas is also significant, the nature of the soil influencing the prevalence of varying types of grasses and low bush. *(H. Frauca)*

Top right:
Rivers. Thousands of kilometres of rivers criss-cross the continent, many with big red gums on their margins. Rivers have much to offer various birds—birds which fish in the water, or find their living in the big gums, or catch insects close to the water's surface. And the water itself means life to many. *(J. Burt)*

Centre right:
Billabongs. To camp by a billabong is to ensure an early morning festival of bird song. Billabong is an Aboriginal word, the very sound of which is a reminder that these waters and the birds which live about them were here before white man set foot on the land. A reminder, too, that the people here before must have been great and knowledgeable bird watchers. *(J. Burt)*

Bottom right:
Seacoast and islands. Here we may sight completely different families of birds, as binoculars swing across the panorama of land and sea. Trips to near coastal islands often reveal nests and retreats of birds who seek to escape some of the hazards of the mainland. And between the sea and the tree-covered land, are the sandy beaches, with a bird population of their own. *(J. Burt)*

Top left:
Alpine complex. A lucky country indeed, offering snow-covered mountains as an added bonus to all the natural wonders of a sun-kissed terrain. In Tas. where there are many hectares of mountain country like this, there are found birds peculiar to the region, with interesting and subtle differences from their mainland relatives. *(H. Frauca)*

Top right:
Rocks. Rocks, of any shape or size, have their own charm, and they make provision for their own galaxy of wildlife, sheltering and shading birds and animals, providing crevice nests for birds of prey, and being the sole haunts of a number of species who seek no habitat other than rocky country. *(H. Frauca)*

Bottom:
Desert complex. On the red desert sands, in the early morning when the shadows are still long, there will be tiny footprints as evidence of who has been there, disproving the assumption that the desert has no life. This is country that can spring to life after rain. But there is life here, somewhere not far away, all of the time. *(J. Burt)*

CASSOWARIES CASUARIIDAE

The cassowary, although one of Australia's rarer birds, has a reputation because of its several distinctive features.

These include its size—it reaches a head height of 1·6 m—its bright colouring, and its potential danger as an attacker.

Few people, even enthusiastic photographers and observers, are able to glimpse the bird in its natural state. This is because the area it inhabits is restricted to the rain forests in north-eastern Queensland.

The fact that it is likely to attack if it feels it is being molested is another reason why many Australians would not go out of their way to observe its behaviour. Its size and strength, plus its very powerful legs, each equipped with a long, lethal, blade-like, inner toe, make it possibly our most dangerous bird. There are at least two accounts of people having been killed by a cassowary.

Cassowaries are flightless, a rarity shared only with the emu among land birds in Australia, and with very few species in other parts of the world. Indeed, many of its physical features are shared with the emu, the one Australian bird to better it in size.

The cassowary's physical make-up is different from that of normal, flying birds. The usual flight feathers of the wing are replaced by long, black spines or quills.

Another unique characteristic is the large, hard knob on the crown of the head, called a casque, sometimes aptly referred to as a "crash helmet". When the cassowary lowers its head, the casque becomes a shield or armour plate, and is useful in enabling the bird to barge through heavy forest undergrowth.

Although unable to fly, these birds are compensated in being able to run very fast, even through the densest forest. They also swim powerfully and swiftly, a useful talent in the rain forest with its many creeks and watercourses.

In spite of its danger potential, it is by nature cautious and shy, more likely to flee than attack. Cassowaries are heard rather than seen, their call being a loud, booming grunt.

The female is slightly larger than the male, this being the only difference in appearance between the sexes. The male incubates the eggs, which are light green in colour, rough on the outside, and large. The nest is made up of sticks, leaves, and other forest debris. Often it is built against a large tree in heavy, secluded jungle. The breeding season is usually confined to July and August.

The cassowary eats jungle fruits, stalks, and miscellaneous vegetable matter. Its manner of feeding is to toss the food into the air, then gulp it in one swallow.

It was not always restricted to the area in which it is found today. The destruction of tropical rain forests have greatly limited its habitat. Much earlier, it is known to have lived further south, and a smaller bird of the family, Bennett's or Dwarf cassowary, now not seen at all in Australia, is said to have been found in New South Wales. Today, as with the emu, only a single species survives in Australia. Cassowaries are also found in New Guinea and some adjacent islands.

Cassowary, *Casuarius casuarius*. (1·5 m. Rain forests. Fairly common in restricted area.) The feathers of this big, colourful bird are rainproof, a useful protection in the wet, tropical forests. A prominent Australian tree genus, *Casuarina*, was named after the cassowary. The rather unique foliage of these trees (the Sheoak and Buloke) was felt to resemble the bird's feathers. *(L. Robinson)*

EMUS DROMAIIDAE

The emu is Australia's largest bird and the world's second largest after the ostrich.

As well as its place of honour in the Australian Coat of Arms, the emu shares with the kangaroo a growing popularity with tourists and bush lovers. The sighting of a flock of emus is regarded by travellers as evidence that they are now in the bush, "away from it all". The emu is seldom, if ever, seen in settled areas. It is not equipped to survive where man, and his dog, live in numbers.

There have been times in Australia's history when fears for the bird's survival were well founded. Pastoralists regarded it as vermin, claiming that it knocked down fences, ate out large areas of grassland, and fouled the land as it grazed. It was hunted and destroyed in large numbers.

In Queensland, when the battle raged against the notorious prickly pear, the emu was charged with being a spreader of the cacti and a price put on the bird's head.

Then man had brought the fox to the continent, adding to the emu's natural predators. These included the bigger hawks, such as Wedge-tailed eagles, and dingoes, enemies which would take both emu eggs and young.

Today the emu seems to be holding its own in those parts of its natural habitat still untouched by man, and flourishing in National Parks and other areas where steps are taken for the big bird's protection.

These birds, found only in Australia, have many quaint and appealing characteristics of their own. They run with a peculiar, ungainly gait at a deceptive speed. A mature bird, escaping from real or imagined pursuers, can sustain a speed of 40 km/h.

They are naturally inquisitive, and this trait is frequently evidenced in the bush, when beak, head, and some neck will appear, like a submarine periscope, from behind sandhills or clumps of bush.

The bird suffers in time of drought, because its diet is based mainly on green grass and plant growth. It also consumes caterpillars, grasshoppers, and large insects. In fact the claim that it will "eat anything" is hardly an exaggeration.

The eggs are dark green, with a rough surface. Because of their size (they weigh approximately 750 grams), they are a worthwhile item of food for predators and sometimes hungry bushmen. Emu eggs have been collected and sold as souvenirs, often with man-made markings added.

The average clutch of eggs is nine, though numbers vary considerably. The male sits on the eggs, incubation taking about eight weeks.

Baby emus are beautifully striped at first, then gradually moult into adult colouring. The striped pattern makes a most effective camouflage. A feature of the birds' behaviour is that the parents will flee from an attacker, leaving the babies unprotected except for this natural concealment.

Although earlier there were others in the family, today there is only one surviving emu species.

Emu, *Dromaius novaehollandiae*. (2 m. Open grasslands, scrubs. Fairly common.) Emus, being non-flyers, have a flat breast bone instead of the usual keel-like bone which supports the wing muscles of flying birds. The female is slightly larger than the male, who will lose 5 to 10 kg during his long sit on the hatching eggs. (*L. Robinson*)

PENGUINS SPHENISCIDAE

The penguin could well be described as the bird least like a bird. It is flightless, it spends more time in the water than it does on land, it normally swims under, rather than on top of, the water and, when ashore, it has an upright stance. At one stage in history, some people were happy to classify penguins as fish, not because of the way they swam, but so their flesh could be eaten on Friday!

But birds they are. Certainly they have adapted beautifully to the climatic and geographical conditions under which they dwell. They are sea-going birds, found only in the Southern Hemisphere, mainly in cool to extremely cold climates.

The Little penguin is the only member of the family to breed in Australia. All other penguins seen are visitors or stragglers, which have wandered during their non-breeding season, or been carried to the southerly shores of the continent by wind or tide. Some members of the family are not seen at all in Australian waters.

At Phillip Island, in Victoria, the "Penguin Parade" is a popular tourist attraction. Every evening during a stage of the penguins' breeding cycle, an audience collects at the water's edge, where the little personality birds waddle ashore to the burrows they left earlier in the day for their fishing expeditions at sea.

Perhaps it is something about penguins suggesting a burlesque or take off of humans themselves that endears them to people. Scientists, observing penguins in remote fields, report that the birds appear to "play games" among themselves.

The penguin family embraces birds of assorted sizes and habits, with minor differences in colouring and markings. All penguins have a general pattern of black or dark above and white below.

A penguin's wings, though not used for flying, have evolved into powerful flippers or paddles. The penguin in fact "flies under water", using its wings as oars, and it is the most powerful and efficient swimmer of all birds. When at rest, it cannot fold its wings back against its body as other birds do. Frequently it sleeps with its beak tucked behind a flipper.

The feathers are small, scale-like particles, densely covering the body. The bones are solid. Penguins are equipped with powerful eye muscles to assist in underwater hunting. Spines or protruberances on the tongue and palate help the penguin to grip and hold its prey. The bill is large and powerful.

It has short legs, set far back on the body. The tarsus, or shank, is particularly short and uncovered. The feet are short and flat, the toes webbed.

The tail is mainly inconspicuous, the body plump, streamlined, torpedo-shaped. Together with the legs, the tail seems to form the rudder or steering apparatus in the bird's swimming. Unlike ducks and similar water birds, the penguin does not use its feet at all for propelling itself through the water.

King penguin, *Aptenodytes patagonica*. (90 cm. Southern seas. Very rare.) It is the second largest of penguins and the largest seen in Australia. This penguin's egg does not touch the ground, but is held and hatched against the tarsus, or shank, under a fold of skin. The bird is thus a mobile, self-contained incubator and brooder. Both sexes help, the egg or chick being exchanged rapidly to prevent freezing. *(B. Allwright)*

At sea, the penguin is an efficient hunter, and its diet consists of fish, crustacea, and squid. It can remain under water for long periods.

Parent birds, on coming ashore, feed their young by regurgitating the food. The chick first strikes at the parent's bill with its own, uttering cries as it does so. The adult then opens its bill, the chick inserts its beak, and snatches at the regurgitated food. The process is repeated until the chick is well fed.

An interesting sidelight concerning penguins is that they were not discovered by Europeans until about the year 1500. There is no mention of them in old literature and, according to the Oxford English Dictionary, the name "penguin" was not recorded in English until 1588.

Top left:
Gentoo penguin, *Pygoscelis papua.* (75 cm. Southern seas. Very rare.) The eggs of the Gentoo are said to be the most popular choice among sealers and poachers. These penguins live in colonies by the sea, usually in a grassy or vegetated area, the sites being changed every two or three years as grasses are trodden down. Gentoos are very fast swimmers. *(B. Allwright)*

Top right:
Adelie penguin, *Pygoscelis adeliae.* (75 cm. Southern seas. Very rare.) It nests among ice slopes, where the only available nesting material is small stones. Like other penguins, it has to contend with predators on land (such as skuas) and at sea (leopard seals). But the weather is the main natural enemy of the Adelie, many birds succumbing to blizzards. *(B. Allwright)*

Centre:
Little penguin, *Eudyptula minor.* (40 cm. Coastal areas. Common.) Also called Little blue penguin and Fairy penguin, it is the smallest of all penguins. Its range appears to be gradually reaching further north along both the east and west coasts. Nests under a bush, rock, or tree root, or in a burrow. Its enemies include Pacific gulls, tiger snakes, dogs, and cats. Water rats and large lizards take eggs. *(I. McCann)*

Bottom:
Rockhopper penguin, *Eudyptes chrysocome.* (60 cm. All southern coast, and north to Fremantle. Frequent straggler.) The crest at the back of the head is usually at disarray as a result of the wind. It is the most aggressive of penguins, savagely attacking intruders. There is much fighting among males in rookeries at the start of the breeding season, both to win mates and for nest sites. *(B. Allwright)*

Above: Royal penguin, *Eudyptes chrysolophus*. (70 cm. Southern seas. Very rare.) There is a heavily-populated rookery of this species at Macquarie Island. Larger than the Rockhopper, Royals have rather rounded heads. Observers report that, because of the light area around the eyes, when wet from swimming the bird's face becomes owl-like. *(B. Allwright)*

ALBATROSSES AND MOLLYMAWKS DIOMEDEIDAE

Albatrosses are the big birds of the oceans, best seen by man from a ship at sea.

The family embraces the two large species called "great albatrosses", one of which, the Wandering albatross, has the largest wing span of all birds. Specimens have been found with a span measuring up to 4 m, and a 3 m span is considered average for full-grown birds.

There are, in addition, four species of albatrosses found in Australian waters which are sometimes referred to as mollymawks. These are of medium size, have dark upper surfaces to back and wings, a shorter tail, and mainly all-white body.

Except for the Sooty albatrosses, the colouring is predominantly white underneath, which, it is believed, is less easily seen by fish than a darker plumage, and aids the birds while hunting either in the air or swimming on water.

It is on the wing that these birds are most impressive. They have a wonderful talent for using wind energy to conserve their own. Many observers have watched them for long periods without any wing movement being displayed.

They will rise into the wind, wheel and glide downwards, gaining speed, bank with a wing tip all but touching the water, then gain height into the wind again. They follow ships for days at a time, often circling or crossing the vessel.

On windless days, more wing movements are needed to keep the birds in the air, and often they are content to rest on the sea. Take-off on such days proves difficult, entailing a scrambling, splashing run on the surface. Likewise landing can be a clumsy or even a dangerous performance. On windy days, both take-off and landing are performed without difficulty.

These birds are seen mainly in southern seas, which they occupy to an approximate northerly limit of 20°S, except for three species which occur in the north Pacific and one found near the equator.

Albatrosses fly long distances, as banding records repeatedly show. A bird found 110 km north of Fremantle in the early autumn, had been ringed as a nestling at an island 480 km south of New Zealand in mid-September the previous year. It is thought that this particular bird might have circumnavigated the globe via South America.

The bill of the albatross is large and hooked. A distinctive feature is that the nostrils occur as small tubes at the side of the bill.

The legs of all species found in Australia are pale or flesh-coloured. The three front toes are fully webbed, but the hind toe is so small as to be barely visible, and even this "pimple" is absent externally in the larger albatrosses. Except for the Light-mantled and Sooty albatrosses, the tails are short and rounded.

Diet of the albatross includes fish, crustacea, cuttle fish (including left-overs from the meals of porpoises, which albatrosses will follow), and frequently galley waste tossed from ships.

White-capped albatross, *Diomedea cauta*. (1 m. Southern seas, coastal waters. Common.) Also called Shy albatross, but not shy by nature and known to try to take bait from fishing lines. Flies fairly close to the surface, flaps oftener than larger species. It does not range far from land, and is the only albatross to breed in Australia. *(M. Carter)*

Top:
Wandering albatross, *Diomedea exulans.* (1·35 m. Southern seas. Fairly common.) This bird is famed for its great size and its ability to remain in the air for long periods. It often follows ships and may stay in the wake of one vessel for several days. It nests every second year. A superb aerialist, it is clumsy on land, waddling ungracefully. *(B. Allwright)*

Centre:
Royal albatross, *Diomedea epomophora.* (1·4 m. Southern seas. Rare.) The largest of all albatrosses. Rather like the Wandering albatross, with which it is often confused, but apart from physical differences it is inclined to frequent waters closer to land. It nests every second year. It makes a musical trilling whistle with its bill raised skywards. *(M. Bonnin)*

Bottom:
Black-browed albatross, *Diomedea melanophris.* (90 cm. Southern seas, ranging north. Common.) Sometimes referred to as a mollymawk. The marked brow gives the bird a frowning or scowling appearance. Albatrosses are mainly silent birds, this one especially so, except in its mating displays when it brays and grunts. They are fast and skilful flyers and follow ships. *(W. Kulikowski)*

23

Top:

Yellow-nosed albatross, *Diomedea chlororhynchos.* (75 cm. Southern seas. Common.) This mollymawk is particularly numerous along the southern coast of W.A. It is rather shy and generally not inclined to follow ships. Likes more temperate seas than other albatrosses. Another non-breeding visitor, its breeding grounds being in the south Atlantic and south Indian oceans. *(J. Gould)*

Bottom:

Grey-headed albatross, *Diomedea chrysostoma.* (80 cm. Southern seas. Fairly common.) Usually solitary and an outstanding flyer, it likes to follow ships for food waste. The sexes are alike. On their breeding grounds, in sub-Antarctic islands, they are heard braying. The chicks, if attacked or too closely approached, will spit out stomach oil to defend themselves. *(W. Kulikowski)*

Top:
Light-mantled albatross, *Phoebetria palpebrata.* (85 cm. Southern seas. Very rare.) One of the sooty albatrosses. Excellent aerialists, they are seen hanging motionless in mid-air while inspecting the sea or a ship beneath them. There are records of this species still breeding 20 years after a first banding. *(B. Jamieson)*

Bottom:
Sooty albatross, *Phoebetria fusca.* (85 cm. Southern seas. Very rare.) Sexes are alike, with males possibly slightly larger. These birds, with a wing span of approximately 2 m, the height of an average household door, are often regarded as the most beautiful and efficient flyers of all sea-birds. The tail can open to assist in steering. *(J. Gould)*

PETRELS, SHEARWATERS, AND PRIONS PROCELLARIIDAE

This large family covers a range of birds of varied sizes and characteristics. All are birds of the sea, where they instinctively are at home. They come ashore only to nest and to raise their young, and even these activities are conducted under conditions difficult for the birds. Hazards arise through their ungainliness and inability to adapt on land, making them easy prey for predators.

They meet these difficulties by mainly nesting in out-of-the-way places and, in many cases, by visiting their nests only at night.

The nests are in crevices between rocks or in burrows. The method of burrowing for these birds is to first loosen the soil with the bill, then to rake out the burrow with a backward movement of one foot. After several strokes this way, there is a changeover to the other foot. An exception to this way of nesting is made by the fulmars, which rest on rock ledges.

Although there is quite a variation in size among members of the family, only the Giant petrel exceeds 60 cm in length. All petrels share many physical features. There is an individual bill, curved at the upper front, with a single tube for the nostril which is divided internally. The plumage is black or dark, and white, with the exception of the attractive blue-grey upper plumage of the prions.

The hind toe becomes a sharp claw or nail. The leg colouring, an important aid to identification if the bird is in hand, varies from flesh white or pink to black and bright blue.

The stories behind the names of the birds in the family are of interest. The name "petrel" comes from Saint Peter, the apostle who walked on the water. These birds, and particularly the Storm-petrels, often giving the impression of doing likewise. "Shearwater" comes from the low, swift gliding flight of these birds, when they often skim the surface of the sea.

The name "Muttonbird" is believed to have been used first in Norfolk Island in 1790, a year when the settlers were without meat until hordes of petrels arrived to breed, and mass slaughter of these birds followed.

Today there is a thriving muttonbird industry in Australia, but it is well controlled and the birds appear to be on the increase. Only young birds are taken, the eggs and adult birds being strictly protected.

Millions of muttonbirds (Short-tailed shearwaters) come down the east coast of Australia in the spring, prepare their burrows, lay their eggs, and raise their young, according to a strict time-table. Each female lays one egg and the total incubation period is about ten weeks.

Enemies of the muttonbirds include gulls and ravens, and cats, foxes, and tiger snakes. The snakes eat the chicks when very young, but the birds quickly grow too big to be menaced in this way and thereafter hospitably share their burrows with the snakes.

In the autumn the mature birds leave, to be followed later by the young, for their wintering quarters, the Aleutian Islands.

Prions have been called "whalebirds", because of their habit of surface feeding in the same area where whales are feeding, and on the same food, shrimp.

Southern giant petrel, *Macronectes giganteus*. (90 cm. Southern seas. Fairly common.) Easy to identify because of its size, it is the only petrel to feed on land as well as on the sea. Mainly a winter visitor in Australia. One found alive near Goolwa, S.A., had been banded at the South Orkney Islands less than three months before. (*White phase: T. Pescott*)

Top:
Southern giant petrel, *Macronectes giganteus*. (90 cm. Southern seas. Fairly common.) *(Dark phase: R. Worden)*

Centre:
Northern giant petrel, *Macronectes halli*. (85 cm. Southern seas. Rare.) It is only recently (1966) that this bird has been officially distinguished from the Southern giant petrel, which it closely resembles. However there are several significant differences in colour pattern, it is smaller, and it commences to breed earlier. The giant petrels compare in size with some albatrosses, but do not have the graceful flight of those birds. *(T. Pescott)*

Bottom left:
Antarctic fulmar, *Fulmarus glacialoides*. (50 cm. Southern seas. Uncommon.) This gull-like petrel flies with good manoeuvring. It is quarrelsome and belligerent, and will spit stomach oil at an intruder. The sexes are alike. One of its calls has been likened to the cackle of a domestic rooster. It follows ships for galley waste and frequents whaling stations for offal. *(B. Allwright)*

Bottom right:
Antarctic petrel, *Thalassoica antarctica*. (45 cm. Southern seas. Uncommon.) This petrel prefers the more southerly regions, and it often settles and rests upon icebergs. Does not follow ships as a rule, but will congregate when a whale is killed. They are good flyers, always landing smoothly. *(B. Allwright)*

Facing page, top:
Cape petrel, *Daption capensis.* (40 cm. Southern seas. Common.) This bird is even more helpless on land than other petrels. However it overcomes this disability by alighting only on high cliffs or icebergs, where taking off consists simply of dropping into air. On the other hand, it settles and floats on the sea in an easy, erect attitude. It also dives expertly, either from the air or from the water's surface. *(L. Robinson)*

Facing page, bottom:
Snow petrel, *Pagodroma nivea.* (35 cm. Cold waters. Very rare.) This species rarely leaves the colder, ice regions. However there is a skin in the Gould Collection at the National Museum, Melbourne, which is marked as coming from Australian seas. Opinion now is that the bird is unlikely to be seen north of 50°S latitude. *(B. Allwright)*

Top:
Great-winged petrel, *Pterodroma macroptera.* (40 cm. Southern seas. Common.) Birds in this genus are sometimes called gadfly-petrels. This species is well named, having a wing span of about 1 m. It breeds in islands off W.A., nesting either on the surface or in burrows. It is a noisy bird at its breeding places, one of its calls resembling the braying of a donkey. *(G. Mathews)*

Centre:
White-headed petrel, *Pterodroma lessonii.* (40 cm. Southern seas. Fairly common.) Has the typical gadfly-petrel flight, ascending to heights of 30 m. Despite its size, it is often attacked and killed by Southern skuas, and also by cats. It is strictly nocturnal on land, not usually heard until an hour after sunset, but then it becomes noisy. It is a non-breeding visitor. *(Antarctic Division photograph by J. Warham)*

Bottom:
Gould petrel, *Pterodroma leucoptera.* (30 cm. Tropical and sub-tropical seas. Fairly common.) The only Australian breeding station of this species is on Cabbage Tree Island, off Port Stephens, N.S.W., where the birds have to contend with the adhesive seeds of the *Pisonia* trees, in which they often become entangled and die. The eggs are laid in late November. Both parents assist in incubation. *(J. Gould)*

Top:
Fairy prion, *Pachyptila turtur.* (25 cm. Seas, shoreline. Fairly common.) Prions are good divers and excellent flyers, with a distinctive fast darting and twisting movement. They will fly close to the sea, rise with the wind as if helpless before it, but are well able to cope with storms. The Fairy prion breeds on islands off Vic. and Tas. *(M. Soper)*

Centre:
Medium-billed prion, *Pachyptila salvini.* (25 cm. Seas, beaches. Common.) It nests on islands in the sub-Antarctic zone. The young chicks are frequently trapped by snow, and then fall victims to skuas and gulls. In Australia, they are most common in W.A. waters. *(T. Pescott)*

Bottom:
Antarctic prion, *Pachyptila desolata.* (25 cm. Southern seas. Fairly common.) Also called the Dove prion. They are often picked up on southern Australian beaches after being washed ashore following storms. They breed in the colder south. The Thin-billed prion, *Pachyptila belcheri,* is similar except for a narrower bill. *(Antarctic Division photograph by J. Warham)*

Top:

Wedge-tailed shearwater, *Puffinus pacificus*. (40 cm. Seas, shoreline. Common.) It nests on islands at several points on both the east and west Australian coastlines. The nest is in a chamber at the end of a long burrow, in rock crevices or in coral sand. Both parents assist in incubation. It has a wailing cry, giving it the occasional name of the Mourningbird. *(C. Webster)*

Centre left:

Fleshy-footed shearwater, *Puffinus carneipes*. (40 cm. Seas, shoreline. Fairly common.) It is pugnacious when handled, struggling angrily and attacking with its beak. Is a good flyer and appears less awkward on the ground than other shearwaters. The only Australian nesting sites are in W.A. waters. A small colony of these on the mainland was wiped out by foxes in 1938. *(N. Chaffer)*

Centre right:

Sooty shearwater, *Puffinus griseus*. (45 cm. Southern and eastern seas, coastline. Common.) Its Australian breeding sites are all in N.S.W. or Tas. waters. It nests in a grass-lined chamber at the end of a tunnel, 1–3 m in length. One egg is laid. Large numbers of birds may be seen off the breeding island in the evenings, awaiting the darkness. *(G. Mathews)*

Bottom:

Short-tailed shearwater, *Puffinus tenuirostris*. (40 cm. Southern coasts. Very common.) The muttonbird of Tas. The sexes are alike, but the males are slightly larger, with a heavier neck. Because of scientific interest and their commercial exploitation, these birds have been studied extensively. It is the only shearwater to breed solely in Australia and the high numbers could make it Australia's most prolific bird. *(K. Stepnell)*

Top:
Little shearwater, *Puffinus assimilis.* (30 cm. Southern seas. Fairly common.) This is the smallest shearwater found in Australian seas. The sexes are alike. It is apparently non-migratory and is found at its haunts for most of the year. It is strictly nocturnal in shore habits. It has a fast, whirring flight, with rapid wing beats. In Australia, breeds only in W.A. waters. *(J. Gould)*

Bottom:
Fluttering shearwater, *Puffinus gavia.* (35 cm. Southern seas. Fairly common.) Resembles the Little shearwater in many ways. It is believed that there are two races of the species in Australia, the birds occurring west of Vic. being of the race *huttoni.* The bird spends much time on, or fluttering close to, the water. It flies with fast wing beats, swims and dives well. *(M. Soper)*

STORM-PETRELS HYDROBATIDAE

This is a family of small, delicate birds, very closely related to other petrels, and noted for their abundance in number and their distinctive flying technique, staying close to the water and bouncing over each undulation of the waves. They also flutter and patter along the surface like "walking on water".

One difference from most other petrels is that the nostril of the storm-petrel is undivided.

The birds in this family generally feed on crustacea, cephalopods, fish, and surface-floating waste from whaling stations. They mostly take their food from the surface while fluttering or paddling. None of them dive. Some, notably the Wilson storm-petrel, frequently follow ships, feeding in their wake.

There are altogether twenty-one species of storm-petrels, with only four listed as appearing in Australian waters. Three others, the Grey-backed, the Black, and the Leach storm-petrels are regarded as stragglers.

Only one species, the White-faced, breeds in Australia. Strangely, this bird is rarely seen on land, coming ashore at night and being well out to sea again before sunrise, and as well, its activities are restricted on moonlight nights. It leaves Australia during the non-breeding season, apparently migrating to the Indian Ocean.

It breeds in all States except Queensland, with its largest breeding ground situated at Mud Island in Port Phillip Bay, Victoria. In the summer of 1960, it was estimated that there were 8000 burrows at this site.

The White-faced nests in a chamber at the end of a burrow, measuring anything from 45 cm to 120 cm long, with an opening too small for a hand to be inserted. Nests are often hidden in growth, such as pigface, which help to protect the burrow.

One egg is laid, pink at first, then turning white, often speckled with red-brown markings. Sometimes eggs are laid on the surface, but these are wasted and not incubated.

Both parents assist in incubation, taking turns in periods of from three to nine days. The total period of incubation is approximately fifty-six days, chicks hatching from about mid-December.

The young are abandoned by day when two to four days old, and after that are normally fed every night by either parent. They are able to fly at about seven or eight weeks. Enemies include gulls, skuas, and tiger snakes.

Banding at nesting sites has shown that birds return every year to the same spot.

White-faced storm-petrel, *Pelagodroma marina.* (20 cm. Seas and shoreline. Common.) When the long legs are held up in flight, they project well beyond the squarish tail. It is a strong, fast surface flyer. Its first eggs are laid from early October. They are attracted to lights, easily caught, and quite docile to handle. *(K. Stepnell)*

Top:
Wilson storm-petrel, *Oceanites oceanicus.* (15 cm. Seas. Common.) Often regarded as the world's commonest bird. Although a non-breeder in Australia, it is seen in greater numbers here than the White-faced storm-petrel. It breeds in the cold Antarctic zone. In spite of its large numbers, it is easily overlooked because of its smallness and its low-flying practice. *(Antarctic Division photograph by W. Dinsle)*

Bottom:
Black-bellied storm-petrel, *Fregetta tropica* (left). (20 cm. Southern seas. Fairly common.); White-bellied storm-petrel, *Fregetta grallaria* (right). (20 cm. Southern seas. Rare.) These species are difficult to identify with certainty. The Black-bellied breeds in the sub-Antarctic region and is seen usually in the winter in the Southern Ocean south of Tas. The White-bellied breeds on south Pacific and south Atlantic islands, and winters in the tropics, being fairly common in the Coral Sea. *(G. Broinowski)*

DIVING-PETRELS PELECANOIDIDAE

Diving-petrels do not possess the typical petrel long wings and legs, but tend to shortness in these and in overall length. The nostril tubes are separated and open upwards, which apparently prevents water entering the nostrils when the bird is diving.

Their food consists of crustacea and small fish. Another difference from other petrels is that these birds do not eat cephalopods.

They dive excellently and can swim under water like penguins, using their wings to propel themselves. Then, with the same action, they can leave the water and take to the air without any change in the rhythm of the wing beat. However, their flying talents are restricted. They flutter their wings rapidly and their flights are short. The sexes are alike.

The feet are webbed and there is no hind toe. On land, because of the way their legs are set back, it is necessary for these birds to perform a take-off run before gaining the air.

Found only in the Southern Hemisphere, diving-petrels bear a marked similarity to the Little auk of the Northern Hemisphere.

A further characteristic is the early stage in life at which these birds can begin to breed, some starting as early as their second year. The nest is in a chamber at the end of a tunnel about 45 cm long, often among plants. One egg is laid, both parents assisting in hatching and brooding, with the chicks needing a longer period of attention than is usual with burrow nesters. One of the parent birds covers the chick for the first ten days of its life, a practice believed to be necessary because the head of the young bird is quite naked of down on hatching.

The adult birds do not circle their breeding colonies before landing, but will go directly to the ground in a tumbling descent, then race to their burrows. In this way they often become prey to skuas, their main ground enemy, which will await their arrival at the nesting sites. The enemy most encountered at sea is the leopard seal.

There are four species of the diving-petrel family, with only one being found in Australia. A single bird of another species, the Georgian diving-petrel, was found in New South Wales in 1958, but this is the only confirmed sighting of the species in Australia.

Diving-petrels are seen usually in flocks and they do not migrate. Their sitting posture on the water has been described as grebe-like.

Diving-petrel, *Pelecanoides urinatrix*. (20–25 cm. Southern seas. Common in limited area.) Also called Common diving-petrel. In Australia, it breeds only on coastal islands in Vic. and Tas. waters and is rarely seen elsewhere. At sea, these birds will rise suddenly in a group from the water, very much in the manner of flying fish. *(E. Whitbourn)*

GREBES PODICIPEDIDAE

The grebes are the personality birds of bush billabongs and inland lakes. An interested observer might come quietly up a bank or a rise and see, not just a sheet of water, but a surface with birds floating on it. Most likely they will be grebes, the friendly little fellows who will stay on after ducks and other birds have flown.

On being approached, they too will disappear, not by flight but, as if by magic, diving expertly, remaining out of sight for some time, then eventually coming up at a spot well removed from where one is watching.

Their scientific name, *Podiceps*, means "rump foot", and refers to the fact that the feet are placed a long way back on the bird's body, near the rump. They are needed back there, for the grebe has no tail to speak of and the feet are on call for steering aid when the bird is moving in the water or the air.

As well as lacking much tail, the grebe has wings that are short and rounded, further restricting its ability to fly. Indeed they rarely if ever fly in the daylight, preferring to do a "night-time flit" if they feel it necessary to change their abode, which could be at such times as when the food supply and vegetation of a well-used spot has run out. Their night flight would be slow and wobbly, because the air is not their domain.

When diving, the grebe employs the method that was utilised by the designers of the submarine. It spreads its feathers, so the air held between them escapes and is replaced by water, aiding it to sink.

Another talent which it displays on the water is its "skittering", the rapid movement across the surface made with feet and wings, when it might look as if it is running before taking off.

The nest is built on a floating raft of water weeds, on a small island or a mound away from the bank, or on a reed bed. Usually from four to six eggs are laid. The nesting birds have a practice of skilfully and rapidly covering the eggs with water weeds or vegetation, which they do by grasping and twisting the grass or weed with their beaks, then placing it in the required position. In this way the eggs are hidden from intruders, or protected from the sun or weather.

On hatching, the chick immediately is able to swim. However it soon learns that this talent is unnecessary in the early stages, and instead rides instinctively on its parent's back, clinging like a steeplechase jockey even when the adult bird goes into a dive.

Little grebe, *Podiceps novaehollandiae*. (23 cm. Inland waters. Common.) May be seen in many and varied places, from large lakes to farm dams. Their preference is for fresh water. The short legs are ideal for swimming, but of little use on land. It is also called a dabchick, and has close relatives in many parts of the world. (G. Weatherstone)

Top:
Hoary-headed grebe, *Podiceps poliocephalus.* (30 cm. Inland waters. Common.) The hoary head in this case is not a sign of old age, but on the contrary is best seen when the bird is in full breeding regalia. Very similar to the Little grebe, but does not share its cousin's objection to salt water. This is an Australian bird although a similar species occurs in New Zealand. *(T. Pescott)*

Bottom:
Crested grebe, *Podiceps cristatus.* (43 cm. Inland waters. Rare.) Also called Great crested grebe. The prominent, ruffed collar appears in the breeding season, when the crest also enlarges and the bird performs extensive displays. Unlike the smaller grebes, has a loud call, described as "heh!" Mainly carnivorous, it eats fish, crustacea, and water insects. *(J. Wightman, Ardea)*

PELICANS PELECANIDAE

What is the pelican's secret? How is it that today, as through the ages, the pelican succeeds in attracting the notice of people everywhere?

Perhaps it is just that these birds possess so many of the qualities that mankind finds likeable, or even lovable. Here we have the comical and the grotesque, combined with dignity and attractiveness, indeed with beauty, for a pair of pelicans floating on calm waters on a still evening is certainly a picture that delights.

Pelicans bring pleasure to every bird observer, keen or casual. They are the inspiration of the poet and the author, of the photographer, the artist, and the cartoonist.

The pelican is quite unlike any other bird and possesses more distinctive features than most. There is the large bill, the huge front pouch, the extensive wing span. It has the practice, when flying, of drawing back its head into its body, and its action in the air is to give a few beats of its big wings, following this with a long glide. Or it will soar for a long time with no wing movement whatever.

The pelican is so unique that it is easily identifiable. When seen clearly, it will not be confused with any other bird.

The wing span of a fully grown bird starts at about 250 cm. The water-carrying capacity of the pouch is over 10 litres. It will soar at heights of over 3000 m, often in flocks of 100 or more. And if these figures all concern the size and activities of full-grown birds, it should be noted that in the first three weeks of its life, a pelican chick grows to six times its original size.

There are eight species of pelican found around the world. The one species seen in Australia is distinct and individual. It is predominantly a white bird, with black markings. They are found throughout Australia, in coastal waters and inland, in salt waters and fresh. They feed mainly in shallow water, the diet including fish, crustacea, and tadpoles.

The nests are not elaborate and sometimes are just a bare hollow in the sand. Usually some nesting material is used, such as water weeds, gum leaves, and feathers. Pelicans have been known to nest in low, dense bushes.

Normally the clutch is of two eggs. They are not good sitters and if disturbed will desert the nest and not return for some time, leaving the eggs or chicks an easy meal for predators, such as ravens or gulls. Pelicans are deserving of care and protection. Because of this tendency to temporarily shun their nest when disturbed, it is recommended that, in the breeding season, observers be content with viewing the nesting colony from a distance, perhaps through binoculars.

After hatching, the young will stay in the nest for a time. Later they will unite with other chicks from near by to form a crèche. The "safety in numbers" policy no doubt helps in their protection and also aids the chicks in maintaining warmth.

Pelicans are not given to loud calling and the only sound they make is an infrequent grunt.

An old legend concerning the pelican stated that, rather than let her young go hungry, the parent would feed them with her own blood, acquired by removing breast feathers with her bill. The legend probably arose from one species having a blood-red tip to the bill. Because of this, the pelican is often chosen as a children's hospital emblem.

Pelican, *Pelecanus conspicillatus*. (1·5–2 m. Coastal and inland waters. Common.) Pelicans will feed in a close circle, constantly moving to stir the fish but preventing their escape at the same time. The sexes are alike. On hatching, the chicks are naked, pink, and grotesque. Many former breeding colonies have been wiped out, but the birds seem to have made a comeback, and possibly are retaining their numbers. *(A. Clements)*

GANNETS AND BOOBIES SULIDAE

Of the four species of this family which occur, and breed, in Australia, the name "gannet" is given to the variety living in the southerly seas area, while "boobies" is used for the other three species which are found in the sub-tropical and tropical zones.

The birds came to be called boobies because seafarers regarded them as dull wits (or boobies), and John Gould, when he came to Australia and saw these representatives of the family, said the Australian gannet "out-boobied" all others. They were so stupid that he was able to catch five of them by hand before the others thought to escape from him.

Gannets and boobies are big birds of the sea, not of the deep ocean, but of shallower, coastal waters. Perhaps their most noticeable characteristic is their diving talent. They will plunge into the sea from great heights, 20 m or more. With their long, pointed bills, it could be thought that they hit the water and spear a fish in the one action, but this is not their practice. The dive takes them under the shoal or the single fish which is their target, and they will grasp their prey in their beaks from underneath as they rise.

Their bodies have no brood patches and the practice in incubation is for the sitting bird to place its heavily-webbed feet over the eggs. Instead of the usual nostril opening on the bill, the birds have a small aperture at the joint of the jaws, under the eyes, and it is this opening which is used for breathing. The opening is closed when the bird dives. The air sacs under the skin of the neck and head are another peculiarity. These fill with air before a dive, softening the blow as the bird hits the surface.

The gannet nests on a mound, built about 25 cm high, of seaweed and available vegetation, held firmly in position by hardened excreta. The nests are placed about 1 m apart, just out of the beak range of the neighbouring nest holder.

The boobies do not nest so elaborately. The Masked and Brown boobies often make no nest at all, the egg being laid in a depression in the sand. On other occasions they might place some vegetation or pebbles around the cavity. The Red-footed booby nests in trees or bushes.

In all species, whether one egg is laid or two, only one chick is raised. There are elaborate nesting displays by the mating birds and calling at the nests.

Gannet, *Morus serrator*. (1 m. Southern seas and shores. Common.) Also called Australian gannet. In their plummeting dives, they hit the water with an impressive splash. Sometimes a flock of these will "round up" fish into a concentrated shoal preparatory to diving for their meal. Diet of fish includes pilchards, mackerel, and barracouta. (*L. Robinson*)

Top:
Red-footed booby, *Sula sula*. (75 cm. Northern seas, shorelines. Fairly common.) The long tail and sleek body are good identifiable characteristics. It has the largest eyes of any of the boobies, and this is probably a contributing factor to its being more nocturnal in habits. It is quite vocal as it comes in to settle and in this species the voices of male and female are alike. (*J. Gould*)

Centre:
Masked booby, *Sula dactylatra*. (75–85 cm. Northern seas and shores. Fairly common.) The heaviest of the Australian boobies. Observers say that the young chicks in the nests on the ground have an interesting method of shielding themselves from the sun. They will turn away from it, and lift up their tails so that their heads are in their own shadows. (*I. Bennett*)

Bottom:
Brown booby, *Sula leucogaster*. (75 cm. Northern seas and shores. Fairly common.) Differs from other boobies in that it will be seen fishing at times in quite shallow water. The calls of the sexes are different, too, the male giving a high screech, and the female a louder, low-pitched note. (*H. Frauca*)

CORMORANTS AND DARTERS

PHALACROCORACIDAE AND ANHINGIDAE

Although the birds in these families are well adapted for life in and about water, the feathers are not waterproof. Consequently, after swimming or diving for some time, the birds find it necessary to dry off, and are often seen with their wings stretched out sideways, looking like someone's washing on the line, or a parson blessing the people.

One reason advanced for this lack of water-proofing in the feathers is that it is compatible with a lack of buoyancy, that quality which in some other birds helps them to float. In other words, nature actually aids cormorants and darters to reach the bottom when in the water, and it is on the bottom that they do much of their feeding, remembering that they are birds of the shallow waters and not of the ocean's depths.

Other physical features of the cormorant are the sealed nostrils, with breathing openings at the base of the bill, under the eye, as with gannets. The bill is long, sleek, and with a large strong hook at its extremity.

The legs are placed well back, so that the birds stand nearly upright like penguins, and indeed the pied species are often mistaken for penguins when seen from some distance.

Cormorants are generally plentiful in Australia as in many other parts of the world. Altogether there are twenty-nine species, five of which are found in Australia. Of these, most have their haunts inland, some are found in lesser numbers in coastal areas, while one variety can be regarded as a coastal species.

When in flocks, cormorants will fly in changing formations, giving rise to the legends that they form letters in the sky.

Often "shag" is used as an alternative name. In Australia, shag and cormorant are interchangeable, although in some parts of the world the two names are used separately to distinguish species.

Cormorants are most efficient catchers of fish, this talent frequently bringing them into disfavour with fishermen, who resent the competition. But on the side of the birds it should be pointed out that some of the species never take fish that would be utilised for human consumption. On the contrary, they eat enemies of both fish and fishermen.

The darters—the birds with the long neck with the kink in the middle—share many of the characteristics of the cormorants. But the beak is pointed, not hooked, there are marked differences between the sexes, and whereas cormorants seldom raise their voices loudly, the darter has a loud and rowdy cackle, describing which frequently extends the imaginations of its hearers. As birds of prey, darters are very efficient.

Cormorants appear to prosper in numbers and to succeed well in changing their place of abode and breeding, following interference with natural habitat. The fact that many species can exist and feed in either fresh or sea water is an advantage, and another reason the bird continues to prosper is the number of eggs in a clutch, frequently four, sometimes up to six.

The cormorant's neck is long, its tail feathers are stiff, and its feet are large and webbed, ideal for paddles to propel it in the water when it has to pursue its prey.

Darter, *Anhinga rufa*. (1 m. Inland and coastal waters. Fairly common.) This bird swims with only its head and long neck protruding, like a snake. It has a habit of devoting long periods to sitting in trees near the water, or for flying around and around a particular spot before landing. Their method of fishing is to spear the fish with their beaks, shake it off, and then eat it. (*F. Lewitzka*)

Above: Black cormorant, *Phalacrocorax carbo*. (85 cm. Inland fresh waters. Common.) The largest of Australian cormorants. It has greedy habits, the diet consisting of fish and sometimes smaller water birds, and it will eat until it is too heavy to take off. Usually nests in high trees, taking the highest position in rookeries where it competes with other birds. *(L. Robinson)*

Right:
Little pied cormorant, *Phalacrocorax melanoleucos*. (60 cm. Mainly inland waters. Common.) This is the smallest of Australian cormorants. Another distinguishing feature is that the head is more rounded than in others. These cormorants are often seen alone, or if feeding conditions are ideal, will be in flocks of hundreds. The sexes are alike, except that the male is slightly larger. (*I. McCann*)

Below:
Little black cormorant, *Phalacrocorax sulcirostris*. (60 cm. Inland, occasionally coastal waters. Common.) Flocks of these will herd fish into shoals. Breeds only in fresh water localities. Likes to nest in paperbarks, lining the nest with strips from these trees. Outside Australia, this species is found only in areas adjacent to the continent and in Malaysia. (*G. Chapman*)

Above:
Yellow-faced cormorant, *Phalacrocorax varius*. (80 cm. Inland and coastal areas. Common.) Also called Pied cormorant. It is not seen in Tas. This species are powerful flyers, keeping near the water when flying into the wind, but higher with assisting wind. These are frequently seen in very large flocks. (*G. Chapman*)

Left:
Black-faced cormorant, *Phalacrocorax fuscescens*. (60 cm. Southern coastal waters. Fairly common.) Breeds in secluded places, and is not found outside Australia. It has the ability to stay under the water for long periods, and plunges of up to 40 seconds have been observed. (*R. Good*)

43

FRIGATEBIRDS FREGATIDAE

The philosophy of frigatebirds would appear to be that other birds of the sea owe them a living, for they frequently feed on pirated, disgorged food. Even on the land they are scavengers, stealing food and nesting material whenever they can rather than hunting up their own.

These are birds of the northern tropical waters, spending most of their lives on the wing. Their method of hunting is to harry other birds—boobies, terns, and tropicbirds among them—in the air, unsettling them so that recently-captured fish is disgorged and dropped, and then quickly taken by the expert frigatebirds. These birds are magnificent aerialists and this talent aids them considerably in their piratical life, both in acrobatic manoeuvres in stealing prey and in their soaring expeditions when a food source is sighted.

They are not equipped with well-waterproofed feathers, so are not given to settling on the water for any length of time. And because they spend the greater amount of their time in the air, their "land legs" have not developed, so that when settling on the land, they prefer a place from which take-off will be easy, such as a tree, where the height will give them some start in altitude.

Although both legs and feet are small and their bodies of only medium size, the birds are characterised by long slim wings, long forked tail, and a long hooked bill. The feathers are mostly black. The male bird has an area of bare skin on the upper breast, which can be blown up like a big, red balloon.

Altogether there are six species of this bird, two of which are seen in Australia. Of these, one is a breeder on coastal islands, the other a rare, non-breeding visitor.

As well as their talent for piracy, the birds are quite capable of taking food from the sea's surface on the wing, and sometimes adeptly catch flying fish in the air.

Both sexes take part in making the nest, in incubation, and in brooding the young. Only one egg is laid, in a nest made of sticks and vegetation, cemented with excreta.

Island observers report that in the early evening these birds will soar capably and magnificently to great heights, becoming mere dots in the sky. In direct flight, they can cover long distances, although more is known of their journeyings in the old world than has been discovered to date by Australian observations.

Although they live by attacking and harrying other birds, they seem largely to enjoy absence of enemies in the bird kingdom themselves. There are accounts of nesting birds being heavily infested with ticks about the face and neck.

Nesting is in colonies, with the nests about 30 cm in diameter, from 10 cm to 20 cm high and usually spaced 75 cm apart. The adult voices at the nesting sites have been described as grunts and rattling sounds.

Lighthouse keepers report that these birds have been known to kill themselves by flying directly into the beacon light.

Bottom left:
Lesser frigatebird, *Fregata ariel*. (75 cm. Northern seas. Common.) Nests on islands all along the northern Australian coastline. In some places were called "rain brothers" by Aborigines, as they were believed to appear before rain storms. Usually seen only in the tropical zone, but occasionally are carried south by winds and have been sighted in Port Phillip Bay, Vic. *(J. Gould)*

Bottom right:
Greater frigatebird, *Fregata minor*. (1 m. Northern seas. Uncommon.) There is some difference in the sexes in this species, the female being 10 cm or more longer than the male and sometimes almost twice as heavy. There is a report of a breeding bird being found with a band indicating that it was at least 34 years old. *(G. Mathews)*

TROPICBIRDS PHAETHONTIDAE

This is a small family of three species, two of which are found in Australia. One of these, the White-tailed tropicbird, is a rare, non-breeding visitor.

Tropicbirds have some characteristics found in other birds to which it bears no relationship. The shape of the head, the overall appearance, and some of its calls are similar to those of the tern.

Perhaps its most distinctive feature, and the one for which the species seen in Australia are named, is the extension of the centre tail feathers, called streamers. These are something like the spiked tails of the Rainbow-birds of inland country.

Another physical feature is shared with the gannet and the pelican, which are of the same order as tropicbirds. This is the placement of air cells under the skin in the front of the body, a protective measure to lessen the effect of impact as the bird strikes the water when diving.

Short and fast wing movements, added to long soaring glides, enable the birds to fly great distances and they are seen far out to sea. They also have the ability to plummet into the water from as high as 15 m and to stay submerged for periods of almost half a minute. They feed in the water on squid and fish.

In southern Australia, breeding activities are restricted to the summer months, while further north the birds breed throughout the year. In some States where breeding does not occur, tropicbirds may be seen at times as itinerant visitors.

The nests are placed to catch some shade, rather than for elaborate shelter. They are simple and labour-saving for the bird, often an unlined depression in the sand.

Normally one egg is laid, off-white with colourful markings. Both birds take shifts in the incubation programme. Calls, described as harsh and penetrating, are made by birds when approaching the nest, and these may be answered by the occupying bird.

Because of its very short legs, the tropicbird is almost immobile and helpless on the ground, a sitting target for predators. Of these, the sea-eagle is the main enemy. Storms also account for losses and there is some evidence that extreme heat will distress the birds.

This bird is also known as the Bosunbird, a name given to it by sailors. There are two theories for this name. One concerns the prominent tail streamers, the sailors saying that the bird carried a marlin spike in its tail. The other theory was that one of the bird's calls resembled the sound of a bosun's pipe.

Above:
Red-tailed tropicbird, *Phaethon rubricauda*. (45 cm. Tropical and warm seas. Fairly common.) The length stated does not include the red tail feathers, or streamers, which are from 30 cm to 35 cm. Sometimes, because of wear and tear, or as a result of accident, the streamers are absent, especially during the breeding season. These birds are said to be extremely tame when nesting. *(A. Wells)*

Right:
White-tailed tropicbird, *Phaethon lepturus*. (40 cm. Northern seas. Rare.) The tail streamers add 30 cm to the bird's total length. As well as being smaller, this species frequently follows ships at sea, not a usual practice of the Red-tailed. Male birds have elaborate wrestling displays at nest sites, sometimes ending in the death of a participant. *(G. Mathews)*

BITTERNS, HERONS, AND EGRETS ARDEIDAE

This family of long-billed birds of the shallow waters may be divided into two sections—first, the bitterns, secondly, the herons and egrets.

The bittern is the bird credited with providing the sound effects which backgrounded the bunyip legends. These stories began with the Aborigines and were enthusiastically taken up by early settlers in Australia when they first heard the bittern's call. This is a loud, repeated booming, sounding across the country, and likened to the noise of gunfire or the bellowing of a bull. The noise doubtless fitted in with pictures sketched in the imaginations of the newcomers to this land of strange and mysterious creatures.

Today, many regard the boom of the bittern with affection, even though they rarely chance to see the bird which makes the noise.

Three species of bitterns occur in Australia, varying in size but all having the distinctive long neck and stiletto-like bills. They have a peculiar stance, adopted as a natural camouflage when they think there is a likelihood of their being observed, in which they remain quite motionless, neck outstretched and bill pointed skywards.

There are eleven species of herons and egrets seen in Australia, with the White-necked heron the one endemic species.

Distinctive characteristics of these birds are the long bills and their long, curving necks. All of them fly, like pelicans, with the neck curved back against the body. The deliberate flight is pleasing to behold. The legs may dangle on take-off, but soon assume the typical position, held out straight behind the body. In the shorter-legged Nankeen night heron, only the toes are visibly extended.

The delicate plumes, which are seen in both sexes at times of breeding, form another outstanding feature, especially in the egrets. Previously these were in demand for the adornment of ladies' hats, and the trade accounted for mass capture and slaughter of the noble birds.

Herons and egrets are found in the wetlands or in places presently carrying water after flooding or rains. An exception is the Cattle egret, a comparative newcomer to Australia, which does not seek out wet areas, and which looks as though eventually it might be found wherever cattle are grazing. These birds were first released in Australia as recently as 1933, when a small number were freed in Western Australia. However, it was some years after this before they began to be seen in numbers, and it is thought that they may have found their way to the continent in the ordinary course of events, as the species is explorative.

Herons and egrets are gregarious and often several species are seen in each other's company, perhaps with other kinds of water birds. Good sightings are obtained from a stationary car or from a chosen position near a lagoon or swamp. A pair of binoculars and a little patience can lead to a rewarding and entertaining viewing session.

Brown bittern, *Botaurus poiciloptilus*. (1 m. Swamps. Fairly common in limited areas.) It is found only in south-eastern Australia and in the extreme south-west of W.A. It will repeat its booming call up to a dozen times and may be heard over a distance of 3 km. When disturbed, flies low over surrounding swamp growth and is quickly lost. (*J. Gould*)

Top left:
Black bittern, *Ixobrychus flavicollis*. (60 cm. Ponds and river margins. Possibly fairly common.) The sexes are similar, but the male is the more deeply black. Because of its nocturnal habits and its liking for the densest vegetation, this is a bird difficult to observe. Perhaps these same features assist the bird to survive. (*J. Purnell*)

Top right:
Nankeen night heron, *Nycticorax caledonicus*. (60 cm. Swamps, vegetated coastal inlets. Fairly common.) This attractive bird, found in most of Australia, is usually seen at dusk, flying to its feeding places, where it seeks yabbies, frogs, small fish, and insects. During the day it will roost in trees in the vicinity of water. Nests in colonies, often in large numbers. (*F. Lewitzka*)

Centre:
Little bittern, *Ixobrychus minutus*. (30 cm. Swamps. Rare.) The scientific name means "little reed roarer", and, as with other bitterns, it is heard rather than seen. It is well camouflaged in its natural habitat, where the strongly made nest consists of reeds and swamp vegetation. It is the smallest of the three bitterns seen in Australia. (*J. Gould*)

Bottom right:
Cattle egret, *Ardeola ibis*. (45 cm. Animal grazing areas. Common and increasing.) These will stand or walk with wings drooping and body hunched as though they are malformed or unwell. However they are sprightly enough to catch insects disturbed by grazing cattle and frequently to perch on the animals' backs, and they are proving adaptable to varying conditions. (*J. Wessels*)

Top:
Pied heron, *Hydranassa picata*. (45–50 cm. Coastal swamps. Fairly common in limited area.) This is a bird of the tropics and is found only in the far north. It is aggressive and belligerent, calls loudly on the wing and is known to practise piracy, forcing other birds to disgorge food. *(A. Wells)*

Centre:
Mangrove heron, *Butorides striatus*. (45–50 cm. Coastal swamps. Fairly common.) In the past it has been called a bittern and it certainly resembles this species, even to the practice of "freezing" to make observation difficult. Its haunts are only in tropical and sub-tropical areas and it is not seen in the southern States. *(G. Chapman)*

Bottom:
Reef heron, *Egretta sacra* (dark phase). (60 cm. Rocky coasts. Fairly common.) Frequents the entire coastline of Australia, except the Great Australian Bight, where the absence of water birds puzzles observers. It nests on small rocky islands, on the sand, or on cliff edges. The white and dark phases of this bird are seen, and breed freely, together. *(J. Ferrero)*

Left:

Plumed egret, *Egretta intermedia*. (60 cm. Inland waters, occasionally coastal. Fairly common in restricted area.) The face of this species turns green when mating and the bill reddens. Differs from the Little egret in the greater dimensions of the bill and the more marked differences between breeders and non-breeders. (*W. Labbett*)

Bottom left:

Little egret, *Egretta garzetta*. (55 cm. Coastal waters, inland lakes, rivers. Fairly common in limited area.) The yellow face reddens and the plumes develop at mating time. This species fishes in the shallows, and perches and nests in trees near by. Not to be confused with the larger White egret, though often the two species are seen together. (*T. & P. Gardner*)

Bottom right:

White egret, *Egretta alba*. (1 m. Coastal and inland shallows. Common.) This large egret is found throughout Australia and can be recognised by its size. It does not move as quickly as the Little egret, either when walking or flying, although it is graceful in the air. Nests in trees or swamp bushes and lays 3 or 4 eggs. (*F. Lewitzka*)

Top left:
White-necked heron, *Ardea pacifica*. (75 cm. Inland shallow waters and waterlogged areas. Fairly common.) This heron does not fancy coastal waters. It is very shy and not as likely to be seen as other herons. It nests in trees, often with eggs or chicks visible from below through the loosely built and poorly lined nest. It will catch its food both in the water and on land in wet conditions. *(E. Bound)*

Top right:
White-faced heron, *Ardea novaehollandiae*. (60 cm. Coastal and inland shallows, waterlogged areas. Very common.) In many places this bird is called erroneously the Blue crane. It is often seen at roadsides, especially in wet years, taking off sluggishly when cars approach. It nests in a tree away from water, and has a diet of yabbies, eels, frogs, small lizards, and rodents. *(C. Webster)*

Right:
Great-billed heron, *Ardea sumatrana*. (1·5 m. Coastal swamps. Rare.) This is a large bird of the tropics, believed to be decreasing in numbers. It is said to make loud, growling noises at night when breeding. The bill for which it is named measures 18 cm and is employed to capture its prey in the humid, mangrove swamps. *(J. Gould)*

STORKS CICONIIDAE

Only one member of the stork family is found in Australia, the stately and colourful Jabiru. Although at one time this bird may have been more plentiful and found in more extensive areas than at present, the same shy and elusive habits that it projects today always made it difficult to capture and to study in its natural state.

John Gould, who came to Australia in 1838, reported with regret that he had been unable to meet up with an Australian stork in the wild. He must have been one of the first to report on the big bird's shyness. However, he still left valuable facts and figures about it.

One event that did aid early ornithological studies of this species was that those skilful hunters, the Aborigines, realising how things stood, would capture these birds, not for food, but for barter with the white man. There is a fascinating account of the exchange of a live Jabiru for tobacco.

The method of capture used by the Aborigines was to creep up on the Jabiru while it was resting, reclining on its tarsi or shanks. It was at a temporary disadvantage here in that, if surprised, it took it a few moments to get back to its feet.

The hunters would squirm through the swamp growth, hidden by bush or reeds, or camouflaged to look like bush-growth themselves, then spring on to the resting bird, capturing it by hand and ensuring that it could be delivered alive.

Thus it was that some very detailed and accurate descriptions of the bird's measurements, colour patterns, and factors of its behaviour were recorded at an early date in Australian bird history.

One thing which those old writers did record was that the Jabirus were quite docile in captivity and quickly assumed the status of family pets. Later naturalists subsequently told of young Jabirus being very easy to rear and handle, so long as they had a yard or paddock to move around in.

However there was one point where the earlier observers seem to have had a wrong impression, as evidenced in their reporting on the bird's eating habits. A Jabiru in captivity, where apparently it quickly learns that its meals will be delivered to its liking and on time, develops a fastidiousness about food that could never apply in the wild, where the birds eat what they can catch and like it. And if they cannot catch anything that moves, they will settle for carrion. This is well removed from the accounts of domesticated birds sending back to the chef meat that was not minced finely enough, or fish in slabs too big to comfortably manage.

Feeding is a major occupation for the birds, as they have big appetites and consume much in a day.

It is a privilege to see one of these birds in its natural surrounds and travellers report enthusiastically that a Jabiru among the lilies of a lagoon is a sight not to be forgotten. The green sheen of its head and neck and its proud demeanour have been compared with the peacock, but its plumage patterns, its stately stance, and its tidy movements are distinctly individual.

In the air, it flies very slowly, but can cover long distances and does much soaring and gliding. Its head is large, its neck heavy, its legs long, and the wings massive. The tail, however, is short.

The name Jabiru was first given to a different member of the stork family in South America.

Jabiru, *Xenorhynchus asiaticus*. (1·25 m. Swamps, lagoons. Uncommon.) Also called Black-necked stork. Its nest is a pile of sticks and twigs, lined with grass and rushes. So long as there are suitable, high trees in the vicinity, it will build in them, otherwise it will nest on the ground. It has a standing height of 1·2 m, half of which is provided by its long legs. (*F. Lewitzka*)

IBISES AND SPOONBILLS THRESKIORNITHIDAE

The two birds in this family, ibises and spoonbills, would appear dissimilar in many ways, with probably the outstanding difference being in the shape of the bill. Yet there is common ground here, because in both species the bills play important parts in recognition, in naming, and in character.

The ibis is well known in many parts of the world and was recognised as the sacred bird of the ancient Egyptians. It indeed must have been held in high esteem by these people, as it was mummified and its image painted on walls and papyrus.

One theory is that the ibis came to be venerated because of the shape of its bill. It reminded the Egyptians of their goddess Isis, who was, among other things, moon goddess, and the bill of the ibis has the shape of the crescent moon. Of course a more practical reason for the bird being so respected was that its usefulness became so obvious to these agriculturally-minded people. The ibis ate millions of grasshoppers and insect pests in the fertile valleys of the Nile, areas most important in providing food.

The bill of the spoonbill is that bird's main characteristic. It is long, strong, and broad, with the wide, flat spoon at its extremity. When the spoonbill is feeding, the bill is moved to and fro through the water, which is strained through the bill, leaving the small fish, frogs, insects, and water life which make up the bird's diet.

The ibis feeds more directly by darting its bill into the shallow water or mud, or catching insects in grassed areas. It would be difficult to overrate the value of the ibis as a destroyer of insects. The grasshopper is its main food and it is said that without the presence of the ibis, these pests would rapidly wipe out the country's vegetation.

One of the three species of ibis found in Australia, the Straw-necked, is regarded here as the most valuable insect destroyer of all birds. This species is unique to Australia.

Ibises are often seen flying in formation in big numbers, the flocks sometimes containing both white and black birds and the colours distinguishable even when the birds are at great heights. Sometimes they will break the formation, sorting themselves into new flocks of their own kind, and this redistribution in the air, into black and white, is an impressive sight.

Bird lovers refer to the Straw-necked (black) and White varieties as "cousins". Perhaps this would make the third variety, the Glossy ibis, a second cousin. It is smaller and perhaps more graceful than the other species, and it is seen more in tropical areas, being rare in southern Australia. Another difference is that the eggs of the Glossy ibis are blue-green in colour, while those of the other species are white or off-white.

Bottom left:
Glossy ibis, *Plegadis falcinellus*. (60 cm. Swamps. Fairly common in limited area.) The distinguishing ibis bill in this smaller species is about 14 cm long. It will sometimes avoid the labours of nest building by utilising an existing nest. It has a greater repertoire of calls and noises than other ibises. *(F. Lewitzka)*

Bottom right:
White ibis, *Threskiornis molucca*. (75 cm. Swamps, mud flats. Common.) Also called Sacred ibis and is very similar to the Sacred ibis of Egypt. The name *Threskiornis* comes from two Greek words meaning "sacred bird". The bill measures from 15 cm to 18 cm. The sexes are alike. It is usually seen in water or in wet localities. *(E. Bound)*

Top:
Straw-necked ibis, *Threskiornis spinicollis.* (75 cm. Swamps, irrigated areas, grasslands. Very common.) This important bird is distinguished from the White ibis by its black colouring as well as the distinctive, horny, straw-coloured feathers on its neck, which are seen if close up or if viewing through binoculars. *(F. Lewitzka)*

Bottom left:
Royal spoonbill, *Platalea regia.* (75 cm. Swamps, flood plains. Fairly common.) Found almost throughout Australia, it nests off the ground, at varying heights from low shrubs to tall trees. The spooned bill measures 20 cm in length. The tuft of feathers on the back of the neck is seen only in breeding birds. *(F. Lewitzka)*

Bottom right:
Yellow-billed spoonbill, *Platalea flavipes.* (95 cm. Swamps, dams, flooded areas. Fairly common.) This species is a native of Australia. The common name refers to its noticeable yellow bill, and the scientific name, *flavipes,* emphasises the yellow feet or legs. These birds are explorative and strong flyers. They are often seen with other water birds. *(F. Lewitzka)*

SWANS, GEESE, AND DUCKS ANATIDAE

Most local birds of this world-wide family have some individual interest and appeal.

Early European settlers in Australia were amazed to find that the swans were black. But then what could be expected in a country where Christmas was celebrated in summer heat and the man in the moon was upside down!

The so-called "geese" of Australia are probably more duck than goose. The Pied, or Magpie, goose has a long neck and its toes are only partly joined by webbing (its scientific name is *semipalmata*, meaning half-webbed). The Cape Barren goose, observed by Matthew Flinders, who nearly sealed the bird's doom at the start by reporting how tasty it was, is today one of the rarer birds of the world, even though it might be seen in numbers of a hundred or more in some of its colonies.

In the other duck species there are noticeable differences between drake and duck, except in the moulting season, when the birds lose all of their wing feathers at once and so, for a time, are unable to fly. At this period, the male takes on what is known as an eclipse plumage, a duller coating very much like that of his mate. This means that he is not so noticeable as when wearing his full colours, and gives him some protection from predators at a stage when, as he is flightless, his life could be endangered.

Birds of the family have a wide and varied range of calls, from the quiet quacking of some of the ducks, the whistling of the whistleducks, to the musical honking of the swans.

The Musk duck, too, has its own peculiar call, one of a number of individualities. This unusual-looking bird gets its name from a musky smell, which is confined to the male in the breeding season. As well as an aroma, an air of mystery surrounds the Musk duck. Few observers have seen them fly, although it is obvious that they cross the country from one stretch of water to another. Also they have a talent for hiding their nests, and often the first indication to watchers that brooding has been in progress, is the appearance of ducklings behind their mother.

One factor which unfortunately has menaced the existence of ducks in Australia is the gun—guns not handled by sportsmen but by others who do not observe the rules. An example of what can happen is provided by the Burdekin shelduck. Any fair shooter will confirm that a bird which is tame enough to let you get close to it, which, when it does move, goes off slowly and directly, presenting an easy target, and on top of all else is unsuitable for eating, does not qualify as a game bird. But this attractive and appealing duck has been wiped out in many areas. Once it was common right down the east coast, but now is found only in tropical zones, where it manages to survive apparently because it is out of hunting range.

Pied goose, *Anseranas semipalmata*. (75 cm. Swamps, billabongs, flood plains. Common in limited area.) Also called Magpie goose, this species is sometimes seen in dense flocks, estimated to range from 50,000 to 100,000 in number. Now found only in tropical areas, these birds were once prevalent in the southern States. Efforts are being made to re-introduce them to some localities. *(B. Milburn)*

Top:
Water whistleduck, *Dendrocygna arcuata*. (55 cm. Deep lakes, lagoons. Common in limited area.) Their constant whistling is probably the best identification. Like the Pied goose, this bird ranged over more southerly areas, but is now found only in a limited tropic zone. It is an expert diver, feeding on underwater plants. *(J. Gould)*

Bottom left:
Grass whistleduck, *Dendrocygna eytoni*. (50 cm. Tropical grasslands. Common in limited area.) Also called, among several other names, Plumed tree-duck. It is seen in large flocks, made up of mated pairs. These birds do not dive to feed, but graze on areas sometimes well removed from water. Although mainly tropical, they are found near southern waters in smaller numbers. *(L. Robinson)*

Bottom right:
Mute swan, *Cygnus olor*. (1·4 m. Parks, ornamental waters. Rare.) This is an introduced species and, although prolific in some parts of the world, opinion is that it will never expand in Australia because of competition from the Black swan. *(F. Lewitzka)*

Top left:
Freckled duck, *Stictonetta naevosa.* (55 cm. Swamps, river margins, flood areas. Rare.) This attractive duck is a native of Australia, but fears are held for its survival. Usually it is seen in the company of other species, but is retiring and mainly nocturnal, and rarely sighted. Behaviour studies of the bird are in progress. *(J. Gould)*

Top right:
Cape Barren goose, *Cereopsis novaehollandiae.* (85 cm. Swamps, pastures. Uncommon.) There are signs that these distinguished birds are responding to measures taken for their expansion and preservation. They are natives of Australia, found only in a few southerly areas. As grazing birds, they seldom enter the water, although they are naturally strong swimmers. *(F. Park)*

Centre:
Mountain shelduck, *Tadorna tadornoides.* (70 cm. Lakes, billabongs, pastures, water areas. Common.) These are also called Mountain duck and Chestnut shelduck. These beautiful birds are often seen in pairs in roadside paddocks, usually out of ordinary photographic range. Happily for them, they are not pleasant to eat, and are possibly increasing in numbers. *(H. Frauca)*

Bottom:
Burdekin shelduck, *Tadorna radjah.* (55 cm. Swamps, lagoons, seashores. Uncommon.) The factors which render it a sitting target also make it an excellent camera study. It would be well if future shooting could be restricted to photographers. Films of this bird and its habitat would give delight to thousands of city dwellers. *(F. Lewitzka)*

Facing page:
Black swan, *Cygnus atratus.* (1·3 m. Any areas of water. Very common.) Although swans have some difficulty in take-off, they make a lovely picture once in the air, with the white wingtips showing. They are found in either fresh or brackish water. Average number of eggs in a clutch is 5 and both parents help in incubation. *(G. Gosbell)*

Top:
Black duck, *Anas superciliosa*. (55 cm. All areas of water. Very common.) Perhaps not well named for purposes of identification, this mottled brown duck is the one best known and most commonly seen. It inhabits ponds in parks and gardens as well as waters in the wild. It is quite difficult to approach in the latter zones. (*G. Churchett*)

Bottom:
Grey teal, *Anas gibberifrons*. (45 cm. Fresh or brackish water areas. Very common.) These pretty little ducks breed over most of Australia, except in the dry centre. They float high in the water. When disturbed, the flock will take to the wing, twisting and turning in the air, the white on the wing distinguishing them from the Black duck. (*F. Lewitzka*)

Top:
Chestnut teal, *Anas castanea*. (50 cm. Fresh and brackish waters. Common in few areas.) Similar in behaviour to the Grey teal, and sometimes a few of these are seen in a flock of Greys. Its main stronghold is Tas. Observers studying the bird report that it adapts well to breeding in nest-boxes. *(L. Robinson)*

Centre:
Mallard, *Anas platyrhynchos*. (55–60 cm. Parks and garden pools. Uncommon.) This duck has been introduced into Australia, fortunately in small numbers only, as it could breed freely and easily upset the natural balance among the native duck population. The domestic duck species, the Rouen, is a descendant. *(B. Lovell)*

Bottom:
Shoveler, *Anas rhynchotis*. (50 cm. Inland and coastal swamps. Rare.) Also called Blue-winged shoveler. The long bill, broadening at the extremity, is an additional identification. It seems that these birds have never been seen in great numbers, and they have been fairly easy victims for predators, especially foxes. They nest on the ground and eat both vegetation and small water life. *(G. Chapman)*

Left:
Pink-eared duck, *Malacorhynchus membranaceus*. (40 cm. Inland waters, preferably shallows. Common.) This unique bird, interesting in appearance, is native to Australia. It is subject to large variations in number from season to season. The brooding duck will cover her eggs with down before leaving the nest, completely hiding them. *(M. Bonnin)*

Centre:
Green pygmy goose, *Nettapus pulchellus*. (35 cm. Deep lily lagoons. Common in limited area.) These pretty little birds belong only to the tropical areas and their sighting in the wild is a rewarding experience for the enthusiast. These are essentially birds of the water, rarely coming to the land, and "graze" on surface plant growth or sometimes dive for underwater vegetation. *(F. Lewitzka)*

Bottom:
White pygmy goose, *Nettapus coromandelianus*. (37 cm. Deep tropical lagoons. Fairly common in limited area.) These are confined almost solely to Qld and only limited research has been conducted on their behaviour and breeding practices. Like the Green pygmy goose, they are water lovers, and feeding habits are similar, although apparently they do not dive. *(J. Gould)*

Top left:
White-eyed duck, *Aythya australis.* (50 cm. Deep lakes and swamps. Uncommon.) The white eye is seen only in the male. Also called Hardhead. Its popularity as a game bird, together with habitat destruction, present severe threats to this bird's continued existence. It is an excellent diver, and mainly vegetarian. *(H. Frauca)*

Top right:
Wood duck, *Chenonetta jubata.* (48 cm. Water margins, grasslands. Common.) Also called Maned goose, its bill and long neck and legs being "goose-like" features. This attractive and unique native bird often delights the slower-driving tourist, as the ducks' heads are seen above the banks of dams or roadside pools, especially in wet seasons. They are not shy, and will stand fairly close inspection. *(J. Oxer)*

Centre:
Musk duck, *Biziura lobata.* (Male 65 cm, female 55 cm. Swamps, lakes, rivers. Fairly common.) An unknowing observer, seeing these birds from a bank, will wonder whether he is witnessing the antics of a vigorous turtle or something prehistoric, as they splash on or just below the surface. At other times they will float on the surface in their very distinctive posture, the male's lobe clearly visible. *(F. Lewitzka)*

Bottom:
Blue-billed duck, *Oxyura australis.* (40 cm. Swamps, lakes. Common in limited area.) This is one of the genus of stiff-tailed ducks, so called because the tail feathers are hard and spiny. They are difficult to observe, hiding in thick water vegetation in summer, retreating well into the centres of large lakes in winter. When diving, they frequently remain submerged for long periods. *(G. Chapman)*

HAWKS AND EAGLES ACCIPITRIDAE

Those who travel around the Australian countryside for pleasure or of necessity, will know that the land is rich in birds of the hawk and eagle family. The study and identification of these birds can become a fascinating pursuit. They have a range of characteristics, habits, and plumage patterns which makes each species individual.

Generally speaking, the hawks and eagles may be distinguished from falcons by the hunting methods they adopt. The birds in the first family will fly slowly around for long sessions, keeping a sharp look-out for prey beneath them. And though there are some capable hunters among them, mostly they like to take their food the easy way. Of course, nothing could come easier than something that is already dead, the food of the carrion-eaters. However, these birds of peculiar tastes serve a most useful purpose, clearing away what otherwise would despoil the environment.

Even the Wedge-tailed eagle is not the aggressive and fearsome hunter that many might think he is. The bird's scientific name is *Aquila audax*, which means "bold eagle". He is big and mighty and majestic, but he is hardly bold. Usually the Wedge-tailed will not defend his nest, or eyrie, against man. Research teams report that when they climb a tree to the nest, the birds fly away, leaving the young or eggs.

Nevertheless it is a bird to watch and admire. It is the fourth largest eagle in the world, two sea-eagles and the Monkey-eating eagle in the Philippines exceeding it in size. A Wedge-tailed specimen in Tasmania had an officially measured wing-span of 2·85 m. The bird's size and the fierce look in the eye no doubt account for its reputation, more than for its behaviour.

An interesting feature in many species of this family is the slowness of juvenile birds to change their plumage to that of the adult. The youngsters are often quite different in appearance and, because they reach adult size quickly, it is possible to sight two birds of the one species showing entirely different colours.

Most birds in this family lay surprisingly small eggs. The Collared sparrowhawk lays an egg measuring 38 mm, while the largest egg from the family is that of the White-breasted sea-eagle, measuring about 80 mm.

Crested hawk, *Aviceda subcristata*. (40 cm. Thick forests. Uncommon.) It is found only in coastal areas, mainly north-eastern. It flies silently and ghost-like through forest trees, ascends to great heights and soars, and indulges in aerobatics. Among the trees it is a target for worrying tactics of smaller birds. (*H. Frauca*)

Top:
Black-shouldered kite, *Elanus notatus*. (35 cm. Open country. Fairly common.) This bird likes to hover, often moving up and down over a pin-pointed area. It sits in roadside trees, where its white plumage attracts attention. Sometimes calls like a Silver gull, which could confuse it with this bird, though not if seen closely. *(H. Frauca)*

Bottom:
Letter-winged kite, *Elanus scriptus*. (35 cm. Open country. Uncommon.) The letter, to the imaginative, is "M" or "W", and is important as the mark distinguishing this species from the Black-shouldered kite. It is a valuable catcher of rats and mice, and frequently appears where these rodents are prevalent. Has a wing span of over 90 cm. *(M. Bonnin)*

Top left:
Black kite, *Milvus migrans*. (55 cm. Country areas. Common.) Also called Fork-tailed kite. These birds will assemble around offal heaps and slaughter yards, and are often on the scene at bush fires or where carrion lies. They have a constantly turning and gliding flight. A rowdy bird, often seen in flocks in large numbers. *(H. Frauca)*

Top right:
Square-tailed kite, *Lophoictinia isura*. (50 cm. Lightly timbered country. Uncommon.) The wings have a span of 1·25 m and when folded reach back beyond the long, square tail. This species has recently been seen in some areas where it was not previously sighted. It hunts small birds, often taking nestlings. *(F. Lewitzka)*

Bottom:
Black-breasted buzzard, *Hamirostra melanosternon*. (55 cm. Light and open timbered country. Rare.) This bird is not usually found in the south. As with many birds of prey, the female is slightly larger than the male, otherwise the sexes are alike in appearance. Its name is perhaps unfortunate, as technically there are no true buzzards in Australia.
(P. Trusler)

Top:
Spotted harrier, *Circus assimilis.* (50 cm. Paddocks, open country. Uncommon.) This species will glide over and about fields and crops, carefully examining the ground below for prey, which could be small birds and mammals, including rabbits. Sometimes seen in the company of the Swamp harrier, and the two easily could be confused. *(F. Lewitzka)*

Bottom left:
Red goshawk, *Erythrotriorchis radiatus.* (50 cm. Lightly timbered areas. Rare.) This is a very efficient hunter, catching other birds as large as ducks and cockatoos, and reptiles, including snakes. It is a very fast flyer when hunting, and also soars at high altitudes. The long scientific name means a "barred or streaked red bird of prey". *(J. Gould)*

Bottom right:
Swamp harrier, *Circus approximans.* (50–55 cm. Swamps, meadows. Common.) Unlike the Spotted harrier, it nests on the ground or in marshes. It likes to be near water and its diet sometimes includes small water birds. It will scream loudly as it attacks prey, probably as a "scaring" aid to hunting. *(W. Taylor)*

Top left:
Brown goshawk, *Accipiter fasciatus*. (Male 40 cm, female 55 cm. Dense bushland, preferably with water. Fairly common.) This unusual photograph shows a Brown goshawk devouring prey—hence the eye is seen between the legs of the bird. In this species there is an extreme difference in size between male and female, and great care should be taken in identification. *(A. Wells)*

Top right:
Collared sparrowhawk, *Accipiter cirrhocephalus*. (Male 33 cm, female 40 cm. Dense bushland, preferably with water. Fairly common.) These birds, like the Brown goshawks, hunt by swooping or pouncing on the prey from a hidden point, the catch usually being smaller birds, which may be caught on the wing, and rodents. They nest high off the ground. *(C. Gill)*

Bottom:
Grey (white) goshawk, *Accipiter novaehollandiae*. (Male 40 cm, female 50 cm. Forests, mainly coastal. Fairly common.) Previously there were thought to be two species, but it is now recognised that the bird may be either grey or white, inter-breeding or locality affecting the plumage colour. The white bird in flight can be mistaken for a White cockatoo. *(E. McNamara)*

Top:
Wedge-tailed eagle, *Aquila audax*. (1 m. Country areas. Common.) This noble bird, Australia's largest bird of prey, has been endangered in many places because of fears by graziers that it would kill numbers of lambs. Now it is at last coming to be regarded as a farmer's friend, accounting for large numbers of rabbits. They soar majestically over country and mountains, usually in pairs. *(R. Dorin)*

Bottom:
Little eagle, *Hieraaetus morphnoides*. (45 cm. Forested areas. Fairly common.) This bird is found throughout Australia, except in Tas. and some eastern coastal areas. It flies slowly, and is often attacked by other birds, notably crows. Looks like a smaller edition of the Wedge-tailed eagle, including such features as the fingers in the wings and the "trousers" on the legs. *(E. Bound)*

OSPREYS PANDIONIDAE

The osprey, famous for its fishing skills, is also known as the Fish hawk. It is well equipped for this task, with stout, powerful legs, and sharply-hooked talons and toes, the toes having special spikes beneath them to grip and hold the most slippery of fish. One of the three front toes can be moved around to become a back toe, as with owls, allowing an even firmer hold on the prey.

The bird's catching method, after sighting a fish, is to plunge forcefully into the water, feet first, usually with a noticeable splash. The power of this plunge sometimes takes the bird right out of sight, below the surface, where if necessary it will pursue the fish. Then it will surface with the fish held in its talons, fly to a tree or suitable perch, and eat the fish—bones, scales, and all.

The osprey's flight action when taking off is heavy and laborious, but in the air it glides and soars gracefully.

The osprey builds one of the largest nests seen in Australia and these often attract attention. The original construction requires careful and patient labour, as a huge quantity of sticks and small branches are collected and put into place. The nest is built on year after year, increasing in size. It eventually may reach a height of 150 cm and can be 125 cm in diameter. It is lined with seaweed and may be built on the ground, among rocks, or in trees near to water.

The breeding period is from May to September. The incubation time is thirty-five days and the sitting is done mainly by the hen, the male bird waiting on her and bringing fish to both mother and brood. The male may be seen throwing fish to his sitting mate, who catches it ably.

After hatching, the young will stay in the nest for sixty days or more. When they feather, there is at first a soft rufous border on the back feathers and a more prominent "necklace". However, they soon assume the same plumage as adults.

Ospreys are found in most parts of the world, exceptions being South America and some Pacific islands. The race found in Australia extends to New Guinea, the Moluccas, and the Philippines. It is seen right around the Australian coastline, though rare in Victorian waters. Its favourite haunts are off-shore islands. Occasionally it will fish in suitable fresh-water lakes and rivers, though inland sightings in Australia have been rare.

Osprey, *Pandion haliaetus*. (55 cm. Coasts. Fairly common.) The wingspan measures 1·75 m. Occasionally this skilled fish-catcher is too ambitious in attacking a large fish. It will spear a fish too heavy for it to lift and, firmly hooked to its prey, may be carried under water and drowned. (*T. Modra*)

FALCONS FALCONIDAE

The birds of the falcon family are magnificently made for their main forte, attacking and catching other birds and ground prey. In most cases, they attack their prey in the air, swooping on it at tremendous speed, then grasping it in their talons or striking it with a toe or claws, returning to recover it.

Their speed, killing efficiency, and flight movements combine to make one of nature's masterpieces.

The Nankeen kestrel and Brown falcon employ methods different from these. The Nankeen kestrel will either sight its prey from a perch or will hover over a spot until something is seen. It will continue to hover, wings barely moving, gradually drifting downwards, lower and lower. Suddenly it will drop to quickly pick up its meal.

The Brown falcon does not hover as much or as efficiently, but will soar at a height, looking down for prey, then swoop in for the catch, gaining great speed as it nears the ground. It has a range of harsh and screaming sounds and is a rowdy hunter.

There are thirty-seven species of falcons throughout the world, six of which are seen in Australia. Of these, two species, the Black falcon and the Grey falcon are native, while the Little falcon is also thought to be a distinct Australian species.

The birds of this family avoid nest building when they can and are happy to find a home that somebody else has built and vacated. Deserted ravens' nests are a popular choice, while some falcons are not above chasing out smaller birds in a nest still occupied. If building becomes necessary, it is done with a minimum amount of labour and material, usually sticks. Apart from the Nankeen kestrel, which will lay up to five eggs, the clutch varies from two to four.

As hunters, they are brave and bold, often attacking and killing birds bigger than themselves. They are much feared by other birds and many, varied alarms are sounded when a falcon is sighted. Some species of ducks and parrots particularly are wary of attack and will keep to cover for long periods if they suspect a falcon to be in the vicinity.

The skill of these birds has been exploited, over the years, in the sport of falconry. Possibly the Chinese were the first people to train falcons. In medieval Europe it was a popular and traditional sport, custom demanding that kings used the efficient Peregrine falcons, while common people had to content themselves with sparrowhawks.

Today falconry is still practised in some quarters, with the Peregrine falcon continuing to be regarded as the master hunter. In Australia there are a few followers of the sport and several varieties of birds of prey are used.

As with hawks, careful attention to detail is recommended when observing falcons. Quite a few of them, at a distance or at first look, are easily confused with other birds. The Black falcon, for example, might easily be confused with a crow, especially if seen flying against the wind.

Nankeen kestrel, *Falco cenchroides* (female). (Male 30 cm, female 35 cm. Open country. Very common.) Also frequently called simply Kestrel. It is often seen sitting on posts or roadside telephone wires, but will not stay for a close inspection. When seen below while hovering, appears to be an all white bird and the beautiful brown needs to be seen for identification. *(F. Lewitzka)*

Top:
Brown falcon, *Falco berigora*. (45 cm. Open country. Common.) Also called Brown hawk. The *berigora* is said to be an Aboriginal name for the bird. Its prey includes small animals and reptiles, smaller birds caught while perching or taken from the nest, and insects. This example has had its wings clipped. *(E. Bound)*

Bottom left:
Black falcon, *Falco subniger*. (50 cm. Open country. Fairly common.) Like other birds of prey, occasionally is seen in numbers in a particular area. An example was the abundance of these birds in Vic. in 1952. It preys on the quail, the presence of which could possibly determine this falcon's movements. It is not seen in Tas. *(J. Gould)*

Bottom right:
Grey falcon, *Falco hypoleucos*. (Male 35 cm, female 45 cm. Inland country. Uncommon.) It is most frequently seen in the vicinity of water. It is regarded as one of the rarer falcons, although it could be significant that at places like national parks where experienced observers are in attendance, a number of sightings have been reported. It is not seen in Tas. *(J. Gould)*

Top:
Little falcon, *Falco longipennis.* (Male 30 cm, female 35 cm. Open country. Fairly common.) Often mis-called Sparrowhawk. This is the bravest, strongest, and most skilful of the smaller falcons and hawks, its efficiency for its size matching that of the Peregrine falcon. The plumage varies according to the locality, birds in dry areas being paler. *(T. Pescott)*

Bottom:
Peregrine falcon, *Falco peregrinus.* (Male 35 cm, female 50 cm. Mainly rugged country. Uncommon.) This most efficient hunter is found in varied races throughout the world. It has a preference for rocky country rather than the open plains. It is the fastest of all the falcons and reaches a speed of 280 km/h when swooping. A noble bird, it perches in a very upright position. *(R. Good)*

MOUNDBIRDS MEGAPODIIDAE

Some of the first European men to tread Australian soil, on coming across large mounds in the bush, thought they had found a type of Aboriginal grave. They consulted the Aborigines for further information and took a lot of convincing that what they had found was a bird nest.

These remarkable constructions are made to hold the eggs and to provide the necessary heat for hatching. Poultrymen, or those engaged in hatchery operations, know the importance attached to the maintenance of the correct temperature in an incubator. In a mound, the temperature is regularly tested by the birds themselves and, if not perfectly right, steps are taken to adjust it.

The bird tests the temperature by prodding its beak well into the mound, a sensitive spot in or near the beak instinctively telling it whether the temperature is correct. Necessary adjustments are made by scratching away or adding to the earth and mound material covering the eggs.

Of the thirteen species of mound-building birds, all of which are confined to the Australian continent and islands to its north, only three species are found on the mainland. These vary in size, appearance, and habit.

The mounds vary in size and are built up from year to year. An average Mallee fowl mound would measure 4·5 m in diameter and would be approximately 1 m high.

The egg is laid in a scraped-out cavity prepared by the male. The egg is large and its laying, observers report, is an exhausting task for the hen. Immediately the egg is laid it is covered with mound material by the male. The average number of eggs laid in a season is about twenty, counts normally varying from fifteen to twenty-four.

Although care is instinctively devoted to the eggs by the birds, there the parental responsibilities finish. The young are left to take care of themselves, scratching their way out of the mound on hatching. As usual in the bird world, the size of the egg is related to the advancement of the chick at time of hatching. Mallee fowl chicks are well feathered instead of being fluffy, and are able to fend for themselves from the first day.

Scrub fowl, *Megapodius freycinet.* (40 cm. Tropical rain forests and coastal zones. Fairly common in restricted area.) The incubating mounds near the sea are comprised of sand, shells, and seaweed, while those of the inland forests are comprised of earth and rotted vegetation. This species bears some resemblance to ordinary domestic poultry. *(J. Gould)*

Top:
Brush turkey, *Alectura lathami*. (70 cm. Rain forest, jungle. Numbers appear to be declining in its limited area.) Its existence is threatened by destruction of habitat and by guns. Like other megapodes, it is not adept at flying, although it roosts in trees at nights. These birds are seen in some sanctuaries, where their colouring and their mound-building talents make them popular attractions. *(L. Robinson)*

Centre and bottom:
Mallee fowl, *Leipoa ocellata*. (60 cm. Mallee country. Uncommon, and in limited area.) The attractive colouring blends well with the usually dry, red ground of the mallee country. Material used in the mound construction includes leaves, twigs, bark, and sand. At some mounds, individual birds, especially males, become friendly to regular visitors. In every mallee fowl habitat, foxes are a worrying enemy. *(Bird, J. Burt; mound, H. Wright)*

PHEASANTS AND QUAILS PHASIANIDAE

This large, almost world-wide family of well over 150 species, includes pheasants, partridges, and quails. Surprisingly, Australia has no native pheasants or partridges and, apart from introduced species, quails are the only members of the family represented.

Introduced species of this family include the common domestic fowl, descended from the wild jungle fowls of Asia. An inspection of the birds at a poultry show demonstrates that the hand of man has joined with nature in exploiting the producing potential of these birds.

They have been bred over the years to produce large numbers of eggs and to provide a meat treat for dinner tables, and have made an enormous contribution to world agriculture.

Of course, this has meant that the ability to take care of themselves in a natural environment has been bred out of fowls, and there are few accounts of released poultry surviving for any time in the wild on the Australian mainland.

Pheasants and peafowls manage to survive in some places under natural conditions. Pheasants are regarded as a table delicacy, although some people feel it is a sad thing to kill so pretty a bird to satisfy a gourmet, which is perhaps why the bird's feathers often accompany it to the table.

The quails of this family are the "true" quails, possessing four toes. They are attractive birds, small and plump, with very short tails and rounded wings. Of the three species of native quails listed, the Stubble quail is unique to Australia.

These birds are very nomadic and will disappear from an area during dry periods, then suddenly be present again in great numbers following good rains and the subsequent growth of lush grass.

Usually quails are seen only when flying, which they do with a characteristic, close-to-the-ground action, most often accompanied by a whirring of wings. Although they usually choose to fly only in short bursts, they are well capable of long, migratory flights.

Quail, because of their plumpness and tasty flesh, plus their elusiveness, are highly regarded as a game bird, which in turn restricts their numbers.

Stubble quail, *Coturnix pectoralis* (female). (15–18 cm. Pastures, grassland, stubble. Fairly common.) Early Australian ornithologists, while appreciating the tasty flesh of the bird, pointed out the numbers of insect pests found in the crops of shot quail, and made a strong case for their protection. They nest on the ground in high grass and lay up to 10 eggs. *(I. McCann)*

Top:
Brown quail, *Coturnix ypsilophorus.* (15–20 cm. Grassland, swamp areas. Fairly common.) There are reports that this species is not as plentiful as it was a decade or two ago. The nest on the ground often has longer grass bent over to form a roof. All of the true quails are uncommon in central Australia. *(H. Frauca)*

Centre:
King quail, *Coturnix chinensis* (female). (12 cm. Swampy grasslands. Fairly common in limited area.) The *chinensis* refers to China, one of the countries to which this species or its near relatives extend. Because of its habits, it is a bird rarely seen. Reports say it is hard to flush and that it flies silently. *(H. Frauca)*

Bottom:
Californian quail, *Lophortyx californicus* (male). (25 cm. Islands, limited areas on southern coast. Uncommon.) An introduced species from the U.S.A. The decorative head feather is peculiar to this game bird. In Australia, it is seen mainly on King Island, in Bass Strait. *(T. Pescott)*

Top:
Ring-necked pheasant, *Phasianus colchicus* (male). (75 cm. Restricted to some southern coastal areas.) An introduced species, apparently able to survive under some Australian conditions. In other countries these are cultivated on special farms and then released for hunters. In Australia, it is proving an elusive game bird. *(F. Lewitzka)*

Bottom:
Peafowl, *Pavo cristatus* (male). (75 cm. A few bush areas. Rare.) An introduced species, breeding wild on Rottnest Island, W.A. These birds are well known as ornamental attractions in parks and gardens. The males display gorgeous feathers with tails up to 1 m long. A danger period is moulting time, when they lose much of their plumage. The regrowing of the feathers saps the bird's vitality and often they do not survive this period. *(F. Lewitzka)*

BUTTONQUAILS AND PLAIN WANDERERS

TURNICIDAE AND PEDIONOMIDAE

Buttonquails have much in common with true quails and often are difficult to distinguish from them. The most important physical distinction is that buttonquails have only three toes, compared with the true quail's four. In buttonquails the small hind toe is absent.

Of course this immediately raises the point that a bird's feet are often hardly visible to the observer, especially when the bird is in the air or settled some distance away, so admittedly we are dealing with a family whose identification can present problems and doubts.

There is a close similarity between the two quail families. Their looks, behaviour patterns, and often their habitats are similar, and frequently members of the two families are seen together.

A major peculiarity of the buttonquail family is the reversal of sexual roles. This is not a new liberation movement on the part of the females, and it is more extreme than might be imagined. Apart from the actual mating position and the laying of eggs, every sex and parental act normally performed by male and female is reversed.

The female makes the courtship advances, then she will fight for territorial and other rights. The male sits on the eggs through the incubation period, and he is left to raise the young, while the female might go off like a gay young blade and find herself a new mate. Then the whole courtship procedure and breeding programme is repeated, a new family started on the way and once again the male is left holding the babies.

Another bird similar to the buttonquails is the very interesting little Plain wanderer. It has become rare and fears are held for its survival. Its loss to Australia would be a tragedy.

These have the small hind toe like true quails, but share the practice of buttonquails in reversing sexual roles. Plain wanderers live in the open plains of the semi-dry inland country. When disturbed or suspicious of an intruder, they have the interesting habit of standing right up on their toes and fairly long legs to inspect the surrounding territory. They possess 180-degree vision in each eye, so one look immediately takes in everything around them.

This bird will always run in preference to flying, and will take to the wing only as a last resort. It runs on its toes, then will stop to make a further inspection.

It will be noticed that, in naming birds of the buttonquail family, the word "button" is dropped, hence we see simply Painted quail, and so forth.

Red-backed quail, *Turnix maculosa*. (13–15 cm, female larger. Wet, grassed areas and pastures. Uncommon.) Like some other species, is elusive and rarely seen, particularly as it occupies a limited local area. It has the habit of bending and binding long grass to roof its ground nest. Its voice has been described as a repeated "oom-oom-oom".
(F. Lewitzka)

Top:
Red-chested quail, *Turnix pyrrothorax*. (13–15 cm. Grasslands. Rare.) It has the same nesting habits as the Red-backed quail. Many birds remove the egg shells from their nests after the young have hatched to help hide the nest. Some quails leave the shell but remove the young to a new site. Because of its elusiveness, observation of this bird has been limited. *(F. Lewitzka)*

Centre:
Black-breasted quail, *Turnix melanogaster*. (18 cm, female larger. Grassland in cleared rain forest areas. Rare.) John Gould named these birds *melanogaster*, meaning "black-bellied", from specimens he obtained, as he was never able to observe them in their natural state. They develop and learn to fly very quickly and are able to breed at 4 to 5 months. *(J. Gould)*

Bottom:
Painted quail, *Turnix varia* (male). (20 cm. Cleared forest, sandy areas. Fairly common.) This bird is expert at performing the "broken-wing" act to lead intruders away from its nest or brood. It is a valuable consumer of insect pests. Lays 4 eggs, its breeding season varying according to conditions. *(M. Seyfort)*

Top left:
Buff-breasted quail, *Turnix olivii*. (18 cm, female larger. Rugged tropical areas. Fairly common in very small area.) It is thought to be a local species, closely related to others found near by. Its haunts are in the extreme north-east and its scientific name is after a naturalist of Cooktown, Qld. *(G. Mathews)*

Top right:
Chestnut-backed quail, *Turnix castanota*. (16 cm, female larger. Tropical forests. Common in limited range.) Similar in appearance and movement to Painted quail and Chestnut-backed quail, but the territories of these species do not overlap. Usually seen in flocks of a score or more. Its zone is in the N.T. and the far north of W.A. *(J. Gould)*

Above:
Little quail, *Turnix velox*. (13–14 cm. Open fields. Fairly common.) In this little bird there are slight differences in appearance between the sexes and again the size favours the female. Lays 4 eggs in a ground nest, at a time to suit local conditions. Often emits a loud call at night, and gives a squeaky sound when flushed. *(A. Olney)*

Right:
Plain wanderer, *Pedionomus torquatus* (female). (15 cm. Grassed, dry inland plains. Very rare.) The reversal of the sexual roles is emphasised here by the female being not only the larger, but the more colourful of the pair. Their appearance likens them to "bantam" bustards. Because of its shyness and alertness, and of course its low numbers, it is seldom seen. *(F. Lewitzka)*

80

CRANES GRUIDAE

In the Dreamtime, according to Aboriginal legend, there lived a beautiful girl named Bralgah, who loved to dance. All day long she would whirl around, arms outstretched, legs skipping or kicking sideways as she fluttered about, always lovely and graceful. All day long she danced, and her tasks were never done.

Because of this neglect of important things, as happened to others in the stories from the Dreamtime, one day Bralgah was turned into a bird. But even as a bird, she was still tall and graceful and beautiful, and she still danced.

From the story of Bralgah came the name Brolga, the bird that dances.

This big grey bird, Australia's only native crane, certainly left its mark on Aboriginal life and culture, so that early settlers gave it another name, Native companion.

The Brolga's dancing influenced the choreography of a number of corroborees which have been closely observed by interested Europeans, who noticed that even the dress and make-up of the dancers imitated the big colourful bird.

The Brolga, like all members of the crane family, is a graceful bird. It is equipped with long legs and neck, and a long, sharp bill. It has a small back toe placed just above the joining point of the three front toes. It can sleep on one leg, perfectly balanced, its head tucked under a wing.

When about to fly, it has to run, with a peculiar bouncing gait, to gain speed before taking-off, but once in the air it is an efficient, strong flyer, attaining great heights and covering long distances.

In spite of its place in Aboriginal culture and its earlier greater numbers, it is not the typical Australian bird that some might think. It is, in fact, closely related to cranes from other parts of the world, and an Asian species, the Sarus crane, is also found in Australia. The Sarus crane has been acknowledged as a resident species only in recent years. Perhaps the reason there have not been earlier reports of it is because of its close similarity to the Brolga.

There is no noticeable physical difference between the sexes of the Brolga, except that the female is slightly smaller. Both parents assist in incubation and in the rearing of the young, which are able to leave the nest soon after hatching. Two eggs are laid, off-white in colour, with brown markings, each about 10 cm long.

Bottom left:
Sarus crane, *Grus antigone*. (1·2 m. Near water. Rare, and in limited zone.) The slight variation in plumage and the leg colouring are the only noticeable differences from the Brolga. When flying, feet and legs are extended and the motions of the wings are powerful and rhythmic. Its main call, like the Brolga's, is a discordant trumpeting. *(F. Lewitzka)*

Bottom right:
Brolga, *Grus rubicunda*. (1·2 m. Beside marshes, ponds. Common in limited area, rare elsewhere.) It is seen in large flocks in northern Australia, but nests and breeds in pairs. It stands over 1 m in height, with a wingspan of 2 m. A chance roadside view of the dance of the brolgas is an unforgettable experience. *(K. Stepnell)*

RAILS AND CRAKES RALLIDAE

A number of the birds in the family of rails and crakes are more likely to be heard than seen, and therefore their cries and calls become significant. In the field, the various calls are regarded as distinguishing characteristics, and the birds often co-operate in their identification, their rowdy voices turned on to full volume.

All of these birds, five species of which are found only in Australia, have close relatives in other countries, for this family is represented almost the world over. Because food and living conditions in swamps, the habitats of these birds, varies little anywhere, the birds themselves are similar in build and appearance, and in voice and habit. Some of the more sociable species, such as the Coot, are seen in parks and gardens.

Birds of this family do not resort to flying if they can help it, and when in the air appear out of their element, legs dangling, flight laboured. Yet they must have some flying ability because obviously they make long, migratory flights by night.

The feet are not webbed but are equipped with long, strong toes, perfect for the birds to tread the surface growth of swamp weeds and water grasses. The tails are short and often flick busily. All members of the family have powerful legs, some swim strongly, and a few dive for food. The wings are short and round.

Generally the plumage is dull and quietly coloured, but often enlivened with small, bright patches. The birds vary in size from small to medium, and in shape are hen-like.

The interesting Black-tailed native-hen, more like a bantam than an ordinary fowl, has the reputation of appearing suddenly in large numbers at places where it has rarely been seen before. There are accounts of an occasion in the 1840s when these birds took over the streets and gardens of Adelaide, walking around in thousands and doing extensive damage. It seems that they disappeared as suddenly as they had come. There are also records of their raiding Geraldton, Western Australia, and of a mass appearance in Perth in 1886. More recently, in 1972, they were seen in great numbers in parts of the Eyre Peninsula.

Lewin water-rail, *Rallus pectoralis*. (20 cm. Swamps, reedy areas. Uncommon.) The slender bill is 3 cm long. Occurs in eastern and south-eastern coastal areas. Its voice, changing to meet circumstances, has been variously described as resembling the grunt of a pig, the croak of a frog, and the purring of a cat. (*T. Pescott*)

Top:
Banded rail, *Rallus philippensis*. (30 cm. Swamps, water margins. Common in limited area.) There is variety of colour and size within the species, although sexes are alike. It has three distinct calls to meet varying circumstances, including a "crake" alarm call, and nests on grass in a sheltered spot, with 5 or 6 eggs. *(J. Ferrero)*

Bottom left:
Red-necked rail, *Rallina tricolor*. (30 cm. Swamps, water-courses in tropical forest areas. Fairly common.) Vocal range includes loud shrieks, a staccato "tok-tok-tok", and a more tuneful, repeated sound. Very timid and difficult to get near. Believed to pair off for breeding season and is seen alone at other times. *(J. Gould)*

Bottom right:
Chestnut rail, *Eulabeornis castaneoventris*. (45 cm. Mangrove swamps. Fairly common in small range.) The long scientific name means "a cautious bird with a chestnut belly". Its range is along the centre of the north coast. It nests low in the mangroves and lays 4 eggs. Its voice is described as a raucous and continued trumpeting. *(P. Trusler)*

Top left:
Marsh crake, *Porzana pusilla.* (15 cm. Swamps. Fairly common.) This bird will dive for its food, including water life, insects, and submerged plants. Has a typical raucous "crake" call and a rapid, unpleasant trill. Nests on ground or on water tussock, laying 4 to 6 eggs. *(F. Lewitzka)*

Top Right:
Spotted crake, *Porzana fluminea.* (18 cm. Swamps. Fairly common.) This crake swims well and appears to fly more easily than others, but is typically shy. It has a sharp "crake" call. The nest is near water's edge, often with visible track leading to it, and has 4 or 5 stone-coloured, spotted eggs. The sexes are alike. *(J. Hannant)*

Centre:
Spotless crake, *Porzana tabuensis.* (18 cm. Swamps, small coastal islands. Rare.) Has a "crake-crake" call and a high-pitched individual shriek. Has been observed at unusual spots about Australia, with possibly main concentration in Tas. This is a local representative of a race found mainly in islands north of Australia. *(T. Pescott)*

Bottom:
White-browed crake, *Porzana cinerea.* (18 cm. Mangrove swamps. Fairly common in small range.) Has been seen climbing swamp trees apparently in preference to flying. Vocal range includes individual version of "crake-crake" call, with crying and purring noises. Usually lays 4 eggs, off-white, spotted. Its zone is along the extreme north-east and northern coastline. *(J. Gould)*

Top:
Bush-hen, *Gallinula olivacea*. (25 cm. Swamps, rain forests. Rare.) This bird is shy and watchful and rarely sighted. Occasionally its sharp, repeated call will give away its presence. It builds a rough nest of grass and reeds, lined with moss to receive its 4 to 7 spotted and colourful eggs. *(J. Gould)*

Centre:
Black-tailed native-hen, *Gallinula ventralis*. (35 cm. Swamps, water margins, grasslands. Common, but varying in territories.) Its voice is a harsh cackle and a loud "cark". Nests on ground, 5 to 7 dark green spotted eggs. Aboriginals in some southern tribes who had not seen them before they appeared in great numbers last century, were convinced they were birds brought by the white man. *(T. Pescott)*

Bottom:
Tasmanian native-hen, *Gallinula mortierii*. (45 cm. Swamps, water margins. Fairly common.) Found only in Tas. where it replaces the Black-tailed native-hen. The biggest bird in the family, and flightless. It has a raucous call and a quieter grunt. Can run at a good speed and is said to dive into running water and walk on the bottom against the current. *(R. Good)*

Top:
Dusky moorhen, *Gallinula tenebrosa*. (35 cm. Swamps. Common.) Dives for food, which will include water vegetation, insects, frogs. An "in-between" bird, more timid than Coots but tamer than Swamphens. Often seen with other water birds. The call is a loud, sharp "cark". It often raises 2 clutches of young in a season. *(T. Kendall)*

Centre:
Coot, *Fulica atra*. (40 cm. Open waters. Common.) Its main call is similar to that of the Dusky moorhen, but has a more extensive repertoire. It will dive for its food and is a good swimmer and flyer. Has a habit of jerking its head while swimming. Large numbers will arrive on a sheet of water at night. Builds a large, open nest in reeds or on a low bush, lays 7 to 10 whitish, spotted eggs. *(L. Sourry)*

Bottom:
Swamphen, *Gallinula porphyrio* (foreground). (45 cm. Swamps, wet areas. Fairly-common.) The breast colour is sky-blue in W.A., purple in the eastern regions. Has a typical loud, resounding call or shriek. Swamphens have an interesting feeding practice, using a foot as a hand, holding food firmly between the toes, like a cockatoo. *(E. Bound)*

BUSTARDS OTIDIDAE

The Bustard, or Wild turkey, or Plain turkey, once roamed the continent in large numbers. Today it is unknown in many places which were its haunts, while in other parts it is rare. What brought about this decline in numbers?

First of all the bustard, in a way, is its own worst enemy. It is a big-bodied bird, all meat, and meat which is tender and tasty, and from the time of settlement, it was shot and hunted in great numbers, and the gun has accounted for the decrease in the bird's population as much as any other single factor. A second reason, and another important one, was havoc wrought to the bird by the introduced fox, which roamed many of the same areas.

Another reason, which still applies, is that the territory which the bird ranges is wide and expansive, so that it is most difficult to police the laws made for its protection.

A final consideration is the bustard's limited reproductive capacity. In its annual breeding period, it lays at the most two eggs, sometimes only one. This is laid under open, sometimes harsh conditions, and the egg or chick has to survive against a number of enemies.

Its interesting characteristics include the stout, strong bill, usually pointed slightly upwards. When the bird is flying, the longish neck and legs are extended and its action, though slow, is strong and rhythmic.

The bustard is well camouflaged and observers, on sighting one, often are amazed that they "did not see it before", and are left wondering how many others they may have missed.

The sexes are alike, but the female is smaller. There is an elaborate mating procedure. The male blows up two large air pouches in its neck, the tail is fanned out and thrown forward to meet the head, which tilts back over the bird's body. The wings are outstretched and held low as the bird struts around uttering a loud but not unpleasant call.

The female attends to the hatching and rearing, although the chicks are able quickly to take care of themselves.

Grasshoppers are the main item in a varied and extensive diet, which takes in small reptiles, mice, spiders, grass and vegetation, and the fruit of low-growing bushes.

Bustard, *Ardeotis australis.* (1·1 m. Grassed plains. Uncommon.) This bird is included in some governmental breeding and replacement programmes. Travellers on northern safaris observe it closely by circling it in a vehicle, coming closer as the circles grow smaller, the bird remaining still. *(L. Robinson)*

JACANAS JACANIDAE

Were one to sketch a jacana, somebody examining the result could be excused for thinking he was looking at a caricature drawn to play up the bird's feet, just as photographs of the bird seem to show the feet out of proportion. And a written account of the physical peculiarities of these birds reads like an essay in abnormalities, even though their unusual features are mostly attractive and always advantageous.

Because this bird is happiest when walking on the large leaves of lilies, which grow on or just below the water's surface, it gives the impression of having the ability to walk along on water. As lily lagoons are their habitat, their feet are formed to cope with this practice.

Although the body is small, little bigger than a common starling, the centre toe and back toe each measure 7·5 cm, giving a total foot coverage, front to back, of 15 cm. These large feet have a capacity to cover an area of 200 square cm, so the slight weight of the bird has all this area of lily leaf to support it. As well as the feet, the legs are quite long. When the bird flies, these legs trail out behind it, and are used instead of the tail for steering.

A further feature, and a very noticeable one, is the red comb or crown on top of the head, large and fleshy. This will change colour to yellow when the bird is agitated.

Even the eggs are peculiar. They have an added protection so that they can be tipped into the water without being harmed. If the eggs roll off the nest, they will float and no damage is done.

If danger threatens, the birds can pick up the eggs or the chicks, take them under their wings and remove them to safety. The jacana is the only Australian bird able to perform this act.

They can submerge and stay under water for long periods and they teach the youngsters to do this from the start. The chicks, after a time under water, will poke up their little beaks, snorkel-like, for air, and are thus able to remain submerged.

During nesting time, the parents will slip away from the nest site if suspicious of any intruders, drawing attention away from the eggs or young. They are also able to perform the "broken-wing" act efficiently to help here.

The one species in this family found in Australia is commonly called Lotusbird. It is also known as Lily-trotter and various names peculiar to a locality.

Lotusbird, *Irediparra gallinacea*. (23 cm. Lily lagoons, still water with floating plants. Fairly common in limited range.) Their general zone is the north-eastern coastline. The colourful plumage is outstanding. They have a loud, trumpeting call and a quieter squeaking. *(N. H. P. Cayley)*

PAINTED SNIPE ROSTRATULIDAE

Here we are dealing with a rare bird. Rare, in that in those parts of Australia where it might be seen, the sightings are few and years might pass before the bird shows up in a particular spot again. And rare in that there are only two species of this bird throughout the world. One of these is limited to South America and the other, to which the endemic Australian race belongs, is also found in Africa and southern Asia.

This is a bird difficult to observe and study, first because of this rarity, and because of its furtiveness, its excellent camouflage, and its silence, as it is not a bird which will readily reveal its presence by loud singing or calling.

There are only some superficial, physical resemblances between the Painted snipe and the true snipe family, and they should not be closely compared, or regarded as related.

Painted snipe have their share of unusual features, but none of these is unique. We find a reversal of sexual roles in these birds as observed in the buttonquails. In Painted snipe, this role reversal is particularly noticeable in the physical make-up. The female is not only larger, but, in this colourful and attractive species, is easily the more beautiful of the two. Her colour patterns are clearer and deeper. The wings of these birds have been described as being like butterflies.

The nests are not elaborate and sometimes the eggs are laid on bare ground. These are usually four in number, are creamy or off-white, attractively pencilled in black. The male is left on his own to incubate these and to rear the young. Later his family may unite with others to form a flock.

The flight of Painted snipe is slow and deliberate, and here again we are not looking for a snipe-like flight movement. (True snipe have a distinctive, zigzagging motion through the air.)

On the ground, the birds have a furtive, hunched stance, and a creeping movement, with the head held low and pulled back to the body. The bill is long and rounded, rather than pointed.

They are most likely to be seen, after wet periods, in marshes, swamp growth, or at other water margins. If they are found, they will fly for as short a distance as possible, keeping close to the ground, and hiding themselves again in the nearest available cover.

Painted snipe, *Rostratula benghalensis.* (25 cm. Flood areas, swamps. Uncommon.) With the long bill, they probe for their food in the mud at the water's edge. On the infrequent occasions when the bird is heard, the male chirps, while the female's call is stronger and louder, and is usually sounded at night. *(T. Lowe)*

OYSTERCATCHERS HAEMATOPODIDAE

Oystercatchers are attractive and fascinating birds most likely to be seen along quiet and deserted sandy beaches.

Bird lovers find much to interest them at the beach. Oystercatchers will be seen probing in the sand or on rocks at the water's edge. As they are approached, they will run along for a time, eventually take to the wing, circling over the sea and then returning to the shore, soon finding the way back to their original spot.

The Sooty, all-black oystercatcher may seem out of place on the beach, where most birds seen are predominantly white, like the gulls, or in some shade of buff or brown, like the camouflaged dotterels and others. Some people, seeing a Sooty oystercatcher for the first time, from a distance, believe there is a crow on the beach.

Oystercatchers in Australia are close relatives of those found in Europe, Asia, and North Africa. The Sooty oystercatcher is found only in Australia, another example, like the swan, of a bird found in paler colours in other parts of the world, yet having a black plumage in Australia.

Oystercatchers are distinctive birds, not likely to be confused with others. The outstanding feature is the long, straight red bill, flattening at the end to be chisel-shaped, a very serviceable tool for probing into the sand, for removing shellfish from rocks, and for prising open these shells. They are solidly-built birds, carried by strong legs with a little webbing on the three toes.

The nests are in small cavities simply scraped in the sand, and lined with shells or seaweed, while the eggs are camouflaged to match the colour of the sand and surrounds. The chicks take care of themselves early in life. They are hatched with black bills, which turn to yellow before changing again to the distinctive red of a mature bird.

The Pied is the more common of the two Australian species, although both kinds are sometimes seen together. The diet consists of varied sea life found among rocks and at the water's edge, including crustaceans and shellfish such as cockles and mussels. Experts have stated that the oystercatchers in Australia actually consume few, if any, oysters.

Top:
Pied oystercatcher, *Haematopus ostralegus*. (45 cm. Coastal zones, beaches. Fairly common.) The call is distinctive, a rather pathetic and penetrating piping, often sounded when the birds are on the wing. These are regarded as shore-birds rather than sea-birds and overseas have been seen feeding in inland fields. (*A. Wells*)

Bottom:
Sooty oystercatcher, *Haematopus fuliginosus*. (45 cm. Coastal zones, beaches. Uncommon.) The busy bill measures 7·5 cm. There are no noticeable differences between the sexes. Also called Black oystercatcher. Usually lays 2 eggs and the normal breeding season is from September to mid-summer. (*T. Modra*)

PLOVERS AND DOTTERELS CHARADRIIDAE

This is the first major family of the so-called waders. Members of the family include Australian and migrant breeders, and birds found both in the coastal areas and inland.

The Spurwing, Masked, and Banded plovers are not migratory birds, so they are seen in Australia at their best and brightest. Breeders which nest out of Australia usually are not seen in their gaudier plumage, but rather in the more drab colouring of the off-breeding period, although sometimes they may retain breeding plumage for short periods of their stay.

The plumage of Australia's breeding plovers, while colourful, does provide excellent camouflage, and often one is right upon the birds before being aware of their presence. The spurs on the wing, an interesting piece of equipment and an identifying guide when the bird is in hand, are difficult to observe in the field. A much better identifying feature is the distinctive bright yellow wattle, which may be picked up from some distance and is seen on all three species.

The call of the plover is well known and it is often heard "chut-chut-chutting" both by day and night, when the bird is on the wing and when it is on the ground and an intruder is sighted.

There are two species of plover which breed in the Arctic regions and migrate across the equator to Australia. A third species, the Western golden plover, is only a very rare visitor to this continent.

Among dotterels, the Black-fronted is a common inland bird, while the Red-capped is seen on the beach along many coastlines. These little beach birds are a delight to watch as they twinkle across the sand, unless there are some chicks to be protected near by, when instead of fast-moving feet you may be treated to a show of a badly-injured wing or leg. The dotterel's performance in pretending to be wounded is a masterpiece. It can make itself appear badly mauled as it leads you along the beach, off the sanded area into grass, anywhere but where the young are crouching, already well camouflaged against the sand and surrounds.

The young of the plover also put on a realistic "pretending to be dead" act, and sympathetic visitors may reach down to pick up the "poor little fellow" only to see it suddenly come to life and go streaking away.

Spurwing plover, *Vanellus novaehollandiae*. (35 cm. Wet grasslands, swamps. Common.) The spurs on the wing are a fighting and defensive equipment. The male spurs are larger than the female, and this is the only noticeable difference between the sexes. Usually lays 4 eggs in a rough nest on the ground. Sitting birds are sometimes seen from the roadside. (*M. Seyfort*)

Top left:
Banded plover, *Vanellus tricolor*. (30 cm. Poorly grassed, rough areas. Fairly common.) Lays on the ground in a lightly-lined nest. When disturbed, the birds will run quickly in short bursts, then stand perfectly still. It feeds on grasshoppers, caterpillars, other insects, and some vegetation. Its main haunts are in W.A. (*W. Taylor*)

Top right:
Masked plover, *Vanellus miles*. (35 cm. Wet grasslands, swamps. Common.) A point debated by experts is whether the two forms, the Spurwing and Masked, are indeed two separate species. In some parts of Qld, where the two kinds overlap, they interbreed. Generally the Spurwing is found in southern Australia while the Masked is found in the north. (*L. Robinson*)

Centre:
Red-kneed dotterel, *Charadrius cinctus* (female). (18 cm. Water margins, inland and coastal. Uncommon.) The genus *Charadrius*, called dotterels in Australia, are generally known as plovers in other countries. The Red-kneed has a typical quick running and sudden stopping performance, with an up-and-down head movement as it stops. It is not found in Tas. (*E. Bound*)

Bottom:
Hooded dotterel, *Charadrius cucullatus*. (20 cm. Beaches, occasional inland salt lakes. Uncommon.) This species lays its eggs in a depression in the sand, which is hardly recognisable otherwise as a nest. The 2 or 3 eggs are light brown and spotted. Its inland sightings have been mainly in W.A. A shy bird, it is quick to run or to take flight. (*G. Chapman*)

Top:
Black-fronted dotterel, *Charadrius melanops*. (15 cm. Margins of fresh or brackish inland waters. Common.) The sexes are alike in this, the most common of inland dotterels. It has sometimes been seen swimming. A particularly well-camouflaged bird, either when running or stock-still. *(I. McCann)*

Bottom:
Red-capped dotterel, *Charadrius ruficapillus* (female). (15 cm. Beaches, general. Fairly common.) Care is needed in their identification. The sexes are different and the red cap is not seen in immature birds. It has a head-bobbing action when it stops its sprinting along the sand. On the wing, it has a rapid flight, low over the water. It is often seen with other waders. *(F. Park)*

Top:
Double-banded dotterel, *Charadrius bicinctus.* (18 cm. Beaches, flat coastal areas. Fairly common in limited area.) A non-breeding visitor from New Zealand, its season in Australia is from January or February to September. Its call is a rapid, repeated "twit" and a longer trill. When feeding, its movements are slow. *(N. Chaffer)*

Centre:
Mongolian dotterel, *Charadrius mongolus.* (18 cm. Coastal regions, mud flats. Uncommon.) A non-breeding migrant from Asia. Could be confused with the Double-banded dotterel. It has a loud one-syllable call and a quieter trill. Usually in flocks, and seen mainly from September to March. *(N. Chaffer)*

Bottom left:
Oriental dotterel, *Charadrius veredus.* (25 cm. Bare flats, mud areas, mainly inland. Fairly common within limited range.) This species is bigger than the Large dotterel. The sexes are alike. It comes from Asia to share the Australian spring and summer. Usually in flocks of its kind, it has a swift, darting flight and utters a sharp call when disturbed. *(J. Gould)*

Bottom right:
Large dotterel, *Charadrius leschenaultii.* (23 cm. Coastal regions, mud flats. Fairly common.) A migrant from Asia, its Australian visit is from October to May. It has a quiet, slowly-repeated call and a louder trill. It is seen mainly along northern coastlines. The *leschenaultii* is after J. B. Leschenault (1773–1826), a prominent French naturalist. *(G. Mathews)*

Top:
Australian dotterel, *Peltohyas australis* (male). (20 cm. Semi-arid areas. Fairly common in limited range.) This pretty bird performs, in the dry, bare, or sparsely-treed inland, in much the same way as its relatives do along beaches. It retains a fondness for water and its movements may depend on local rains. It lays its eggs on the ground and will cover them with readily available material when not sitting. *(B. Lovell)*

Centre:
Grey plover, *Pluvialis squatarola.* (26 cm. Coastal. Fairly common in limited area.) A non-breeding visitor from the northern hemisphere. On its arrival in August, it has retained some of its breeding plumage, which it soon loses. It takes on the blacker under-colouring again just prior to its departure in April. *(N. Chaffer)*

Bottom:
Eastern golden plover, *Pluvialis dominica.* (25 cm. Beaches, rock outcrops, wet areas. Fairly common.) From the northern hemisphere, it is clad in some of its breeding plumage for the same limited period as the Grey plover, in whose company it is sometimes seen. It likes to feed on sand banks and mud areas on insects and small life left by receding waters. *(E. Lindgren)*

95

SANDPIPERS SCOLOPACIDAE

This is the second big family of waders. "Sandpiper" is not an Australian name, nor are the others in this family. They are mostly old-world names, charming and pleasant-sounding, like sandpiper itself, and others like whimbrel, sanderling, greenshank, and tattler.

Although these are not native Australian birds,. they at least spend their summers on the Australian continent, leaving the cold of their homes to fly, like the lucky and the wealthy, to the sunshine of another, far-away land.

In dealing with such non-breeding visitors, different and limited means of identification are required.

It is necessary therefore to attach more importance to what there is to see and to hear. The length and shape of the bill is a distinguishing feature and in all of these birds, the bills are longer than the head, and are mainly long, straight, and pointed for digging in the sand or mud, though some are curved one way or the other, at the end.

Regarding plumage, as a general rule the birds' breeding colour would be an overall rich brown, which changes to a quieter grey in the non-breeding plumage seen in Australia.

The birds vary in size from little specimens of 15 cm to the largest bird of about 50 cm, so that no member of this far-flying family is bigger than a crow.

Probably the most fascinating feature of the birds' lives goes unobserved. Only their absence is noticed, as one morning the places where yesterday they were in abundance, now are vacated. The flight away has been unseen, because they fly by night.

After leaving Australia, the birds will fly via islands north of the continent to their breeding places in Siberia in the Arctic Circle, where there will be ice and snow, but almost continual daylight. There they nest, lay their eggs, and rear their young.

Then, when the long days begin to change to long nights, they turn again and begin their flight back to Australia, some 15 000 or 16 000 km away. Unlike jet passengers, they may not sit back and rest on their flight. In fact, it seems they can have little sleep, because at their daytime stopovers, they feed rather than rest. Then as darkness comes, they are in the air again, calling to each other as they fly. And then, one morning, the people who five months ago noticed that the birds had flown, now just as suddenly see that they have come back.

Turnstone, *Arenaria interpres*. (25 cm. Coastal. Fairly common in limited area.) Some observers differ on whether this should be in the sandpiper family or the dotterel family. Its name comes from the habit of turning over pebbles and small stones with its bill. Its plumage pattern is an efficient camouflage along the shorelines. *(G. Chapman)*

Top:
Japanese snipe, *Gallinago hardwickii*. (30 cm. Swamps, flood areas, wet grasslands. Fairly common in limited area.) Nests in Japan at heights above 1250 m. Its arrival in Australia is said to annually coincide with the first full moon in August. Makes a loud "cark" when disturbed, and has a very fast and erratic zig-zagging flight. *(J. Gould)*

Bottom:
Pintailed snipe, *Gallinago megala*. (30 cm. Swamps, wet grasslands. Rare.) Like the Japanese snipe, it is not strictly a wader, as it is much more likely to be flushed from grass than to appear on sand or mud banks. It is also called Chinese or Marsh snipe. Very difficult to distinguish from the Japanese snipe. *(G. Mathews)*

Top:
Little whimbrel, *Numenius minutus*. (30 cm. Dry open grassed areas. Uncommon.) The long, down-curving bill and the pale strip in the crown are identifying points. Has a sharp alarm call and chatters when feeding. Although uncommon, sometimes may be seen in fairly large flocks, flying in strict formation, in the north. *(G. Chapman)*

Centre:
Whimbrel, *Numenius phaeopus*. (40 cm. Swamps, seashores, grass fields. Fairly common.) Its call is a high, distinct whistle, repeated a number of times. Will pick up food, rather than dig or probe for it. *Numenius* is derived from Greek words meaning "new moon", after the crescent shape of the bill. *(N. Chaffer)*

Bottom:
Eastern curlew, *Numenius madagascariensis*. (50 cm including bill of from 15 to 18 cm. Coastal areas, uncommon.) This is the largest bird in the family. Its name is from its call, which is not unlike that of the native Bush curlew of the inland. Feeds on crabs, shellfish, and grubs, probed from the sand or soft patches, with the long bill. *(G. Chapman)*

Top:
Greenshank, *Tringa nebularia.* (32 cm. Beaches, inland water margins. Fairly common.) A very shy and cautious sandpiper with a loud, shrill call. Flight is fast and direct, with the legs extended well beyond the tail. It is seen in Australia from August to April. The bill is slightly turned upwards at the end. *(T. Kendall)*

Centre left:
Marsh sandpiper, *Tringa stagnatilis.* (20 cm. Inland water margins. Uncommon.) Also called the Little greenshank. Usually seen alone or in groups of only 2 or 3. When in the air, its feet protrude well beyond the tail. Unlike the larger Greenshank, it seldom frequents beaches or coastal zones. *(D. Paton)*

Centre right:
Wood sandpiper, *Tringa glareola.* (20 cm. Swamps, river arms, water margins. Uncommon.) The bill is straight, measuring 3 cm. This bird seeks refuge in bushes and will perch on trees, stumps, or posts. Its stay in Australia is usually from August to April. Has a sharp call, repeated three times. *(M. Bonnin)*

Bottom:
Common sandpiper, *Tringa hypoleucos.* (20 cm. Rivers, creeks, running water preferably with boulders and snags. Fairly common within small area.) This species belies its name in many places, being rarely seen in Vic. and S.A. It likes to feed in the more turbulent places in moving streams, and flies low over water. *(M. Bonnin)*

Top:
Grey-tailed tattler, *Tringa brevipes.* (25 cm. Rocky beaches, pebbled shores. Fairly common in small area.) The straight bill, measuring 4 cm, is an identifying feature. The *brevipes* means "short-footed". Its zone is the more northerly coast and it is seen only rarely in the south. *(T. Kendall)*

Centre:
Wandering tattler, *Tringa incana.* (25 cm. Rocky beaches, pebbled shores. Rare.) It is almost impossible to distinguish from the Grey-tailed tattler. One difference, which can be seen only when the bird is in hand, is a nasal groove in the bill, measuring about two-thirds of the bill's length here, only half of the bill in the Grey-tailed. The flight is graceful, but fast. *(E. Whitbourn)*

Bottom:
Terek sandpiper, *Tringa cinerea.* (25 cm. Coastal flats, creeks, estuaries. Rare.) The sleek, upcurving bill measures 5 cm. Keen observers have reported rare sightings in the south, but this bird mainly frequents more northerly coastlines, usually in small groups. It is continually on the move when feeding, with a number of individual head and body motions. *(D. Paton)*

Top left:
Knot, *Calidris canutus*. (25 cm. Coastal area, mud flats, sandbanks. Rare.) This species submerges its head as well as its beak in mud when probing for food. The *canutus* is from King Canute, who rebuked his courtiers in withdrawing from the rising tide. Flies in flocks which invariably keep a close, tight formation. *(D. Paton)*

Top right:
Great knot, *Calidris tenuirostris*. (30 cm. Coastal areas, mud flats, sand banks, occasionally inland. Rare.) Like the Knot in habit and appearance, but a little larger. Its voice is said to be a whistle of two notes. The season in Australia usually extends from August to April. *(D. Paton)*

Centre:
Sharp-tailed sandpiper, *Calidris acuminata*. (20 cm. Coastal and inland mud flats and sandbanks. Common.) A fast-flying bird, usually seen in well-ordered, large flocks. Its legs do not project beyond the tail in flight. Its food, taken leisurely after receding tides or from where water has been, includes insects and worms. Its call is a sharp whistle. *(K. Woodcock)*

Bottom:
Pectoral sandpiper, *Calidris melanotos*. (18 cm. Fresh-water swamps. Rare.) Some notes in its call have been likened to those of the Budgerigar. The short, pointed tail is a distinguishing feature. Its stay in Australia extends from the spring to early autumn. *(J. Gould)*

Top:
Long-toed stint, *Calidris subminuta* (left). (14 cm. Tidal flats, inland swamps. Rare.); Red-necked stint, *Calidris ruficollis* (right). (14 cm. Tidal flats, inland swamps. Common.) The yellowish legs and feet of the Long-toed are a good guide to identification as well as the long toes—the middle toe measures 2·5 cm. Because the Red-necked is seen mainly in non-breeding plumage, the red neck is not a prominent feature. *(G. Mathews)*

Bottom:
Curlew sandpiper, *Calidris ferruginea.* (20 cm. Mainly tidal flats, some inland swamps, lakes. Common.) This bird gives a pleasing chirrup when disturbed, also uses a sharper whistle. Flight is fast and low, with the legs trailing beyond the tail. Some non-breeding birds of the species winter in Australia, otherwise departure time is in early autumn. *(N. Chaffer)*

Top:
Broad-billed sandpiper, *Limicola falcinellus.* (18 cm. Tidal flats, estuaries. Rare.) The *falcinellus* means "little scythe", referring to the long, wide, distinctively-shaped bill. This species was once considered even rarer, but now occasional sightings are recorded. *(D. Paton)*

Bottom:
Sanderling, *Crocethia alba.* (18 cm. Ocean beaches. Uncommon.) A feature of this species is that it has no hind toe. There have been rare inland sightings, but usually likes the sea beaches, where it feeds on the run, chasing the ebbing water. It has a short, shrill call. The sexes are alike.
(G. Chapman)

Top:
Bar-tailed godwit, *Limosa lapponica*. (35 cm. Tidal flats, estuaries, occasionally inland. Uncommon.) The long, slightly upturned bill is an identifying feature. The sexes are similar, with the female slightly larger. When flying, the legs extend beyond the tail. The call has been described as "kew-kew" and, when flying, "kit-kit-kit". *(M. Bonnin)*

Centre:
Black-tailed godwit, *Limosa limosa*. (35 cm. Swamps, lakes, tidal flats. Fairly common within small area.) The long, straight bill measures up to 10 cm. Godwit is an old English name, the origin of which is not known. Its main range is in the north-east, otherwise sightings are rare. Season is from August to March. *(N. Chaffer)*

Bottom:
Ruff (male) or Reeve (female), *Philomachus pugnax*. (25 cm. Inland lakes. Rare.) There have been a few sightings of this bird in the last decade. The outstanding feature of this species is in the male's behaviour in his northern hemisphere breeding zone, where he grows a large ruff or ring of neck feathers. This would not be visible in Australia, out of the breeding season, nor would the birds be heard, as they are silent when not breeding. *(D. Paton)*

PHALAROPES PHALAROPODIDAE

Imagine a bird that nests and breeds in the Arctic zone among other species of somewhat similar appearance, but is different because of its remarkable red markings, eye-catching in the whiteness of those regions, even among myriads of other birds.

And imagine that the brightest of these bright birds on display is not the male bird, like a gaudy peacock or even a barnyard bantam rooster, but instead is the lady of the partnership.

And afterwards, when the breeding season is over, and brightly-coloured plumage gives way to dull, pale, ordinary-looking feathering, and the nights get too long to live with, instinct tells the birds to take to the wing and to fly away, with the goal not necessarily far-away countries, but just the distant sea itself. Then, with thousands of kilometres behind it, the bird comes to rest at last, not on land, but on water, where it settles and sits, bobbing on the waves.

So that this bird will not feel lost or endangered, under the feathering of its breast there is additional and unusual water-proofed plumage, enabling it to continue resting on the sea, bobbing buoyantly about, feeding on the surface, quite content with its lot, whirling and spinning from time to time in its sitting position, actions that help it as it catches its food.

Even its feet are different from those of birds which otherwise look like this one, now that the plumage has paled. The feet of this bird are partly webbed, to help a little more in the image of a sitting duck. And its toes are lobed, like those of a grebe, another bird that sits for hours contentedly on the water.

Phalaropes have all those features—a colourful breeding dress, especially in the female, the reversal of sexual roles, the ability to fly the width of the world and to come to rest on the ocean.

Of course their instinctive settling on the sea's surface makes their occasional Australian sightings so much more a rare event. Certainly the few recorded visits to inland lakes would have been accidents due most likely to birds being blown off their guided course by storms.

Doubtless many bird observers feel that a new discovery of one of these birds along an Australian shore would be an exciting event. Those who have seen and reported them certainly have rendered a valuable service.

Red-necked phalarope, *Phalaropus lobatus*. (18 cm. Southern coasts. Very rare.) Bears some resemblance to the Sanderling and could be a near relative of the sandpiper family. Physical features are the long, thin, needle-like bill and the black legs. As they sit on the water, their bearing is upright, with the head held high. *(K. Carlson, Ardea)*

STILTS AND AVOCETS RECURVIROSTRIDAE

The very long legs of these birds give them undoubted identification. These legs, with other physical adaptations, make the three species found in this family very efficient feeders and waders in the true sense of the word.

In all, the sexes are alike. They all have long necks and long, sharply-pointed bills, varying in the amount of curve, and with some flexibility and sensitivity in the end, enabling them to "feel as they go", and to pick up small living things in the mud or sand.

The feet are webbed, or partly so, the wings are long and pointed, the tails short and square. All share a degree of black and white in the plumage.

The Pied stilt is also commonly called White-headed stilt and Black-winged stilt, names that can be confusing when checking references on the bird.

This species, neat and tidy in its ground activities, somehow looks awkward in the air, its long legs trailing behind its short tail as it flies.

Its breeding season may vary, but is usually August to December in southern States, January to March in the north. It lays four olive-green eggs. It feeds on water worms, shrimps, snails, and other small shellfish, and some seeds. Like the other species in the family, it has a call which is likened to the yapping of a puppy.

The Banded stilt can be identified by the absence of black about the neck. It has a distinctive chestnut colouring about the breast and abdomen, which disappears when the bird moults. It will breed and lay throughout the year, at times dictated by local and climatic conditions. It is rarely seen along the east coast.

The Avocet is distinguishable not only because of the noticeable bill, which begins to curve at about its half-way mark, but also for the red head and neck colouring. Because of this feature, it is frequently called the Red-necked avocet. The nest is a small depression in grass or mud. It lays four yellowish-grey eggs, arranging them in a circle, with the pointed end of the egg directed inwards.

Avocets bob the head when walking. While feeding, the curved bill is swayed from side to side, slashing through the mud or water, aiding the bird to cover wider areas in its search for food. It also swims well, and will up-end to feed—head down, tail up, like a duck.

Pied stilt, *Himantopus himantopus*. (38 cm. Swamps, tidal estuaries, shallows. Fairly common.) The legs of this species measure 20 cm, making it the longest-legged bird, proportionate to its body size, seen in Australia. Its movements are graceful and fastidious. It shakes off any mud that may be clinging to its feet before going to the nest. (*T. Kendall*)

Above:
Banded stilt, *Cladorhynchus leucocephalus.* (40 cm. Salt marshes, shallow lakes, brackish estuaries. Common in some areas.) The bill measures over 7 cm. Its breeding colonies were not discovered until 1930. One of these is at Lake Grace, W.A., and the few other known nesting sites are either in W.A. or S.A. *(M. Bonnin)*

Right:
Avocet, *Recurvirostra novaehollandiae.* (45 cm. Salt marshes, shallow lakes, swamps. Fairly common.) The distinguishing upturned bill measures 9 cm. It will fly in flocks, often quite large. When they utter their yapping call on the wing, there is the peculiar sensation of dogs barking in the air. They also have a trumpet-like call. *(E. Laslett)*

STONE-CURLEWS BURHINIDAE

There are two birds in this family, one a bird of the bush, the other of the beach, each named accordingly.

The Bush curlew is heard rather than seen. Heard, because of its peculiar call, loud and penetrating. Not seen often, because stone-curlews are creatures of the night, with an inborn ability to hide themselves by day.

The bird's grey plumage, streaked with black and white and tinted with varying degrees of buff or brown, is a perfect camouflage among the dead timber, sticks, bark, and dry grass that are found where it dwells.

As well as its natural camouflage, the curlew has the habit of "planting", stretching its long legs out straight and getting down to lizard level, so that it becomes identical with the ground surface.

Some people find the curlew's call eerie, or terrifying, or melancholy. Others, especially bush people, grow to love it.

The Bush curlew in years gone by made a favourite pet for some who did not have near neighbours who might be disturbed by its call. It was a most efficient destroyer of night-time garden pests. Though generally a docile and friendly pet, this is one of the most vicious of birds when defending its young in the wild.

Sometimes a curlew chick might be seen on the ground in a paddock. Should it be picked up, the interloper can expect an air attack of an intensity attained by few other birds. The parent birds will circle low and close, swishing at the intruder, so he is happy to put back the baby where he found it and to make his departure. Unfortunately for the Bush curlew, its survival has become more difficult because of encroaching civilisation upon the open country which it haunts.

The Beach curlew bears a close resemblance to its bush counterpart, and it is reported that its call is similar. It is not found in large numbers and research on it has been limited. Like its country cousin, it possesses a talent for camouflage, which, with its rarity, makes a sighting an uncommon occurrence.

The large yellow eyes are a unique feature of both species.

Left:
Bush curlew, *Burhinus magnirostris*. (50 cm. Open forest, lightly timbered areas. Fairly common, but now in limited range.) Eggs are laid on the ground, sometimes not even in a formed depression. The Aborigines, as well as telling stories of this night bird, have given it names like Willaroo and Weeloo, after the sound of its call. (*D. Mann*)

Below:
Beach curlew, *Esacus magnirostris*. (50 cm. Tropical coasts. Uncommon.) The bill measures over 7 cm and the tail 11 cm. The sexes are alike. It lays one egg, unprotected on the sand. Its "kerloo" call is usually repeated about eight times. Its range extends south to the N.S.W. border in the east, and to the North West Cape in the west. (*J. Wessels*)

PRATINCOLES GLAREOLIDAE

Two members of this family are seen in Australia. First, the Australian pratincole, or courser, which is a native of Australia, and sometimes flies to near countries and islands as a non-breeding visitor. The other species seen is the Oriental pratincole, a non-breeding visitor to Australia from Asia, which is more closely related to pratincoles of other countries than is the Australian pratincole.

The native bird is colourful in its own right, yet is effectively camouflaged and very difficult to see if it chooses to stay still. The sexes are alike.

It possesses a squarish tail, fairly long, thin legs and long, swallow-like wings, which extend beyond the tail when they are folded. It has a small and short beak, but it can "open wide" to catch insects, which it does most efficiently both on the ground and in the air. It is also known as the Swallow-plover, bearing some resemblance to each of these birds.

Although roads and highways and the fast traffic they carry have created a major hazard to the lives of many birds, certain species have more or less adapted themselves to living along with this danger. A few species, of which the Australian pratincole is one, actually seem to have benefited from modern roads and their traffic.

These birds haunt the roadsides, for a beetle or an insect is easy enough for them to see on the bitumen. Or if the insect is there but not clearly visible, it will be stirred up by the first vehicle that comes along, so this bird appreciates the appearance of an occasional car.

The Australian pratincole has several body movements peculiarly its own. Sometimes, as though to draw the attention of its fellows, it will indulge in bobbing or see-sawing actions. In the air, it has a side-slipping flight, doubtless to aid in catching flying insects.

It has white feathers below its tail and underparts, not usually noticeable, but becoming conspicuous when the bird is flying or indulging in its bobbing, which supports the theory that this last movement is performed to draw attention.

The Oriental pratincole arrives in Australia usually in large flocks, about the end of the year, to depart again in March or April. They are sometimes seen in the company of the Australian species, but have a liking to be near water.

Top:
Australian pratincole, *Stiltia isabella.* (20 cm. Plains, ungrassed areas. Common in limited zone.) It can run very fast and in the northern areas of Australia it is nicknamed the "Road Runner", though it must not be confused with the North American bird. Its ground nest is often surrounded by a ring of small stones or gravel. *(T. Kendall)*

Bottom:
Oriental pratincole, *Glareola pratincola.* (20 cm. Plains, ungrassed areas in vicinity of water. Fairly common in north-west only.) The scientific name means "one who resides in a gravelly field". As with the Australian pratincole, the recorded length does not include the folded wings extending past the tail tip. *(E. Lindgren)*

SKUAS STERCORARIIDAE

Very often skuas are made to sound the villains of the piece. In general reading and in field notes, it seems there is nothing good to be said of them. They are pirates and parasites. They steal the eggs and devour the young of smaller sea birds, they harass gulls and terns, robbing them of hard-won food. And they are big and bullying and powerful, so have few enemies to fear themselves.

A first close contact with a skua then is surprising. Here, it seems, is a mild-mannered bird, smooth-feathered and pleasant-faced, no meanness in its bearing, no wild look in its eye. They are, in fact, an interesting bird to observe and study. Unfortunately it is difficult to experience good close-up sightings, but there are excellent museum specimens on exhibition.

Four species are included here, three as being likely visitors to Australia or Australian waters and one a rare vagrant. Two of these, the Great skua and MacCormick skua, are from the Antarctic regions and two, the Arctic and the Pomarine, fly down from the north.

Skuas possess a number of individual features. Often noticeable are the two extended centre tail feathers which protrude up to 10 cm or more and should be seen in adult birds of full plumage.

These are strong-flying, solidly-built birds, of gull-like shape and appearance, except for their normal darker colouring, which is similar to that of an immature Pacific gull. Their practice of attacking other birds in the air, forcing them to drop or disgorge food, which is then taken over by the attacker, is their main characteristic.

It behaves in the way it does because it is the natural thing for it to do, and it does so most efficiently. Having sought out and found its victim, it will attack with the skill of a fighter pilot, indulging in clever aerobatics, manoeuvring skilfully and swiftly around and about the other bird, until food is surrendered. That is all the skua wanted. The other bird is now permitted to go on its way, practically unharmed and unburdened by any heavy load.

For varied diet, skuas will also follow ships, taking food tossed overboard, and they will feed on carrion, found floating or washed ashore.

Great skua, *Stercorarius skua lonnbergi*. (60 cm. Coastal waters. Fairly common.) Also called Southern skua. The largest of the skuas, it migrates from Antarctica to "summer" in the Australian winter, its season normally extending from April to November. Has a wingspan measuring 2·5 m. It is usually at sea, but sometimes comes to shore, especially around anchored ships. A bold bird, there are accounts of it taking food held in the hand. *(I. Bennett)*

Top:
Arctic skua, *Stercorarius parasiticus*. (40 cm. Coastal waters. Fairly common in smaller range.) Its range is mainly the south-east coastline and Bass Strait, and the season is from September to April. It might rest on the water close to beaches, but very rarely does it come ashore. Breeds in the northern hemisphere. *(J. Gould)*

Centre:
Pomarine skua, *Stercorarius pomarinus*. (50 cm. Coastal waters. Fairly common in limited range.) Seen mainly along the mid-N.S.W. coast, rarely elsewhere. It could be confused with the Arctic skua, but it is bigger and more strongly built, and prefers more open waters. Also there is more marked whiteness in the wing of this bird. *(J. Gould)*

Bottom:
MacCormick skua, *Stercorarius maccormicki*. (55 cm. Coastal waters. Rare.) A specimen banded in Antarctica in March 1957 was recovered at Yorke Peninsula, S.A., in May 1958. This appears the only official report on the mainland, although the bird, a close relative of the Great skua, could well be sighted in Australian seas. *(B. Allwright)*

GULLS, TERNS, AND NODDIES LARIDAE

Top of the list in this family happens to be the Silver gull, which is fitting, for it is surely one of the best-known birds in Australia. A bird of the seashore, it appears to be making more and more inland appearances, and in places is as much at home following a farmer's plough as it is behind a fishing boat near the shore.

They are seen in large numbers on the beaches, and come into city and suburban areas.

It takes a seagull some time to assume its full adult colouring, which is why it is often thought that there are two varieties of these birds on the beaches, those with black bills and legs, and another kind with these in red. But the black-billed birds are the young ones, which also show mottled brown and grey feathers on their backs. As the birds mature, the legs and bill become the typical bright red, the back feathers a clearer grey.

The other main member of the gull side of the family is the big, solid Pacific gull. He also is sometimes counted as two birds, the younger ones being of a completely different colouration. The young are the big brown birds seen on the beaches, sometimes mistaken for, and called mollymawks, which are a species of albatross. These immature gulls are seen in numbers, because it takes four years for them to reach maturity.

The Crested tern is frequently mistaken for a seagull along the coast line. Terns, known often as sea-swallows, are generally smaller than gulls, with different shapes in wings and beaks, and with a typical, swallow-like flight. Many terns, like the Crested, have the attractive black cap. Some, like the Sooty tern, very plentiful in the north, are black above and white below.

The in-between species, the noddies, are more closely related to the terns.

All birds in the family are water birds, with webbed feet, seen mainly on the seashores, but with occasional appearances inland. One species, the Whiskered tern, is entirely a bird of the inland. All are noisy and gregarious, many of them nesting in big colonies.

Silver gull, *Larus novaehollandiae*. (38 cm. Coasts, infiltrating inland. Very common.) Its carking call is as well known as its appearance. It nests on the ground in colonies and in places surrounded by water, and lays 2 or 3 eggs. Its food is anything edible, in the widest sense. Many birds with only one leg are seen, victims of encounters with large fish at sea. *(A. Gibb)*

Top:
Pacific gull, *Larus pacificus.* (60 cm. Coasts. Common.)
The heavy bill measures 6 cm. They will carry tightly-
closed shellfish to a height of 10 m, then drop them to
the rocks below to crack the shells. In hidden places,
builds a well-woven nest, measuring 25 cm in diameter.
The diet includes smaller birds, fish, crabs, and carrion.
(L. Robinson)

Right:
Kelp gull, *Larus dominicanus.* (60 cm. Coasts. Uncommon
and in limited area.) Also called Dominican gull. Very
similar to the Pacific gull, it breeds at a few places in
Australia and its range is the south-east coast, small areas
in the west, and in Tas. It is more plentiful in New Zealand.
The young can swim when a week old. *(M. Bonnin)*

113

Top:
Common noddy, *Anous stolidus.* (40 cm. Tropical coastal areas. Common.) This species usually occurs in great numbers. It nests and roosts on islands off the coast. The scientific name means "senseless and stupid", perhaps given because of the bird's misguided trust in man. Observers report that at sea these birds have been seen resting on the backs of turtles. (*J. Ferrero*)

Centre:
Lesser noddy, *Anous tenuirostris.* (30 cm. Coastal islands. Common in local area.) Only known breeding place in Australia is at the Abrolhos Islands off the W.A. coast. The nests, usually in mangroves, are made of seaweed, cemented with excrement. John Gilbert recorded a visit to the islands to admire these birds in 1843. (*J. Gould*)

Bottom:
White-capped noddy, *Anous minutus.* (35 cm. Tropical coastal zones. Very common in limited area.) This species breeds and nests in densely-populated colonies on coral islands, where the calls of both adults and young are sometimes deafening. Very similar to the Lesser noddy, the fork in the tail being a distinguishing feature. (*G. Chapman*)

Top:
Gull-billed tern, *Sterna nilotica.* (40 cm. Inland fresh water, coastal estuaries, lagoons. Fairly common in limited range, rare in Tas.) When feeding, glides down to the surface to grasp food, only the tip of the bill touching the water. Does not dive or become wet. Nests on the ground, laying 2 or 3 eggs. *(T. Lowe)*

Centre:
Caspian tern, *Sterna caspia.* (60 cm. Coastal, occasionally inland lakes and rivers. Fairly common.) The largest of the terns, with a wing span of 1·35 m. When fishing, hovers to sight a surfacing fish, then dives expertly. Fiercely aggressive in defending nest or young. The call is a loud, harsh scream. *(C. Gill)*

Bottom:
Crested tern, *Sterna bergii.* (45 cm. Coastal waters. Common.) Here seen displaying, this species breeds on reefs and offshore islands. Its call is similar to that of the Silver gull, but quieter. When fishing, said to grasp fish behind the head, ascend with it held in the beak, then swallow it in mid-air. *(T. Kendall)*

115

Top:

Black-naped tern, *Sterna sumatrana.* (30 cm. North-eastern coasts. Fairly common.) This species inhabits tropical lagoons and is found from Darwin to the Barrier Reef. It feeds by diving or surface skimming, sometimes after hovering to sight prey. Like other tropical terns, loses many eggs to gulls and other predators. The long streamers of the forked tail are a feature. *(K. & B. Richards)*

Centre:

Roseate tern, *Sterna dougalli.* (38 cm. Northern coasts. Fairly common.) This species nests in colonies on the ground in roughly-made nests, lined with pieces of shell and coral. It lays 2 eggs, of variable shades and patterns. Many eggs are lost to gulls and reptiles. Feeds on fish, which it catches by diving. *(G. Chapman)*

Bottom:

Common tern, *Sterna hirundo.* (35 cm. Coastal estuaries. Rare.) It breeds in the northern hemisphere and has a strong preference for sandbanks and also visiting large lakes with sandy shores. It likes a high post for occasional perching. Most of its recorded sightings are in the south-east. Catches fish below the surface and enters the water with little splashing or disturbance. *(M. Carter)*

Above:
White-fronted tern, *Sterna striata.* (40 cm. Coastal waters. Uncommon.) This species is a non-breeding visitor from New Zealand. It is seen in a limited zone, along the south-east coast to eastern S.A. Graceful in the air, it alights to fish in the surf. In 1959 invaded Vic. in large numbers, a solitary bird being observed as far inland as Wyperfeld National Park in the mallee. *(M. Carter)*

Left:
Lesser crested tern, *Sterna bengalensis.* (38 cm. Northern coastal waters. Common within small range.) A neat and tidy smaller tern, that breeds on tropical islands and nests in colonies. They leave large quantities of eggs lying on the sand in these colonies, in an amazing array of blotched patterns, each seeming to be different. *(G. Chapman)*

Top left:
Little tern, *Sterna albifrons.* (25 cm. Inshore waters, sandbanks. Common, but variable.) Its range is the eastern coastal areas, with occasional visits inland, and a recorded sighting at Goolwa, S.A. Breeding season varies with locality; a summer breeder in the south. Hovers over shallow water for long periods, then will dive and fish efficiently. *(E. Bound)*

Centre left:
Bridled tern, *Sterna anaethetus.* (40 cm. Tropical, sub-tropical waters. Common.) Similar in appearance and in some behaviour to the Sooty, but comes to land to roost at nights. Its call has been described as resembling the yapping of a puppy. Birds hover while seeking food, then pick it up from the surface. *(B. Lovell)*

Bottom left:
Sooty tern, *Sterna fuscata.* (45 cm. Tropical, sub-tropical waters. Very common.) The call of these birds, well known in the tropics, is interpreted as "Wide-awake!" and is not always appreciated when it disturbs people during the night. In the past, there were accounts of the eggs being collected by hundreds of dozens for sale to Qld pastrycooks. *(M. Bonnin)*

Below:
White-winged black tern, *Sterna leucoptera.* (25 cm. Inland lakes and coastal marshes. Uncommon.) A non-breeding visitor from parts of Europe and Asia, seen from September to March. Does not dive, but takes its food in flight low over the water. It also takes flying insects. *(G. Chapman)*

Above:
Fairy tern, *Sterna nereis*. (25 cm. Inshore waters, sandbanks. Common.) Appears to occupy territories where the Little tern does not appear, so that between the two small species the entire Australian coastline is covered. A noisy bird, it nests colonially on islands, rather than the mainland. A large group in northern W.A. is said to number 15 000 birds. *(L. Robinson)*

Left:
Whiskered tern, *Sterna hybrida*. (25 cm. Inland lakes, stretches of water. Fairly common.) This is the country cousin in the tern family, feeding not only on lakes and the farmer's dams, but also in his fields and ploughed paddocks. Not usually seen at all on the seashores. Will take food from water's surface in flight, or will dive. *(E. Bound)*

PIGEONS AND DOVES COLUMBIDAE

Pigeons or doves, the names are interchangeable, vary in size from the plump fruit-eaters to the small and dainty Diamond dove. They vary in their choice of habitat, from dense, humid rain forest, through dry desert and semi-desert country, to the cooler, southerly regions. And they vary in their colouration, from brightly-patterned, showy birds, to birds of soft, delicate, quietly-blending shades.

But though there are contrasts, there are many similarities among the various species of the family. A feature of all pigeons is the whirring of wings on their take-off. A flock of Crested pigeons, a species common in many parts of Australia, make a peculiar, tinkling sound with their wings as they pass overhead.

Most pigeons of any size are well fleshed, and in Australia the number have been greatly reduced because of their "table" qualities. John Gould gave the Wonga pigeon the scientific name of *Leucosarcia*, meaning "white-fleshed", and from the start of settlement the flesh won the bird a reputation.

Another species which has paid the penalty for being a tasty dish is the well-known Bronzewing, although here a warning should go with the naming of this bird as something good to eat. In some areas, the bones are reputed to contain poison from the seeds of the plant *Gastrolobium*, eaten by the birds. And while the birds themselves are immune to the poison, and their meat is considered safe and edible, bones given to dogs may make the animals convulsive and dangerous, killing them in the end.

Another interesting feature in the lives of many pigeons, especially those within the drier areas of the continent, is their drinking habit. Water is very important for a seed-eating bird, and these birds drink to a regular pattern. They arrive at water-holes, dams, or drinking places just before or just after sunset, in great flocks, then drink deeply. It is believed that both the timing of this practice and the mass arrival of the birds, is an instinctive protection against predators.

Early Australian ornithologists began studies and observations of pigeons which have continued over the years. There is still much to learn. Some of the most colourful pigeons live in remote, tropical areas, where research has been difficult.

Also in recent years, some species feared to be extinct, or nearly so, have been found, with sightings not of an odd bird or two, but of huge flocks of thousands of birds.

The Domestic pigeon is a common, everyday sight. This bird, whose origin goes back to an overseas species, illustrates the remarkable adaptability of some members of the family. Then pigeons have been exploited as a commercial table bird, the squab industry raising large numbers for the market.

More fortunate are those pigeons bred as homers, for a sport which, in Australia, attracts many devotees, with numerous suitable routes available for the navigational flights that excite the homing enthusiast.

Domestic pigeon, *Columba livia*. (33 cm. Town areas, occasionally open country. Common.) An introduced species, it is well able to survive and prosper, and appears to be increasing in numbers. It haunts farm homesteads, suburban factory buildings and warehouses, and old stone city buildings. Feral birds go further into uninhabited areas. *(F. Lewitzka)*

Top left:
White-headed pigeon, *Columba leucomela*. (40 cm. Rain forests, wooded areas. Fairly common.) Ranges along the east coast from northern Qld to southern N.S.W. Also called Baldie. During the breeding season, the call is a gentle boom, with an additional cooing syllable appended. It nests in tangled vines or jungle trees about 20 m high. *(F. Lewitzka)*

Top right:
Brown pigeon, *Macropygia phasianella*. (40 cm. Rain forests, wooded areas. Common.) Its zone is mainly that of the White-headed pigeon, on the eastern coast. Also called Pheasant pigeon. Has two calls, one of three notes, the other a short, single coo. This bird can use its tail to assist in moving about the forest. It nests in the trees and lays 1 egg. *(F. Lewitzka)*

Centre left:
Spotted dove, *Streptopelia chinensis*. (28 cm. Towns and cities. Common.) An introduced species, also called Spotted turtledove. It is increasing in numbers, but does not seem to have penetrated far inland, other than to cities. It calls frequently with a soft continued cooing. A scavenger, it likes suburban gardens and compost heaps, and will happily feed with poultry. *(F. Lewitzka)*

Bottom left:
Senegal turtledove, *Streptopelia senegalensis*. (25 cm. Urban areas. Fairly common in local area.) An introduced species. Like the Spotted dove, it is an Asiatic bird. It was originally released in Perth at the end of the nineteenth century and at present is restricted to areas of W.A., but is increasing. Voice is a soft cooing. *(F. Lewitzka)*

Above:
Green-winged pigeon, *Chalcophaps indica.* (25 cm. Heavy rain forests and adjacent scrub. Fairly common.) There are some differences noticeable between the sexes, the male slightly more colourful. Unfortunately this attractive bird keeps to the denser forest areas and observation has been difficult. Its call is a coo, monotonously repeated.
(B. Lovell)

Right:
Common bronzewing, *Phaps chalcoptera.* (30 cm. Open country. Common.) This bird ranges throughout Australia except for the Cape York Peninsula. Its voice is a low, gentle boom. It is occasionally seen in flocks out of the breeding season. It drinks at dusk after a cautious approach to the water. The nest, where 2 white eggs are laid, is usually hidden in secluded thickets. *(P. Munchenberg)*

Top:
Brush bronzewing, *Phaps elegans*. (28 cm. Coastal and inland bush country. Fairly common.) Its zone is not as extensive nor its numbers as large as previously. Its voice, and nesting and breeding habits, are similar to the Common bronzewing, the nests being frail and saucer-shaped, with the eggs sometimes visible through it from below. *(F. Lewitzka)*

Centre:
Flock pigeon, *Phaps histrionica*. (28 cm. Dry grasslands, saltbush plains. Common in certain areas.) This bird, thought to be extinct a decade or two ago, recently has been seen and filmed in large flocks, and possibly is common in its local zones. Mainly seen on the Barkly Tablelands and near areas, with sightings further afield in good seasons. It limits its drinking to a very short period around sunset. *(G. Chapman)*

Bottom:
Crested pigeon, *Ocyphaps lophotes*. (30 cm. Inland wooded and open areas. Common.) Unfortunately is mis-called Topknot pigeon in many places where it is commonly seen. The erect black crest is distinctive. Its call is a single woo, repeated for long periods. This is a conspicuous bird, often seen on roadside posts or telephone wires. It needs to be close to water. *(I. McCann)*

Top left:
Plumed pigeon, *Petrophassa plumifera*. (20 cm. Rocky, high-temperature areas, near water. Uncommon.) Found in the centre and northwards. These dainty birds were hand fed near Alice Springs during drought years. They vary a little in colour and size according to the locality. It is also called the Spinifex pigeon. It runs rapidly or flies with fast wingbeats. *(E. Bound)*

Top right:
Red-plumed pigeon, *Petrophassa ferruginea*. (20 cm. Dry, rocky areas. Uncommon.) Also called Western plumed pigeon, and similar to the Plumed pigeon. It is well camouflaged to match the rocky, spinifex country that it haunts. It nests on the ground by a low bush or spinifex, and roughly lines it with dry grass. If flushed, it takes off with a particularly loud whirring. *(G. Chapman)*

Right:
Squatter pigeon, *Petrophassa scripta*. (28 cm. Open timbered areas. Uncommon.) Likes occasional trees in vicinity, to which it will fly when disturbed. The common name is from its practice of lowering itself to the ground, then remaining motionless, to avoid being noticed. It is also called Partridge bronzewing. Numbers greatly declined following land settlement. *(F. Lewitzka)*

Left:
Chestnut-quilled rock pigeon, *Petrophassa rufipennis*. (30 cm. Tropical rocky outcrops. Fairly common in limited area.) Believed to be confined to the stony areas of Arnhem Land, N.T. In general appearance and behaviour it resembles the White-quilled pigeon, but the absence of the white wing feathers make it a difficult bird to spot. *(F. Lewitzka)*

Bottom left:
White-quilled rock pigeon, *Petrophassa albipennis*. (30 cm. Fairly common in small local area.) Its zones are the Kimberleys and the Victoria River areas of the N.T., the birds in the former having more white in wing. Like the other 5 species of the genus *Petrophassa*, it is a native pigeon. Lays 2 creamy white eggs in a nest among the rocks or on the ground. *(G. Chapman)*

Bottom right:
Partridge pigeon, *Petrophassa smithii*. (25 cm. Open timber. Uncommon.) This species is well named and is the nearest Australian bird to a partridge. It resembles the Squatter pigeon in many ways. The *smithii* is after Sir James Smith, an English botanist (1736–82). Its zone is mainly the top of the N.T. *(F. Lewitzka)*

Top left:
Bar-shouldered dove, *Geopelia humeralis*. (28 cm. Woodlands, scrub, near water. Very common.) Also called Mangrove dove. This bird ranges extensively over northern Australia. Some listeners interpret its call as "hop-off". It lays 2 white eggs in a lightly-made nest in mangroves or a low bush. The breeding season may extend to almost any time of the year, depending on local conditions. *(C. Webster)*

Top right:
Peaceful dove, *Geopelia striata*. (23 cm. Savannah woodlands, open timber. Common.) Its well-known call, perhaps heard differently by various people, has been described as plaintive, sad, evocative. It builds a flimsy nest, so that the eggs often can be seen from below. A ground feeder, eats mainly seeds and some insects. It is not usually seen in the south, or in the south-west of W.A. *(I. McCann)*

Centre:
Wonga pigeon, *Leucosarcia melanoleuca*. (40 cm. Rain forests, tall timber. Uncommon.) Its call, "wonga" or "wonka", is repeated monotonously, and may be heard a kilometre away. This bird is amazingly camouflaged, having a talent to look like a tree stump, and is difficult to see even when experienced observers know it is in the vicinity. *(H. Frauca)*

Below:
Diamond dove, *Geopelia cuneata*. (20 cm. Savannah, open timber. Common.) This delicate little bird is the smallest of Australian doves. Like the Peaceful dove, it is a ground feeder. It has a range of calls which are difficult to describe. It feeds mainly on the ground and has a similar zone to the Peaceful dove. *(Ardea Photographics)*

Above:
Purple-crowned pigeon, *Ptilinopus superbus* (top); Red-crowned pigeon, *Ptilinopus regina* (bottom). (Both: 23 cm. Rain forests, mangroves. Common.) Two very similar species of tropical fruit-eating pigeons. Both build a round platform nest of twigs, in bushes and trees at heights of 3 m and upwards. One white egg is laid, and breeding time is from October to February. *(M. Kröyer-Pedersen)*

Above:
Banded pigeon, *Ptilinopus alligator*. (35 cm. Tropical bushland, jungle, rock outcrops. Possibly fairly common.) A very shy fruit-eating bird, previously thought to be extinct, but now hopes are held for its survival and progress. The *alligator* is after the Alligator River in its N.T. habitat. *(E. Zillman)*

Top right:
Wompoo pigeon, *Ptilinopus magnificus*. (50 cm. Dense rain forests. Common in local range.) This is another pigeon named after the sound of its call. This is a very colourful and distinguished-looking bird, its sighting or an opportunity to photograph it, always delighting tourists and observers. An added inducement is that it is often seen in the company of other pigeon species. It eats wild figs and other fruits. *(E. McNamara)*

Below:
Torres Strait pigeon, *Ducula spilorrhoa*. (38 cm. Rain forests, mangroves, tropical coastal islands. Common in limited local range.) Also called Nutmeg pigeon. This is a well-known, popularised bird, its behaviour and appearance making good film studies. In its bush habitat, inner seeds of fruit it has consumed are seen on the ground around mangroves and wild fruit trees. *(F. Lewitzka)*

Bottom right:
Topknot pigeon, *Lopholaimus antarcticus*. (45 cm. Rain forests, coastal timber areas. Fairly common.) There could be confusion with the name of this bird, the true Topknot pigeon, and the more common Crested pigeon, although strangely, in theory at least, their territories hardly overlap, but dovetail. This is a distinctive fruit-eating pigeon, with a peculiar guttural call. *(F. Lewitzka)*

128

LORIKEETS, COCKATOOS, AND PARROTS PSITTACIDAE

Here is a family that certainly makes Australia a lucky country—a collection of colourful, fascinating, appealing birds, something for all to enjoy, for wherever one travels, some of the parrots, lorikeets, or cockatoos are there.

A traveller's diary will highlight the birds that caught his eye. He checklists them as he goes . . .

Those exciting pink birds, abundant on every roadside, taking off as tourist bus or hire car drives by, often wheeling dangerously close to the windscreen . . . Galahs, the people call them.

Those big, black, slow-moving birds, noticed on our visits to timber forests or flapping over the Northern Territory safari camp, somehow a part of the country's landscape, like the gum trees themselves . . . Black cockatoos.

Those myriad little green and yellow birds, in flocks flashing low over the dry plains, seen from the windows of the big diesel train that crosses the Nullarbor . . . Budgerigars.

The mass of big, clean, white birds, sheeting a green field, clouding and crowding into a big tree, turning it white—not quite all white, as they have yellow crests up and they are letting us know they are there, now the car has stopped . . . White cockatoos.

The frolicsome, friendly red and blue parrots that came to the cabin in the National Park and sat on our shoulders—we have photos to prove it . . . Crimson rosellas.

Those beautiful blue and yellow birds that flew down out of the sky and ate the honey mixture which we held in the plates they gave us at that tourist spot on the Gold Coast . . . Rainbow lorikeets.

Then when the driver stopped for us in the Centre, and we were about to tell him we had seen white cockies in the south, suddenly, through the binoculars, we saw the additional delicate pink . . . Major Mitchell cockatoos.

There are three groups in the family. The cockatoos, mainly bigger birds, with crests and short, square tails. The lorikeets, in all colours, feeding on nectar, and with a brush-like tongue like the honeyeaters. And the parrots, the big collection of long-tailed birds, all kinds and colours, and mainly ground-feeders.

Outstanding among the distinctive family features are the bills, not unlike those of hawks and eagles, but not used to catch large, live prey, for parrots are mainly vegetarians. The feet are equally distinctive, with two toes forward, two toes back. They are employed to hold food and to bring it up to the mouth, so that these birds are interesting and capable feeders.

Rainbow lorikeet, *Trichoglossus moluccanus*. (30 cm. Timber areas, mainly coastal. Common.) These playful and likable birds prefer the flowering native trees, especially eucalypts, banksias, and melaleucas. They have a noisy screech and chatter unceasingly as they feed. Birds in the air will hear others in trees below and will drop in to join them. (*L. Robinson*)

Top right:
Scaly-breasted lorikeet, *Trichoglossus chlorolepidotus*. (20 cm. Areas of blossoming trees and bushes. Common.) As with all lorikeets, the sexes are mainly alike, and these birds indulge in upside down, gymnastic movements when feeding. These are often found with the Rainbow lorikeet and are similar in behaviour. Their nest, in a hollow, is usually high in the tree. *(L. Robinson)*

Bottom left:
Red-collared lorikeet, *Trichoglossus rubritorquis*. (30 cm. Timber areas. Common in limited range.) These are birds of the north and the Kimberleys. Lorikeets fly rapidly, with thrusting movements as though assisted by a hidden force. Some experts regard these as a sub-species of the Rainbow lorikeet, for they are very similar except the slight difference in colour. *(F. Lewitzka)*

Bottom right:
Varied lorikeet, *Psitteuteles versicolor*. (20 cm. Timber, flowering trees. Common.) An aggressive bird, it will chase other birds trying to feed in the same trees. Nests in high holes in trees, lining the nest with bits of bark or eucalyptus leaves, both birds working on its preparation, and 2 to 4 eggs are laid. *(L. Robinson)*

Top left:
Little lorikeet, *Glossopsitta pusilla*. (15 cm. Areas of flower-ing trees, fruit trees. Common.) It feeds on the nectar of various blossoms and on berries and fruits. It assembles in large flocks at feeding points, becomes much involved with this activity and is easily approached at such times. It has a typical screeching call. The mainly green colouring is an effective camouflage. *(F. Lewitzka)*

Top right:
Purple-crowned lorikeet, *Glossopsitta porphyrocephala*. (18 cm. Areas of flowering trees. Common.) These birds are travellers and their routes follow the seasonal blossoming of the gum trees. A small, dainty bird, it is at least as noisy as the other lorikeets. It is the only lorikeet to appear in the south-west of W.A. *(G. Taylor)*

Bottom left:
Musk lorikeet, *Glossopsitta concinna*. (23 cm. Timber, flowering trees. Common.) This bird has a preference for the bigger blossoming gum trees, but will eat berries from a variety of native and introduced plants. It has a typical loud, penetrating call. When breeding, it is seen in pairs, at other times in flocks. As with some other parrots, it exudes a musky odour, after which this species is named.
(L. Robinson)

Top left:
Cockatiel, *Nymphicus hollandicus.* (28 cm. Open inland country. Common.) It is frequently seen by the roadside, often on telephone wires. The thin crest, which measures 5 cm, is a distinguishing feature. Also called Cockatoo parrots and Quarrions and, in W.A., Weeros. Its call is an attractive, repetitive whistle, ending on a higher note. *(B. Lovell)*

Bottom left:
Fig parrot, *Opopsitta diopthalma.* (13 cm. Tropical rain forests, jungle. Uncommon.) This parrot gets its name from the practice of feeding on the seeds of native figs. It is the smallest of Australian parrots and in a genus of its own on the continent, although it has a close relative in New Guinea. Because of its dense and remote habitat, observation of this species has been restricted. *(L. Robinson)*

Below:
Palm cockatoo, *Probosciger aterrimus.* (60 cm. Rain forests, jungle. Common in very small range.) Found only at the tip of Cape York Peninsula. It is the largest and has the most powerful beak of all parrots, with which it cracks open the hard nuts from palm trees. This bird "blushes", the cheek patches turning a more noticeable red when it is aroused or disturbed. The home base of the species is New Guinea. *(L. Robinson)*

Top left:
Glossy cockatoo, *Calyptorhynchus lathami*. (50 cm. Mountain forests, open timber, river margins. Rare.) Its low numbers make observation and research difficult and some fears are held for the survival of the species. It eats the seeds of casuarinas and its haunts are about these trees. The call has been described as a soft caw. *(J. Gould)*

Top right:
Yellow-tailed cockatoo, *Calyptorhynchus funereus*. (60 cm. Rain forests, bush areas, river margins. Fairly common.) Flocks are often seen at groves of tall banksias. It feeds on the seeds of these trees and others, and tears bits from rotting tree limbs to extract wood borers and tree grubs, serving a useful purpose to forestry. A loud, distinctive call and a slow, typical flight. *(L. Robinson)*

Centre left:
White-tailed cockatoo, *Calyptorhynchus baudinii*. (55 cm. Forest areas, open timber. Fairly common in limited range.) It is found only in the south-west of W.A. This species, *baudinii*, is one of four black cockatoos with banded tails. It feeds on pine cone seeds and is seen at pine plantations. Lays 1 or 2 eggs, but usually only one chick is raised. *(L. Robinson)*

Bottom left:
Red-tailed cockatoo, *Calyptorhynchus banksii*. (60 cm. Forests, open timber. Common.) Its rowdy call always advertises its presence. The young male in this species takes 4 years to acquire the full magnificent adult plumage. In the south and south-east, these do not usually appear in the territory of the Yellow-tailed cockatoo, with which it is fairly similar in habit and behaviour. *(L. Robinson)*

Top left:
Gang-gang cockatoo, *Callocephalon fimbriatum*. (30 cm. Dense timber, mountains in summer; open timber, plains in winter. Fairly common in limited range.) John Gould regarded this as the most fascinating of Australian cockatoos, and a sighting of them is always an occasion. They have an individual "talking" murmur when feeding, which often reveals their presence. They are rarely seen on the ground. *(J. Ferrero)*

Top right:
Galah, *Eolophus roseicapilla*. (35 cm. Open areas. Very common.) The whole flock will "change colour" as they wheel, revealing the beautiful pink under-feathers. Many people can recall the day when seeing a galah was an event, but today they are one of the most prolific of country birds. They have continued to thrive, even during drought years, and obviously this is a species suited by land clearance and crop cultivation. *(H. Frauca)*

Bottom left:
Sulphur-crested cockatoo, *Cacatua galerita*. (40 cm. Open timber. Very common.) Also called White cockatoo. The large flocks have scouts perched in high trees to observe any intruders. The name "cockatoo" has come into common usage as a watchman for a sly-grog spot or gaming school. Very noisy and noticeable, the birds are wary and difficult to approach closely. *(K. Stepnell)*

Above:
Major Mitchell cockatoo, *Cacatua leadbeateri.* (40 cm. Dry inland areas. Rare.) There are only isolated spots left where these birds can be seen and bird-lovers appreciate recent governmental moves for harsher penalties for their destruction. Sir Thomas Mitchell was one of the first to admire its beauty and his comments are fittingly remembered by the name. *(W. Moreland)*

Top right:
Long-billed corella, *Cacatua tenuirostris.* (38 cm. Open timber. Rare.) This species seems to be declining in favour of the Little corella. The longer upper bill is a feature to distinguish it from the Little corella, with which it has much in common, including the ground-feeding habit. Its voice, raised when alarmed or disturbed, is a loud, harsh screech. *(L. Robinson)*

Bottom right:
Little corella, *Cacatua sanguinea.* (35 cm. Open timber, water courses, mangroves. Very common.) It is rare in parts of the south and in Tas., but is abundant and thriving and could extend its range. It is a ground-feeder, eating seeds from surface plants and digging for bulbs and roots. *(M. Bonnin)*

Top right:
Budgerigar, *Melopsittacus undulatus.* (18 cm. Open timber, open plains. Very common.) It forms into enormous flocks and is probably the most plentiful parrot in Australia. A feature of their flying is the tight, precise formation, the entire flock wheeling and twisting as one bird, always at high speed. The green and yellow are its natural colouring and additional colours seen on birds in captivity have been introduced by selective breeding. *(L. Robinson)*

Bottom left:
Red-cheeked parrot, *Geoffroyus geoffroyi.* (23 cm. Rain forests, jungle. Common in limited area.) Like the Red-sided parrot, is found only in the forests near the top of Cape York. It was not discovered and recognised as a species until 1913, but is now believed to be fairly numerous in its local zone, although there is still much to learn of its life and behaviour. It sounds a single syllable call, repeated a number of times. *(G. Mathews)*

Bottom right:
Red-sided parrot, *Eclectus roratus.* (33 cm. Rain forests, jungle. Common in very limited area.) Also called Eclectus parrot. This is the only Australian parrot in a genus found mainly in islands north of the continent. An unusual feature is that, contrary to the custom among parrots when sexes differ in appearance, here the female is the brighter of the two. Very noisy, their cries reveal their presence in the dense rain forests. *(L. Robinson)*

Top left:
Superb parrot, *Polytelis swainsonii*. (35–40 cm. River margins, flood areas. Uncommon.) Also called Green leek. It has a limited zone in southern N.S.W. and northern Vic. Nests in a high hollow and lays 4 to 6 white eggs. It is probable that parrots' eggs are generally white because they are more clearly visible in a deep hollow, and since the egg is hidden away, a camouflage is unnecessary. *(L. Robinson)*

Top centre:
Regent parrot, *Polytelis anthopeplus*. (38 cm. Open timber. Fairly common in very limited area, rare elsewhere.) Also called Smoker. Large, and fast flying, they gather seeds from the yellow *Hibbertia*, a wildflower about 50 cm high that grows in the Victorian Mallee, a haunt of these birds. Their plumage makes them difficult to sight on these plants, but discovering them is a rewarding experience. *(L. Robinson)*

Top right:
Princess parrot, *Polytelis alexandrae*. (40–45 cm. Dry plains, spinifex country. Uncommon.) This bird is sometimes found, unaccountably, well away from water. Because of the remoteness of much of its territory, the largely un-inhabited areas of the Centre and W.A., fairly limited research has been undertaken. It is said to perch lengthwise along limbs of suitable trees. *(L. Robinson)*

Bottom right:
Red-winged parrot, *Aprosmictus erythropterus*. (30 cm. Open timber, mangroves. Fairly common.) This beautiful bird is wary and hard to approach. Often when it is disturbed, it takes to the air, screeching loudly, and the first glimpse of them, regretfully, is of their departure. For nests they choose hollows not too high off the ground, but going down deeply into the tree trunks. *(J. Ferrero)*

Above:
King parrot, *Alisterus scapularis.* (40–45 cm. Coastal forests, river margins. Fairly common.) This bird likes large trees, and timber milling considerably restricts its habitat. The sexes are noticeably different in some of the calls as well as in plumage. Its food is mainly seeds and it will show up in open areas if the right food is about. *(L. Robinson)*

138

Above:
Elegant parrot, *Neophema elegans.* (20 cm. Open country. Fairly common.) This bird has benefited from land clearance and is extending its range. Its preference is for ground seeds, so it haunts grazing areas. It nests in holes in trees, usually at some height. Its call is said to be a sharp twitter, quite like that of the Crimson finch. *(L. Robinson)*

Top right:
Bourke parrot, *Neophema bourkii.* (20 cm. Mulga country, sandy areas. Common.) Its flight is fast, low, and direct, with the whirr of the wings evident from near by. It has regular drinking habits, going to watering places before sunrise and at dusk. It nests in small trees and lays 4 or 5 eggs. *(B. Lovell)*

Bottom right:
Blue-winged parrot, *Neophema chrysostomus.* (20 cm. Inland plains, some coastal zones. Common.) It has a characteristic tinkling call on the wing. It will nest in any hollow, in tree, log, or post. Believed to migrate to the mainland from Tas. Its feeding habits are like those of the Elegant parrot, with which it is easily confused. *(L. Robinson)*

Above:
Orange-bellied parrot, *Neophema chrysogaster*. (20 cm. Tidal rivers, sandy areas, grass patches. Rare and in limited zone.) This bird, so rare that very limited knowledge of it has been acquired, appears to have bases on some Bass Strait islands, from where it flies to both Tas. and the mainland. It has a distinctive, quick drop to the ground to terminate flight. *(F. Lewitzka)*

Top right:
Scarlet-breasted parrot, *Neophema splendida*. (20 cm. Open country, dry areas. Rare.) In spite of the array of colour, for some reason it is easy to overlook. Although shy, it will not move far when disturbed, apparently depending on its natural camouflage. The common colouration of the male (left) is a solid orange-yellow belly. *(L. Robinson)*

Centre right:
Turquoise parrot, *Neophema pulchella*. (20 cm. Grassy valleys with near timber, rock outcrops. Uncommon.) This is another parrot with a limited range. Previously its range was more extensive and its numbers greater. Needs timbered areas for shelter and nesting. A ground-feeder, it eats mainly seeds and grass. *(L. Robinson)*

Bottom right:
Rock parrot, *Neophema petrophila*. (20 cm. Rocky and sandy areas, with saltbush and samphire. Coastal islands. Common.) Its territory appears to begin where that of the Orange-bellied parrot leaves off, continuing from the S.A. border, west along the south coast, to the west coast of W.A. It is rarely seen inland. It nests in rock crevices. *(L. Robinson)*

140

Right:

Ground parrot, *Pezoporus wallicus.* (35 cm. Coastal heaths, swamps. Rare.) The long tail measures 20 cm. With a quail-like plumage pattern, it is well camouflaged and hard to locate. It is also nocturnal in habit, which, with its rarity, makes it a bird seldom sighted. It retreated from previous habitats as settlement extended, with a big depletion of numbers. The longer legs enable it to run rather than to move with the usual parrot waddle. *(G. Chapman)*

Below:

Night parrot, *Pezoporus occidentalis.* (24 cm. Dry inland area, spinifex country. Very rare.) This is the bird of mystery. Is it, or is it not, extinct? There have been occasional and fairly recent reports of sightings, apparently without official confirmation. Quests by dedicated ornithologists have to date proved fruitless. It nests near clumps of porcupine grass. A new confirmed sighting would delight all bird and nature lovers. *(J. Gould)*

Top:
Crimson rosella, *Platycercus elegans.* (35 cm. Forests, coastal scrub. Common.) The sexes are similar in appearance and the green birds seen are immatures, not attaining adult plumage until a year old. These are sociable birds and thrive in National Parks, camps, and reserves. Their food includes seeds, soft fruits, nectar, and some insects. The breeding season extends from September to February. *(L. Robinson)*

Centre:
Green rosella, *Platycercus caledonicus.* (35 cm. Timbered areas. Common in limited zone.) This rosella is found only in Tas. and some islands of Bass Strait. In winter, large flocks will gather in the hedgerows found in that area. The calls have been likened to various musical instruments. It is closely related to the mainland rosellas. *(L. Robinson)*

Bottom:
Yellow rosella, *Platycercus flaveolus.* (35 cm. Red gum forests, river margins. Fairly common.) Its limited zone is mainly the Murray and its tributaries, extending into inland N.S.W. It can be heard chattering as it feeds in the red gums, sometimes when high up and hidden by leaves. There is a loud, harsh screech, reserved for alarm calls. *(L. Robinson)*

Top left:
Pale-headed rosella, *Platycercus adscitus.* (30 cm. Open timber. Common in limited range.) Like the other 7 rosella species, it has its specialised territory: along the east coast from northern N.S.W. to the tip of Cape York. It has benefited from forest clearing and land cultivation. Its flight and behaviour patterns are similar to the Eastern rosella. It has a preference for Scotch thistles. *(H. Frauca)*

Top right:
Western rosella, *Platycercus icterotis.* (25 cm. Open timber. Common in limited area.) As the name suggests, its zone is in W.A., where it is seen on roadsides and in farmed paddocks, in the south-west of the State. It is sometimes seen in the popular Kings Park, Perth. This is the smallest of the rosellas. It will lay from 3 to 7 eggs. *(L. Robinson)*

Left:
Eastern rosella, *Platycercus eximius.* (30 cm. Open timber, settled areas. Very common.) These lovely birds are common sights in most of their south-easterly range, with occasional appearances in suburban gardens. They have a fairly fast flight, spreading the tail before swooping to a landing. The nest is anywhere in available hollows and will lay up to 9 eggs. *(H. Frauca)*

Left:
Adelaide rosella, *Platycercus adelaidae*. (35 cm. Open timber. Settled areas. Common.) Appropriately enough, often seen in suburban Adelaide. Its preference seems to be for populated areas, and it is also sighted on roadsides, around farms and orchards, and in parklands. It will feed on grain left scattered about and will drink from farm troughs. Its calls are like those of the Crimson rosella. *(H. Wright)*

Below:
Northern rosella, *Platycercus venustus*. (28 cm. River and creek margins. Timber country. Rare.) Its beautiful and distinctive colour patterns make it one of the attractions in its zone, the N.T. and Kimberleys. Unfortunately it is most difficult to observe and its numbers appear to be decreasing. It lays up to 4 eggs. *(L. Robinson)*

Top left:
Twenty-eight parrot, *Barnardius semitorquatus.* (40 cm. Open timber. Common.) Related to the Port Lincoln parrot, but larger and confined to the extreme south-west of W.A. The common name is based on its three-syllable high-pitched whistle. The narrow red band on the forehead and the greenish belly are distinguishing features. *(F. Lewitzka)*

Top right:
Cloncurry parrot, *Barnardius macgillivrayi.* (35 cm. River margins, open timber. Uncommon and in restricted range.) This is a species on which so far only limited knowledge is to hand, and the exact limits of its range are undefined. It likes the big gum trees found along rivers and creeks. The young have a yellow band in front which disperses early in their life. *(L. Robinson)*

Centre right:
Mallee ringneck, *Barnardius barnardi.* (35 cm. Dry inland and mallee country. Common.) It is normally seen in pairs or in small flocks, in mallee country or where other euca-lypts flourish. It does not share the adaptability of the Port Lincoln parrot and the range is more limited. *(E. Bound)*

Bottom left:
Port Lincoln parrot, *Barnardius zonarius.* (38 cm. Open timber. Common.) As the name suggests, it is very common around Port Lincoln and the Eyre Peninsula, S.A. Often seen on the roadside, it is one of the easier birds to photo-graph, and makes an excellent study. It may also be observed in woodlands and most types of open country. *(L. Robinson)*

Top left:
Red-capped parrot, *Purpureicephalus spurius*. (35 cm. Forests of big timber. Common within limited range.) It likes the jarrah and the other tall trees of the south-west of W.A. which is its zone. A long upper mandible is especially suited to cracking the hard nuts from these trees, for access to the seeds. Also eats nectar and, unfortunately for its own well-being, fruit from orchards. (*L. Robinson*)

Bottom left:
Red-rumped parrot, *Psephotus haematonotus*. (25 cm. Open timber, town areas. Common.) Also called Red-backed parrot and Grass parrot. The "Grassies" of the schoolboy, it is well known in southern Australia. Likes open grass-land and low bushland, with a fondness for regrowth of lopped gum trees. They are friendly and will walk or waddle away rather than fly. They have a little tune of their own, which they give voice to when flying. (*I. McCann*)

Below:
Paradise parrot, *Psephotus pulcherrimus*. (30 cm. Light timber country, with termite mounds. Very rare, existence doubtful.) The sad facts are that there has been no confirmed sighting for almost half a century. Knowledge of them comes from the old bird books, in which warnings were sounded about the likelihood of the bird's disappearance. If trapping for aviaries contributed to its fall in numbers, it is tragic, as the bird rarely survived in captivity. (*J. Gould*)

Top:
Blue-bonnet, *Psephotus haematogaster*. (30 cm. Open timber. Common.) This is the only representative of the genus *Psephotus* in which the sexes are alike in appearance. Not perhaps well-named, as it is the face, not the bonnet or crown, that is blue. Also called Bulloak parrot and will be found in casuarina clusters. Frequently seen on roadside trees from a stationary car. *(P. Munchenberg)*

Centre:
Naretha parrot, *Psephotus narethae*. (25 cm. Dry open areas, casuarina clusters. Uncommon and in very limited area.) Also called Little blue-bonnet. This species is aptly named after one of the stopping places on the Indian-Pacific Railway. Naretha, on the western fringe of the vast Nullarbor, is from an Aboriginal word meaning "salt bush". The bird's range extends along the edge of the Nullarbor, eastwards to approximately the S.A. border. *(F. Lewitzka)*

Bottom:
Mulga parrot, *Psephotus varius*. (30 cm. Mulga scrub country. Common.) The differences between the sexes is very noticeable. These are the friendliest parrots seen in the drier country. If disturbed, they might fly up into trees, but will be down again very soon if the way is clear. Eats seeds of porcupine grass, guinea flowers and seeds, and blossoms from local trees. *(G. Taylor)*

147

Top:
Golden-shouldered parrot, *Psephotus chrysopterygius*. (25 cm. Light timber country, with termite mounds. Very rare.) This is another bird certainly in danger of extinction. A feature of its behaviour is that it builds its nests in functioning termite mounds and lives satisfactorily with the termites. A third creature comes to the party, a moth, whose larvae eat the droppings of the young in the nest and whose breeding cycle matches that of the parrots. *(L. Robinson)*

Centre:
Hooded parrot, *Psephotus dissimilis*. (25 cm. Tropical light timber country, with termite mounds. Common in small local area, otherwise rare.) This is another species which nests in termite mounds, and regarded by some observers as a sub-species of the Golden-shouldered parrot. Its small zone is in the vicinity of Pine Creek, N.T. It lays 5 eggs to a brood and produces 2 broods each year, but is in a country where nature's bird marauders abound. *(L. Robinson)*

Right:
Swift parrot, *Lathamus discolor*. (25 cm. Forest areas. Common.) This bird of numerous colours and shades breeds only in Tas., in a season extending from November to January. Then it crosses Bass Strait to winter in Vic., following the blossoming of eucalypts. Has a tinkling musical call which it sounds on the wing. It is a fast and erratic flyer. It feeds on the outer branches of the gum trees and is easily approached. *(L. Robinson)*

CUCKOOS AND COUCALS CUCULIDAE

The Australian cuckoos, though related to those overseas, have no call that resembles the popular call of the old-world birds, such as that of the bird in the cuckoo-clock, the call after which the cuckoo was named.

Best known in the Australian family is the Pallid cuckoo, whose song, while at first cheering people by foretelling the coming of spring, later can irritate them considerably. This mating call goes up the scale, is repeated by day and by night, so that its repetition sends some people near to screaming point.

The hen remains silent when it is time for the pair to get together on their big act of deception, when they "con" innocent birds of the bush neighbourhood to incubate their eggs and to brood their chicks for them.

Having observed the surrounding territory and its bird population—honeyeaters, mudlarks, trillers, robins, flycatchers—and worked out where these other birds are nesting, the male bird will attract their attention. He might do this by his aggravating song, or by his hawk-like flight, just the thing to bring out other birds to chase him. He ensures that they are kept well occupied and away from their nests for a time.

Meanwhile, back at the nest, the female cuckoo arrives and busies herself putting one of her own eggs in the nest. Because the rightful owner can count her eggs, the cuckoo will remove one of the eggs already there. When the owner returns, she finds the same number of eggs as when she left, and suspects nothing amiss. The female cuckoo will repeat her performance in several nests in the locality.

The baby cuckoo, when it hatches, has two important physical characteristics: strong legs, and a tender spot just below its neck. As soon as anything else touches this spot, the nestling will thrust with its legs until whatever is irritating it, another baby bird or an egg, is thrown from the nest. Thus, very soon the baby cuckoo is the only surviving member of the clutch. So the foster parents have just one baby to bring up.

In Australia, all members of this family are parasitical like this, with the one exception of the Pheasant coucal, a bird different in several ways from the cuckoos.

Top:
Pallid cuckoo, *Cuculus pallidus*. (30 cm. Open timber, urban areas. Common.) This is a bird that "gets around", so much so, that all of its movements are not clear to observers. In the warmer inland it is present throughout the year, but in the coastal areas of the south-east, arrives only at the start of spring. This species is not seen outside Australia. *(G. Weatherstone)*

Bottom:
Oriental cuckoo, *Cuculus saturatus*. (30 cm. Rain forests, forest margins. Uncommon.) This is a non-breeding visitor from the northern hemisphere, and is usually seen from November to April. Identification could be difficult; the plumage likely to confuse it with the Barred cuckoo-shrike and the shape with the Pallid cuckoo. *(E. Zillman)*

Top:
Fantailed cuckoo, *Cacomantis pyrrophanus*. (25 cm. Forests. Common.) The name is from its practice of fanning its tail as it comes to ground. The flight of cuckoos should provide family identification, with their distinctive undulating movement through the air, as they make a few strokes with the wings, then fold them for a short glide. *(M. Bonnin)*

Centre:
Brush cuckoo, *Cacomantis variolosus*. (23 cm. Rain forest, mangrove areas. Fairly common in limited range.) One feature which does not endear it to bird lovers is that a favourite hired foster-parent is the well-liked Rufous fantail. The voice is a slow, mournful scale descent, distinguishing it from the Fantailed cuckoo. *(G. Chapman)*

Right:
Chestnut-breasted cuckoo, *Cacomantis castaneiventris*. (23 cm. Rain forests. Rare.) The dense habitat and its secretive habits have made studies of this species most difficult. Apparently nothing is known of its breeding practices, other than that it is parasitic and does not build a nest. The call is a comparatively quiet and short downward scale. *(J. Gould)*

Top left:
Little bronze cuckoo, *Chrysococcyx malayanus*. (15 cm. Rain forest, mangrove areas. Fairly common.) The genus to which bronze cuckoos belong consists of approximately 12 species, 4 of which are found in Australia. This bird's range is mainly limited to the northern coastlines. It usually chooses warblers as foster-parents for its young. *(J. Gould)*

Bottom left:
Golden bronze cuckoo, *Chrysococcyx lucidus*. (18 cm. Forests, open timber. Fairly common.) This species covers vast areas in migratory flight, some birds leaving the continent for northern islands. Like other cuckoos, it is a valuable pest destroyer. These birds have strong stomachs and will eat hairy caterpillars which other birds will not touch. *(M. Kröyer-Pedersen)*

Centre right:
Horsfield bronze cuckoo, *Chrysococcyx basalis*. (18 cm. Open timber, coastal zones. Common.) Another mobile bird, is found throughout Australia, except in the dry centre and dense forest areas. It usually calls from a position on top of a tree and the call has been interpreted as "see-you", repeated with a down-the-scale inflection. A pinkish egg, with red spots, is usually laid in the domed nests of wrens or thornbills. *(G. Chapman)*

Bottom right:
Black-eared cuckoo, *Chrysococcyx osculans*. (18 cm. Dry areas, mallee, mulga. Uncommon.) Feeds on or near the ground, flies low, and usually perches on low branches or in small trees. For its host, chooses a builder of a cup-shaped nest, such as a Speckled warbler. Known to migrate to some northern islands, but all of its movements are not clear. A group making a sound recording of this bird's call found that it called throughout an entire night. *(G. Chapman)*

Top:
Koel, *Eudynamys scolopacea* (female). (40 cm. Tropical and sub-tropical forest areas. Common.) This species breeds in Australia, placing eggs in nests of friarbirds and other large honeyeaters. It migrates to islands northwards from May to August. It is a fruit-eater, both from wild trees and cultivated orchards. It sings a distinctive little musical tune, and also has a "coo-ee" call. *(H. Frauca)*

Centre:
Pheasant coucal, *Centropus phasianus.* (60 cm. Tropical, sub-tropical heathlands, grasslands, swamp margins. Common.) The long tail gives this bird a pheasant-like appearance. This is the only Australian representative of a group of 27 species. It builds a roofed or hooded nest, open at each end, so that the head protrudes on one side and tail on the other. *(C. Webster)*

Left:
Channelbill cuckoo, *Scythrops novaehollandiae.* (60 cm. Tropical, sub-tropical forest areas. Fairly common.) This big bird causes a mass attack when he goes out to decoy birds away from their nests. It fans out its tail, giving it a majestic appearance. The female chooses nests of crows, currawongs, and magpies. The Aborigines believed that the arrival of this bird foretold stormy weather. *(J. Gould)*

BARN OWLS TYTONIDAE

Barn owls are distinguished from other owls by the noticeable facial disc or mask. All owls have a unique feathered pattern in the face, but in the barn owl this is very clearly outlined to form the heart-shaped disc. These are birds of the night, ill equipped for daytime foraging or hunting, in fact helpless in the face of daytime attacks and harrying from smaller birds.

Four species of barn owls are found in Australia. The most common, called simply Barn owl, is very noticeable if seen openly in the daytime because of its pale colouring, so it must find a secretive roosting place for its daylight hours.

Barn owls are so called because of their habit of roosting in or near barns, where the rodents which are their main source of food are readily available. These birds always like to be near a food supply. They find it difficult to adjust to varying diets and often will die if a food source is suddenly cut off. Mice are their favourite food item and in times of a plague by these rodents, the owls are likely to appear suddenly in great numbers. They are magnificently-equipped hunters, able to swoop down silently to snatch the prey in capable claws.

The Barn owl is also known as the Delicate owl, a name justified for the sheer delicate beauty of their plumage. The blending of soft brown with the dotted whitish shades makes a lovely combination.

The Masked owl is in many ways a larger edition of the Barn owl. Though not as prolific, it is seen in many parts of the continent, including the Nullarbor Plains, where in the absence of trees it will roost in caves.

The Sooty owl is restricted both in its range and in numbers. Its facial mask is a little rounder and not as heart-shaped as in the others, and it has the shortest tail of any member of the family. It also has very fixed ideas about being boss in its own selected territory.

The Grass owl, though not so rare as the Sooty, also must be regarded as uncommon. This bird provides a fine example of physical adaptability, the differences from other owls being most marked, and certainly to the bird's advantage. It has long legs, clean of feathers, on which it can stand and view the surrounding areas, thus being aided in finding its own prey and in dodging would-be predators, like the fox and dingo.

A behaviour feature of all owls is the disgorging of pellets. On catching prey, the bird will consume all of the animal caught, but in the hours that follow, the owl's digestive system will sort out what is good and nourishing from waste material, such as bones and fur. Then at some time during the following day, the bird will open its beak widely and disgorge this waste, neatly bundled in a pellet. A subsequent examination of the pellet will reveal exact details of the owl's diet. Pellets disgorged by barn owls are distinctive in that, as well as being tidily wrapped, they have an additional mucous covering, which dries to form a protective skin.

Barn owl, *Tyto alba*. (30–35 cm. Savannah country, farmlands. Common.) This is an Australian representative of a species found almost the world over. The sexes are alike in appearance but the female is slightly larger than the male. Because of their value as a rodent destroyer, agriculturists find it worthwhile to preserve the big, older trees on their properties, with suitable nesting hollows. (*F. Lewitzka*)

Top left:
Masked owl, *Tyto novaehollandiae*. (38–45 cm. Savannah country, arid areas with roosting caves. Uncommon.) The large disgorged pellets found under a roosting place will indicate the presence of this species. They are popular in some localities as rabbit destroyers. There are accounts of fierce bluff displays by pairs of these birds when threatened. (*T. Waite*)

Bottom left:
Sooty owl, *Tyto tenebricosa*. (38 cm. Wet forest areas. Rare.) They have a varied repertoire of calls, from the soft and melancholy to a loud screeching. Proportionate to size, they have the largest eyes of the barn owls. The diet includes ring-tailed possums and gliders, rodents, and large insects. (*J. Gould*)

Bottom right:
Grass owl, *Tyto longimembris*. (35 cm. Swamp areas, heathlands, grassed areas. Uncommon.) The sexes are similar, with the female larger. It hides during the day in clusters of grass. The eggs are a little less rounded than is usual with owls. Study of this species has been limited and there seems to be no recording of its voice. The species has relatives in India and Africa, and the Australian race has extended to New Guinea. (*J. Orrell*)

OWLS STRIGIDAE

People who work late at night, who prefer to stay up rather than to go to bed, or for some reason are at their best when others are asleep, are popularly known as night owls, a tribute to those efficient, fascinating, big birds of the night.

For those in this category who would like to put some of the time to a study of birds, the owl family is recommended as one which would provide exciting and rewarding hours.

The mere presence of one of these birds, indicated by its call, arouses interest. A detailed study of its characteristics and personal traits proves an engrossing subject.

An owl's eyes face forward and this, with its flat face, gives it binocular vision. An owl must move its head to see anything at all that is not directly in front of it. Its head moves easily, as it has a flexible neck which allows the head to twist around so that the bird can look over its back. It can also swing its head back again quickly. There is the story of the small boy who ran around and around a perched owl, convinced that the bird's head was following him in unbroken revolutions. The owl's reverse head turns were performed too quickly for the lad to observe them.

The owl has very sensitive ears. Frequently owls depend on their hearing alone to catch their prey. Unlike the ears of most other living things, the ears of the owl are not placed on the same plane, one being set at a lower level than the other.

An owl has peculiar feet. It can reverse one toe, so that it has either three toes in front and one behind, like most other birds, or it can have two in front and two behind, like parrots and cuckoos.

But perhaps it is the calls of the owls that add zest to night "observation" of these birds. (Observation is an operative word, as owls are best studied and most likely to be seen and heard on bright, moonlight nights.)

The call of the Boobook is one of the most typical night noises of the Australian bush. It is friendly, musical, appealing. It often calls close to a camp or dwelling, so the call is easy to record, and one that will repay the trouble taken. A playback, bringing the bush into a living-room, is an unfailing source of delight.

Perhaps the most notorious night noise of the bush is the scream of the Barking owl. This is described as being very much like a woman shrieking in dire distress and, when not anticipated, produces fear in its hearers. The bird also has a call resembling the barking of a dog, hence its name. And it has an attractive "wook-wook" call, repeated twice, and heard often.

The Powerful owl's call is a deep, echoing, "woo-hoo", to some, uncharacteristic of the personality of this big, determined hunter.

Owls nest mainly in hollows and lay two to three rounded white eggs. The eggs of the Powerful owl are unusually small for such a large bird.

Boobook owl, *Ninox novaeseelandiae*. (35 cm. Open timber. Common.) Also called Mopoke, both names being interpretations of its call. Early settlers, on first hearing this call, thought it was an Australian cuckoo, and of all Australian bird calls, the Boobook's is perhaps most like the old world cuckoo. Has a typical soundless flight and catches small birds, mice, and insects. *(A. Gibb)*

Top left:
Barking owl, *Ninox connivens*. (43 cm. Inland timber areas, savannah country. Fairly common.) Also called Winking owl. Its barking call is realistic enough to awaken people in the country and have them wonder about a disturbance in the kennels. It is a most efficient hunter and is large enough to account for rabbits and small hares, as well as rats, mice, and varied birds and animals. *(L. Thorpe)*

Top right:
Rufous owl, *Ninox rufa*. (50 cm. Tropical forests. Uncommon and in limited area.) The sexes are similar in plumage pattern but the male is larger. It lives in three distinct northern zones, out of the Powerful owl's territory, but because of the remoteness, is rarely sighted. Its call is similar to that of the Powerful owl, but quieter. *(E. Zillman)*

Bottom right:
Powerful owl, *Ninox strenua*. (65 cm. Damp timbered areas. Uncommon.) The male is slightly larger than the female and does the hunting while the young are being reared. It is felt that a prevalent parasite might restrict the population of this big bird. It likes to perch by day in a thinly-leafed tree permitting fairly clear viewing and easy take-off. *(I. McCann)*

FROGMOUTHS PODARGIDAE

These birds are often referred to as Frogmouth-owls. But they are not in the owl family, nor even related. Certainly they are owl-like in some respects. Similarities include the big eyes, the silent flight, and the preference for night life.

But frogmouths are related to other birds, such as kookaburras, swifts, rollers, and rainbowbirds. The scientific name *Podargus* refers to gouty, not very useful feet, and is appropriate enough, because this is the major difference between these birds and those of the owl family, remembering the efficient, sharply-hooked feet of the owls.

The Tawny frogmouth is the species of this family seen most in Australia. In fact, almost throughout the land, it is a common country night bird. It suffers tragically from roadside deaths. It is a ground feeder, and the bitumen roads present ample sources of food supply.

The name "frogmouth" is apt, and a sketch of the limited area about the bird's mouth and eyes could well pass for a drawing of a frog. The bill is broad and flat, most unbird-like, and capable of opening widely.

Yet although they have this large mouth opening, or gape, frogmouths do not eat insects on the wing, like nightjars and swifts. They take moving things off the ground, such as spiders, centipedes, beetles, frogs, crickets, mice, and small lizards.

The flight of the Tawny frogmouth is low and slow, but powerful enough, although it does not cover long distances.

The nest is roughly made on a tree fork from gathered sticks. The eggs are white and the sitting bird adopts a typical, flattened or reclining attitude while on the nest, its mate sitting in the same tree or in another near by. The birds would not be easy to spot in the daytime. The frogmouth's camouflage is one of nature's wonders. These birds can sit or crouch along the branch of a dead tree, blending perfectly into the overall picture. They "freeze" as part of the act, and not only do their greyish plumage shades blend perfectly, but their very outline seems part of the tree, resembling a broken limb or a knotty bough.

If approached closely, the birds might bluff for a while, giving out a loud hiss with threatening, wide-open mouth. The same mouth is capable of giving a sharp nip.

There are three species of the genus *Podargus*, all of which are represented in Australia.

Tawny frogmouth, *Podargus strigoides*. (40 cm. Open timber. Common.) This bird is seen here in its camouflage act, which from even a close range resembles a broken limb. It will hold this position until it is approached to even less than a metre. (*L. Pedler*)

Top right:
Tawny frogmouth, *Podargus strigoides.* (40 cm. Open timber. Common.) Usually some bristles are present around the big, broad bill. Their preference is for large trees for daytime roosting. It lines the roughly-made nest with eucalyptus leaves and lays 2 or 3 white eggs. *(F. Lewitzka)*

Bottom left:
Papuan frogmouth, *Podargus papuensis.* (55 cm. Tropical forest areas. Uncommon and in limited area.) Similar to the Tawny frogmouth in behaviour and appearance, but larger, being the biggest frogmouth. It has a more extensive range of calls. It covers a very extensive area in New Guinea. *(G. Chapman)*

Bottom right:
Marbled frogmouth, *Podargus ocellatus.* (35 cm. Rain forests. Uncommon and with limited range.) This bird also belongs mainly to New Guinea and research on it has been restricted. It is said to vary its diet of insects and small animals with occasional fruit. Its call has been described as a repeated "kooloo". *(H. Frauca)*

OWLET-NIGHTJARS AEGOTHELIDAE

This is an owl-like bird, made to sound a relative of the big birds of the night by its name. But this is not a bantam owl and, like the frogmouth, is not even related to the owl family.

The frogmouths and the true nightjars are its near relatives, and with them it shares many of its physical features. However, it possesses enough characteristics of its own to have won for itself the distinction, in Australia, of making a single species family.

Nocturnal, with the night bird's typical large eyes, it spends the sunlit hours in a hollow in a tree or a similar enclosed cavity. Occasionally during the day it may be heard uttering its call from this lair, but in the daylight it has not the impact of the sad-sounding wail of the night.

It hunts both in the air and on the ground. The procedure for catching insects on the wing is to fly at the prey with open mouth, snatching them in. On the ground it is fast and agile, and though it goes on to roads and highways after its prey, it is not a frequent road casualty.

An important part of its equipment are the bristles around the beak. These are a useful aid to hunting, helping to ensnare flying insects. Also these bristles serve a purpose in enabling the bird to gauge the size of a hollow, the "cat's whiskers" which measure the room available for entry.

The Australian species is said to have originated in New Guinea, where the birds are very common and are found in several species. In Australia, Owlet-nightjars are possibly more common than is believed. They range over almost the entire continent, wherever there are trees big enough with hollows for them to hide in.

Birds who shun the daylight naturally are not often observed, although this species will show itself if disturbed. They may be viewed, if their roosting tree is known, by giving a few taps on the tree. The bird will come to the opening of its hollow to see who is knocking.

It is the smallest of Australian night birds. Other distinctive features include the lengthy barred tail, which provides another way of distinguishing the bird from an owl, and the nostrils, which are in slits at the tip of the beak. The legs and feet are pink.

The scientific name, *Aegotheles*, is a Greek word meaning "goat-sucker", and refers to a folklore which told of these birds taking milk from goats in the small hours of the night.

Owlet-nightjar, *Aegotheles cristatus*. (23 cm. Open timber, forests. Common.) As it hunts both on the ground and in the air, its food is any small insect that flies or crawls. A likely reason for their shunning daylight is that on any appearance in the open, they are attacked by other birds, who obviously take them as members of the owl family. (*K. Woodcock*)

NIGHTJARS CAPRIMULGIDAE

Nightjars roost on the ground by day and hunt in the air by night. They are seldom seen in their daytime haunts, not that these places are especially secluded or hidden away. Rather the birds themselves are hidden right on the open ground, for these are masters of camouflage.

They roost or crouch, the big eyes closed to mere slits, their entire plumage blending with the ground or its covering.

The eggs they lay—on the ground, too—are marked or coloured to match the habitat, so if a sitting bird is disturbed and takes to the wing, the interloper will be unaware that an egg is there.

And to complete the range of camouflage perfection, when the eggs hatch, the young, who are most in need of a protective colouring, are so much in tune with their surrounds as to be almost invisible.

The nightjar has other attributes suited to its own life-style. It has the pointed wings of birds which chase and catch their prey in the air, able to twist and turn in pursuit. The eyes are especially large for night functioning, like those of owls or stone-curlews.

The call of night birds is an important feature of their behaviour pattern, because, even with their better-than-ordinary night vision, they still have to advertise their presence or locate their mates in the darkness, and a loud, distinctive call is surely the best way of doing this.

The three species of this family all have calls of the necessary strength and individuality. The White-tailed nightjar earned itself the name of Choppingbird, because one of its calls is likened to the noise of somebody chopping wood or hammering nails.

The call of the Spotted nightjar is often interpreted as a series of loud caws and gobbles, while the White-throated nightjar sings a lovely mating song during the breeding season, which is usually from August to December.

The distribution of nightjars generally is almost world-wide. The notorious American bird, the Whippoorwill, which generally annoys the citizens in its territories as the Pallid cuckoo does in Australia, is a member of the expansive nightjar family.

As with Owlet-nightjars, the scientific name refers to the legend of goat-sucking birds. This name, Caprimulgidae, is a combination of Latin words, whereas the name used in the case of Owlet-nightjars was Greek.

A further point of interest with nightjars is the way their eyes, caught by a spotlight at night, will glow back with a brightness like two balls of fire, to the extent of astounding night-time bush walkers.

White-tailed nightjar, *Caprimulgus macrurus*. (26 cm. Tropical coastal areas, rain forest, water margins. Common.) Also called Large-tailed nightjar, as well as other names referring to its chopping call. The tail measures up to 15 cm. It lays 2 eggs on the ground, without recourse to nesting material or scratched-out cavity. (*E. Lindgren*)

Right:
White-throated nightjar, *Eurostopodus mystacalis.* (35 cm. Dry sclerophyll forest. Fairly common in own zone.) Generally its area covers those parts of Australia not inhabited by the Spotted nightjar. Lays only 1 egg, off-white marked with purple and brown, but will sometimes have as many as 3 broods in a season. The chick can run and almost take care of itself on hatching. *(H. Frauca)*

Below:
Spotted nightjar, *Eurostopodus guttatus.* (30 cm. Dry open timber, mallee. Common.) It has a very extensive range, covering almost the entire continent, excepting Tas. and a few eastern coastal areas. It likes an abundance of ground litter. The birds of the two species in the genus *Eurostopodus* do not have bristles about the mouth. *(G. Taylor)*

SWIFTS APODIDAE

Swifts are birds of the sky. They do not, in fact cannot, rest or move freely on the ground. Their legs and feet are not equipped for ground movement, but the toes are clawed for clinging to vertical surfaces. If one of these birds should be stranded on the ground through some circumstance, it is quite incapable of taking-off in flight.

It has to flutter and work itself along to the first tree, post, or upright thing it can find, then proceed to scramble up, grasping with beak and claws, working itself higher and higher until it reaches a height at which it can let go and become airborne.

One question debated is whether the Spine-tailed swift does roost in Australia. There are some who say that the bird does not "land" at all during its Australian stay, while others assert that it will roost or settle at deserted, unseen spots on high tree trunks or against cliff faces.

It is the sky that is their domain, and certainly they live most of their lives in the air, hunting and eating, even mating on the wing.

The Spine-tailed swift, the one most often observed in recent investigations, is no longer than 20 cm, but has a wing span of over 50 cm. Its wings, when folded, project 8 cm beyond the tail.

These birds are often connected in people's minds with swallows, but there is no relationship here. There is similarity in some of the flight patterns and both groups catch insects on the wing.

However, swifts are related to frogmouths and nightjars, although there is little similarity in appearance. They share with nightjars the physical habit of flying with the beak open to catch flying insects, although swifts are not nocturnal hunters. Also swifts are capable of much greater sustained flying speeds than frogmouths and nightjars.

The Grey swiftlet is the only member of the family to nest and breed in Australia. The nests, built in colonies along cave walls and roofs, are made of saliva from the bird's mouth, mixed with vegetation. Most build their nests this way, but one overseas species, the Edible-nest swiftlet, uses saliva only, and as the name implies, the nests are recovered and sold for human consumption.

Grey swiftlet, *Collocalia spodiopygia* (left); Uniform swiftlet, *Collocalia vanikorensis* (right). (Both: 11–12 cm. Tropical coastal cliffs and ranges. Grey: Fairly common in limited zone; Uniform: Rare.) They are seen in large flocks over the ranges and jungle, and are fast on the wing, reaching estimated speeds of 200 km/h. Their colonies contain hundreds of nests and the flight into the nesting caves is bat-like. *(G. Mathews)*

Top:
Glossy swiftlet, *Collocalia esculenta.* (9 cm. Tropical coastal cliffs, cleared forest areas. Rare in limited area.) Its range is perhaps even more limited than those of the other tropical swiftlets. The species which do not breed in Australia are believed to mate and nest in New Guinea, migrating to the continent at irregular times. *(J. Gould)*

Right:
Spine-tailed swift, *Chaetura caudacutus* (top); Fork-tailed swift, *Apus pacificus* (bottom). Spine-tailed: (20 cm. Sky over forests. Common.) Flocks are often seen before storms. The spines are a continuation of the tail ribs and project 2 or 3 cm. The powerful wings beat rapidly in flight, with variations of gliding and diving. Fork-tailed: (18 cm. Sky, mainly inland. Common.) This bird is likely to fly anywhere over the continent if food is available and weather conditions match its flight patterns. *(G. Broinowski)*

KINGFISHERS ALCEDINIDAE

King of kingfishers in Australia is the kookaburra, needing no introduction because it makes such a good job of introducing itself. Its laughter, at sunrise and sunset, and often at other times during the day, is heard throughout the bush, in towns, and in many suburban areas.

Traditionally this laughter is a bush noise, and if kangaroos are used to show a bush setting in a visual medium, then the kookaburra's laugh is the first choice when setting is indicated by sound.

While the kookaburra is the most well-known member of the kingfisher family, rarely in his natural environment does he catch fish. However, he catches many other living things, a lot of them categorised as pests, and particularly he is known and valued for his snake-catching skill. If snakes are about with young, more than likely a kookaburra will find them, and he and his brood will quickly account for a big proportion of the snake family. They will also devour rodents, lizards, yabbies, a variety of insects, and the young of other birds.

The kookaburra's appeal is not limited to his voice. He is a handsome fellow in his own right, with some colourful plumage and a distinctively shaped body and bill. He is often seen on telephone wires or roadside trees, sitting motionless, watching for a movement on the ground below. There are limitations to his activities, and because of his weak legs and feet, he is not seen manoeuvring about the thicker bush or among branches like parrots and other birds. Nor are the wings suited to long flights.

Some other eye-catching birds in the kingfisher family must rate as among the most beautiful of birds in striking blue or green, in combinations of these colours, and with some subtle tones of red and quieter shades.

There are more than eighty species of kingfisher the world over. Ten kinds are found in Australia. Only two of these are known as "true" kingfishers. These are the Azure kingfisher and the Little kingfisher, of the genus *Ceyx*. In this group, the bills are long, the tails short, and the birds are distinguished by having only three toes, two in front and one behind. These are well named as "fishers". They live along creeks and rivers and their food is water life—small fish, crabs, yabbies, tadpoles, and insects.

Members of the family will kill their prey, whether reptile or fish, by holding it in the powerful beak and hitting it hard against a tree branch.

Azure kingfisher, *Ceyx azureus*. (18 cm. Inland waters. Fairly common.) A shy bird, and to sight it closely, one must move slowly and quietly and stay hidden. Catches fish by diving efficiently. Will watch for prey near the water, with a jerking or bobbing head movement. Excavates its nest in soft soil or sand along the bank of a stream. (*C. Webster*)

Top:

Little kingfisher, *Ceyx pusillus*. (12 cm. Mangrove areas, water courses in tropical rain forests. Uncommon.) The smallest of Australian kingfishers, it is a smaller version of the Azure kingfisher, and is even shyer and more difficult to sight or photograph than the former. Has a very limited range in the far north, occasionally sighted in the Darwin area. *(G. Chapman)*

Centre:

Kookaburra, *Dacelo gigas*. (45 cm. Open timber, town edges. Very common.) Also called Laughing jackass. When sounding its popular laugh, tilts its head skywards and moves its tail up and down. The tail is similarly moved as it settles after flight. Adapts well to civilisation and many birds are fed regularly in backyards. *(J. Ferrero)*

Bottom:

Blue-winged kookaburra, *Dacelo leachii*. (35–38 cm. Northern coastal and inner-coastal timber areas. Common.) Rather similar to the Kookaburra in appearance and behaviour and its call sounds like an unsuccessful attempt to imitate the other's laughter. Frequently steals eggs and young from near-by nests and is continually harassed by other birds. Nests in hollows, high in trees, and lays 3 or 4 white eggs. *(R. Fletcher)*

165

Top left:
Sacred kingfisher, *Halcyon sancta*. (20 cm. Mangroves, open timber, creeks and rivers. Common.) Visits the south to breed in the spring and summer, announcing its arrival with a ringing four-syllable call, a repeated "ki". These breeders are believed to migrate to New Guinea and Indonesia, while the birds which breed in the north will remain throughout the year. It catches prey both on land and in shallow water. *(A. Young)*

Top right:
Forest kingfisher, *Halcyon macleayii*. (20 cm. Coastal and inner-coastal timber areas. Common in limited area.) They build mainly in the nests of tree termites, a tunnel with an egg chamber at the end. The white patch on the wing is the most distinctive mark of this species, but can be seen only when the bird is in the air. It may be seen throughout the year in the tropical north; mainly a spring–summer migrant further south. *(A. Clements)*

Left:
Red-backed kingfisher, *Halcyon pyrrhopygia*. (22 cm. Mallee scrub, savannah areas. Fairly common.) This bird tunnels a nest along the soft-soiled bank of a watercourse, or in a sand-dune. It is not a fish-catcher and can exist away from water. Its diet includes insects, spiders, small lizards, scorpions, and centipedes. Usually sits alone in a tree, watching for prey, then will dart suddenly. *(F. Lewitzka)*

Top left:
White-tailed kingfisher, *Tanysiptera sylvia.* (30 cm. Rain forests. Uncommon and in limited area.) Favours lush tropical country and migrates from New Guinea to northern Australian areas to breed, tunnelling into a termites' nest low on a tree or on the ground to lay its eggs. Its call is said to be like that of the Sacred kingfisher. The two central tail feathers extend up to 18 cm in the male bird, a little shorter in the female. *(L. Robinson)*

Bottom left:
Mangrove kingfisher, *Halcyon chloris.* (24 cm. Mangrove areas, open timber, creeks and rivers. Fairly common in limited range.) This species does not come south. Its call, of two notes only, is regarded as the feature best distinguishing it from the similar Sacred kingfisher. Like the former bird, it nests in tree holes and termite nests, laying 3 white eggs. *(N. H. P. Cayley)*

Bottom right:
Yellow-billed kingfisher, *Halcyon torotoro.* (18 cm. Mangroves, rain forests. Rare.) The limited range is at the extreme tip of Cape York. Its call is a loud, sad trilling. It will pounce on insects, small lizards, rodents, and swamp creatures from a low branch, usually hunting alone. It nests in tree termite nests, laying 3 white eggs. *(E. Zillman)*

BEE-EATERS MEROPIDAE

It is a pity that these birds, in Australia as in other parts of the world, are called bee-eaters, as this name could unduly concern apiarists. The name commonly used for the single Australian species, Rainbowbird, is more apt, because here is a beautiful bird, showing a range of eye-pleasing rainbow colours.

Rainbowbirds, great insect-catchers, will select a small working area. The long, pointed wings make them excellent aerialists, able to twist and change direction or altitude to catch an evasive insect. Their diet takes in moths, dragonflies, beetles, wasps, grasshoppers, and all kinds of flying insects. Most certainly bees do not form a disproportionate part of their diet.

The nesting procedure is of interest. The nest is in a burrow or tunnel, for which they choose soft or sandy soil, preferably along the bank of a watercourse or a raised earth formation, as on the side of a graded road. In making the burrow, the drilling is done with the bill and the earth removed with the feet. The soil removal is done most efficiently. There is no heap of dirt left, no tell-tale mound as is left behind by some burrowers or by a post-hole digger. This would be a "give-away" to predators. As it is the hole is small and so shaped to be well hidden.

The choice of the direction this hole faces is important. Invariably it is directed away from prevailing winds, so that dust and rain cannot blow in. The birds must possess an inbuilt awareness of local climatic conditions.

The bird ranges all over Australia, except for the extreme south-east and south-west. They migrate to the south, arriving there in the early spring in small flocks, heralding their arrival with a distinctive call. In the early autumn, they will leave as suddenly as they arrived, headed back to the warmer north.

Rainbowbirds are likely to occur in large numbers in places where they have not been prominent before. There is a report of a mass appearance in Darwin in the early 1960s. In Victoria they were seen in the springtime of 1974 in greater numbers than usual and in places they had not previously visited.

Rainbowbird, *Merops ornatus*. (20 cm. Open timber. Common.) The two long tail feathers are generally a distinctive feature, extending beyond the normal length of the tail for nearly 3 cm in the male, a little less in the female. However these sometimes become frayed as the breeding season progresses, or the birds could lose them. (*H. Frauca*)

ROLLERS CORACIIDAE

Rollers get their name from the practice of rolling in the air when in flight, sometimes indulging in a routine to match that of a stunt pilot, with rolls, loops, and dives. Their dives would be especially exciting if performed at an air pageant, because the "pull-out" is left until the last split second.

Because of these antics, they have been described as the clowns of the air, as though they performed to entertain spectators or themselves. Perhaps the second thought is not far off the mark, as their aerobatics are regarded as part of a display flight and ornithologists believe that often the aerial manoeuvring of birds is a cementing of relationships in the mating programme.

The birds of the single species seen in Australia are called Dollarbirds, because when they spread their wings in flight, two silver shapes or dollars are revealed.

Rollers are in the same general group as kingfishers and bee-eaters, and all share a number of features. The most noticeable would be the bright colouring and rollers, though not as brilliant as the beautiful Rainbowbird and some of the kingfishers, are nevertheless attractive birds, with blue-green colouring, bright red legs and bill, and a red circle around the eyes.

Another interesting characteristic shared by these three families is one that easily could go unnoticed. It is that the three front toes, for some of the way, are jointed together.

This feature, which must solidify the foot, is found in two of the toes of the kangaroo.

The Dollarbird comes to Australia to breed in the spring and summer. Its range mainly is in the far north and north-east, coming south into Victoria, with occasional appearances in Tasmania.

It favours country where tall trees abound and will spend most of its days in the tops of these. The birds will perch on an open or dead branch, leaving to chase flying insects, their main food. As evening approaches, this activity will increase, and they will be seen doing their twisting and turning, hawking over the trees until nightfall.

Occasionally they will come to the ground to vary their diet with such things as beetles, slugs, termites, and centipedes. Also they will be seen clinging to the side of a tree, with their strong beaks pulling out larvae from under the bark.

Dollarbird, *Eurystomus orientalis*. (30 cm. Woodlands. Fairly common.) Also called Broad-billed roller. The sexes are alike. Its call is hard, cackling, and unpleasant, usually heard only when flying. In the winter, they leave Australia for New Guinea and other northern islands as non-breeding visitors. *(E. Lindgren)*

PITTAS PITTIDAE

In official Australian bird checklists, this family heads the order of birds known as Passerines. Passerines make up more than half of the over 8,000 bird species of the world. In Australia, their count is roughly 350 out of an approximate overall total of 750 species.

Perhaps the most important single distinguishing feature is that the foot of such birds has three toes pointed forward and one toe pointed back. When the bird perches, the hind toe locks into place and the bird, even if asleep, cannot fall from its perch.

In the families of non-passerines, the arrangement of the toes varies considerably. For example, waterbirds and seabirds have webbed feet. Some birds have no hind toe or just a mere pimple representing the hind toe. Others, like parrots and cuckoos, have two toes facing forward and two pointed back. Owls can vary their toe directions, from having three pointed forward and one back, to two pointed each way, thereby adjusting the gripping facility of the foot. Frogmouths, kingfishers, and rollers have two front toes joined for part of the way. Other birds still, like the herons, have the back toe joining the leg at a higher level than the front toes.

Passerines are often referred to as "perching birds", but the name is not ideal for distinguishing purposes as some of the species within the group prefer to roost on the ground.

Pittas are not often seen in Australia for several reasons— their low numbers, their very limited range, the remoteness of their habitat, and their elusiveness.

Three species are found, only one, the Buff-breasted pitta, being present in any number. They are birds of the dense, hardly-accessible rain forests, where they dwell and feed mainly on the ground.

The nests, on the ground or places low in tree or bush, are domed, with an entrance at one side and a built-up ramp. There are usually four eggs in a clutch. These are creamy-white, marked in brown or grey.

This species is also called the Noisy pitta, and its loud and clear call is the one revelation that the birds are in the vicinity. The regular call is a three-syllable ejaculation which brings varied interpretations of what the bird is saying. Reported phrases heard are "Get to work", "What's the time?", and "Have a bath". Some observers claim that the bird possesses a ventriloquial talent, the voice seemingly coming from a different direction from that in which the pitta is located.

Although most of its activities are at ground level, the bird sometimes goes high into trees to sound its call, but even this is done with an odd touch, as it climbs rather than flies to the tree-top.

Their food consists of insects and small reptiles, caught on the forest floor, and tropical snails, which are held in the beak and beaten on to rocks to smash the shells.

A fourth species, the Blue-winged pitta, is a rare vagrant from Malaysia with only a few sightings on the north-west coast.

Buff-breasted pitta, *Pitta versicolor*. (20 cm. Rain forests. Fairly common in limited range.) The small range is the north-eastern coastal zone. It has become more elusive than ever in its breeding season, October to January, and its nest is difficult to find. The eggs are glossy, creamy white, with an assortment of markings. *(F. Lewitzka)*

Above:
Black-breasted pitta, *Pitta iris*. (16 cm. Tropical rain forests, mangroves. Uncommon.) This is also aptly called the Rainbow pitta. Its range, so far as is known, is limited to the top of N.T. and northern W.A., and some coastal islands, including Melville Island and Groote Eylandt. *(F. Lewitzka)*

Left:
Blue-breasted pitta, *Pitta erythrogaster*. (18 cm. Tropical rain forests. Uncommon.) Its limited zone is at the top of Cape York. Believed to migrate to New Guinea. The breeding season is from October to January when, like the Buff-breasted pitta, it builds a dome-shaped nest, well hidden. Lays 3 or 4 creamy or buff eggs, with purple markings. It moves very quickly over the forest floor and sounds a sad, two-syllable call. *(J. Gould)*

LYREBIRDS MENURIDAE

The once-plentiful lyrebird, with the arrival of settlers became the victim of mass slaughter, both for the fun of the hunt and for the commercialisation of the tail feathers, and possibly came close to extinction.

Happily today there is a different story, as steps are taken towards protecting this fascinating bird. One major move has been the "artificial" extension of its breeding range. Lyrebirds were taken across Bass Strait from Victoria and are successfully established in Tasmania. In other places, they have been introduced into National Parks and into smaller, safe areas.

In Sherbrooke Forest, near Melbourne, Victoria, the lyrebird is seen and heard at its best, and here it is a popular tourist attraction and a continued source of local interest. Fortunately their calls alone are an attraction, because they are shy and elusive birds, often heard and not seen.

Lyrebirds—the name comes from the shape of the instrument, sometimes seen in the bird's tail—are found only in Australia. There are two species, the Superb lyrebird, and the Albert lyrebird, the latter found only in north-eastern New South Wales and south-eastern Queensland.

The outstanding physical feature of the bird is the tail of the mature male, made up of a total of sixteen striking feathers. Among other significant features are the powerful legs and big clawed feet, with toenails approximately 3 cm long. The wings are short and rounded and the bird is not a great flyer. Though it roosts and nests high up, away from ground enemies, it will reach these heights by springing from bough to bough, rather than by flying. It will return to ground level by gliding, using its wings as brakes as it nears the ground.

The male conducts an impassioned, pre-mating courtship. His behaviour is typically masculine, sometimes pleading and coaxing, at other times full of bounce and business. The hen is just as typically female, utilising the wiles of her sex, playing hard-to-get, neatly timing her eventual response. In the male's display, the long tail is thrust forward over the bird's head, hiding his body under an umbrella of beautiful feathering, silvery-white and wispy, the whole act performed against a brilliant musical background. The loud, challenging mating music changes, as the performance proceeds, to rounds of clever mimicry, in which a variety of sounds of the bush may be heard, especially those of other bird species.

Bottom left:
Superb lyrebird, *Menura superba*. (80–90 cm male, 45–50 cm female. Thick, tall forest, fern gullies, mountain areas. Fairly common in limited range.) Its brilliant mimicry imitates such varied calls as the cockatoo's screech, the whip of the Whipbird, and the Kookaburra's laugh. Apart from bird calls, it imitates dogs barking and the sawing of timber. A sub-species, called the Prince Edward lyrebird, is found in N.S.W. and Qld. *(I. McCann)*

Bottom right:
Albert lyrebird, *Menura alberti*. (80–90 cm male, 50–60 cm female. Fairly common in very limited area.) The *alberti* was given by John Gould in 1850 to honour Prince Albert, consort of Queen Victoria. Like the Superb lyrebird in many ways, but males will display on fallen logs, rather than on mounds in cleared places. *(J. Gould)*

172

SCRUB-BIRDS ATRICHORNITHIDAE

The family of scrub-birds, confined to Australia, consists of only two species, one of them rare and the other exceedingly so. Yet these small birds have contributed much to the pages of Australia's bird history.

They make their mark mainly through their various vocal characteristics. These include a very rich, loud song voice, a marked talent for mimicry, and a ventriloquial quality that can be most misleading to an observer trying to pinpoint their presence. All of their vocal gifts are tied to a peculiar development in the muscles of the voice box, and it was suggested at the time of their discovery that this gave them an affinity with the lyrebird and the two families were thus placed near to each other.

Their original discoverers were John Gilbert and an assistant, James Drummond, who found the birds in the Drakesbrook area of Western Australia in 1842. Gilbert, a co-worker of John Gould and a dedicated ornithologist who gave his life in his devotion to bird study in Australia, sent specimens to John Gould, then back in London. The bird fascinated Gould. He called it the Noisy scrub-bird, thereby disappointing Professor A. Newton, who felt this lacked imagination and that such a bird was entitled to a name more striking and romantic. Yet today the bird still bears Gould's original vernacular name.

Then in 1865, another species of the family was excitingly discovered right on the other side of the continent, in a limited range in north-eastern New South Wales and south-eastern Queensland. This discovery was made by two collectors, James Wilcox and John Macgillivray,

who did not recognise the bird. It was forwarded to Dr E. Ramsay, of Sydney, who identified it as a slightly smaller scrub-bird. Because it showed a reddish colouring in its plumage, he called it the Rufous scrub-bird.

In the years that followed, there were occasional sightings of this bird, but the Noisy scrub-bird was feared to be extinct. Then in 1961, probably the most exciting chapter in the history of the bird was written when, near the south coast in Western Australia, the species was rediscovered by a group of dedicated ornithologists.

Scrub-birds, because of their elusiveness, their quiet colouring, and the dense country they occupy, are exceedingly difficult to locate and to sight. They rarely fly, doing so only as an extreme measure when disturbed.

Bottom left:
Noisy scrub-bird, *Atrichornis clamosus*. (23 cm. Covered ground areas in coastal bushland. Very rare.) Runs fast through the low bushes, like a small mammal. The name *Atrichornis* means "a bird without hair or bristles" and *clamosus* means "noisy". (*J. Gould*)

Bottom right:
Rufous scrub-bird, *Atrichornis rufescens*. (16 cm. Covered ground areas in rain forests. Rare and in limited range.) The nests are dome-shaped, with a side entrance, and lined with a wood-pulpy substance, set hard, but wet when first placed in position. Some of the limited range is in a National Park area and the species seems to have chances of survival. (*J. Gould*)

LARKS ALAUDIDAE

Larks are prominent birds in the old world. A naturalist visiting Palestine in the middle eighteenth century to report on the birds of the Holy Land, said simply that "there were larks everywhere". Africa is regarded as the larks' home base and it is said that the number of species lessens as the family extends its range from that country. In Australia, only one species made the distance. This is *Mirafra javanica*, the little Bushlark.

However, with the coming of settlers, the lark population was reinforced by the introduction of the Skylark, some of which arrived in Melbourne in 1857. It is a bird that adjusted well to Australian conditions, not interfering with the balance of nature as do some introduced birds, but adding enchantment to the surrounds and the skies.

Both of these species are similar to the Pipit, but there are differences to aid identification. The Bushlark is heavier, shorter, and has a stouter bill than the Pipit, and can be distinguished from the Skylark by its smaller size, the absence of a crest, and by the darker undercolouring. Its song on the wing, though resembling the Skylark's, is rather thinner. The Bushlark is seen in varying plumage shades in different parts of Australia.

The Bushlark has an individual, undulating flight. It sings while on the wing, sings on moonlight nights, and has some reputation as a mimic. In various localities, especially in South Australia, bird enthusiasts have found an added interest in noting the names of other birds mimicked by the Bushlark.

The Skylark, too, has a distinctive flight, coupled with its much-loved song. It will set forth, climbing higher and higher, the wings quivering as it sings melodiously. It keeps rising, until it is just a spot in the sky, still singing. It appears to hang hovering there, then it starts to descend, possibly with a different song now, gathering speed as it falls, until when about thirty metres from earth, it will break off its song and plummet down in a dive which makes one wonder whether the bird will safely survive.

Although common, it is not easily observed except when in the air, for as well as possessing excellent camouflage, it will hide itself behind grass or growth if approached.

Bottom left:
Bushlark, *Mirafra javanica*. (13 cm. Grassed paddocks, marshy areas. Common.) It has benefited from land settlement and clearance. Unlike many other small birds, larks will run with a "left, right" foot movement, instead of hopping on both feet at once. Also called Singing bushlark and Horsfield bushlark. (*G. Mathews*)

Bottom right:
Skylark, *Alauda arvensis*. (18 cm. Grassed paddocks, farmed areas. Common.) An introduced species. As with the Bushlark, the sexes are alike. The expression "skylarking" does not refer to the behaviour of this bird. Rather it is a pun on the bird's name, most likely introduced when sailors were "larking" (frolicking) atop high masts or rigging of ships. (*J. Gould*)

SWALLOWS AND MARTINS HIRUNDINIDAE

These are attractive birds, worthy of notice, delightful to watch in the air, and making a worthwhile contribution to man's well-being as insect destroyers. Their handsome plumages are generally black above, white or grey underneath, with some red markings.

The names "swallows" and "martins" carry a wide meaning and sometimes are interchanged among birds of the family. The main difference between the two is that swallows have a long, forked tail, whereas the tails of the martins are shorter and only slightly forked.

The White-backed swallow, as its name implies, breaks away from the general description of being black overall on the top, and its white head, back, and throat are its best identifying features. They build tunnels in sand banks, about 60 cm deep and 5 cm in diameter, and as well as nests, these are used for resting or "hibernating" in cold weather, out of the breeding season, when the birds will gather in large numbers and drop into a torpid state.

The common Welcome swallow builds its cup-shaped mud nest on verandahs and porches, in sheds and under bridges, in caves and in mine shafts. These birds are often seen sitting on wires along the roadside, which seems to indicate that this perching base ideally suits their small feet. Swallows are connected in people's minds with the spring, and that is when they are most often seen. Their winter movements in southerly districts are not always clear.

The other swallow listed is the very rare (in Australia) Barn swallow, of which there have been isolated appearances in the north.

Two species of martins belong to Australia. Of these, the Tree martin is distinctive in its liking for trees, in which it usually nests, choosing a ready-made hollow, although it might on occasions lessen the size of the opening with mud packing. Its habits are like those of the Welcome swallow, with which it often associates.

The other species, the Fairy martin, is also common, except in the north. A distinctive feature is the white patch on the rump or rear of the bird. These take more trouble with their nests than do the Tree martins, plastering their mud structures to a well-chosen, protected wall or overhanging area.

White-backed swallow, *Cheramoeca leucosternum*. (15 cm. Open spaces, with near by sandbanks. Common.) The forked tail makes up half the bird's length. Found mainly in inland areas, in small flocks, it twitters rather noisily in flight, a louder voice than that of the Welcome swallow. As with all members of the family, the sexes are alike. (*J. Gould*)

Top left:
Welcome swallow, *Hirundo neoxena*. (15 cm. General populated areas. Common.) The nests are made by mud segments being reinforced with grass or straw, then lined with materials such as hair, feathers, and grass. The call is an individual, one syllable tweet, which, in a flock, makes an accumulation of sound. It lays 3 to 4 white eggs, attractively spotted. *(K. Stepnell)*

Top right:
Barn swallow, *Hirundo rustica*. (15 cm. Northern towns. Rare.) Because of its similarities to the Welcome swallow, perhaps some visits to Australia have gone unnoticed. It is a non-breeding visitor from the northern hemisphere, so it would moult while in Australia and could be seen without the long feathers of the usually forked tail. *(J. Gould)*

Centre:
Fairy martin, *Petrochelidon ariel*. (12 cm. Open spaces, near water. Common.) This is the smallest bird in the family. It is very active in the air, swooping and darting after small insects. The nests are bottle-shaped, with a narrow entrance and lined with leaves and grass. Because of this, the bird is sometimes called Bottle swallow. *(M. Seyfort)*

Below:
Tree martin, *Petrochelidon nigricans*. (13 cm. Open timber, settled areas. Common.) Its flight is both acrobatic and tidy and it is an efficient insect-catcher in the air. Often seen in very large flocks, especially on summer evenings, just before settling down to perch in trees for the night. It lays 4 or 5 off-white, spotted eggs. *(H. Frauca)*

PIPITS MOTACILLIDAE

Although this family embraces both pipits and wagtails, it is noticeable that in Australia today it has only a single representative, the Pipit.

Three wagtails are often listed as stragglers or rare visitors to Australia—the Blue-headed wagtail, the Yellow-headed wagtail, and the Grey wagtail. They are birds of combined plumage colouring of black, grey, white, and yellow, with the Blue-headed wagtail possessing a blue-grey crown. They were given the name "wagtail" from a habit of wagging or bobbing the tail up and down, a practice indulged in to a lesser extent by the Pipit.

It is important to note that these birds are unrelated to the popular Willie wagtail which is in the family of fly-catchers, and has a different tail movement, wagging its tail from side to side.

Ornithologists consider it strange that the family Motacillidae is not more largely represented in Australia, where the conditions seemingly are most suitable for them. The Pipit, however, thrives here and is often seen. Its plumage, though devoid of bright colouring, is nonetheless appealing and a challenging photographic study.

It is frequently seen on the roadside. Even when moving after being disturbed, a Pipit normally will not go far. It may run along the ground for a short distance, or if it should rise, the flight will be short, then the bird will drop suddenly to the ground again, where it finds its own feeling of security.

Its preference is for open grasslands, where it may be seen quite alone, or in pairs, or sometimes in sizeable flocks. It will be seen sitting on low rocks, or on fences, but rarely perched in trees. It spends most of its hours on the ground.

In the spring, the Pipit is seen rising high into the air, like a Skylark, but it does not have the lark's continued song. It shares the mimicry talent of the Bushlark, blending the tunes of other birds with its own songs. On the ground, it utters only shorter chirps.

The Pipit may be confused with the birds of the lark family. It can be distinguished from the Bushlark by its tail-bobbing habits, and by its lighter, longer body and its more slender bill. The tail bobbing also distinguishes it from the Skylark, as does its longer tail, the lack of a crest, the absence of the quivering wings when ascending, and the quality of the song.

Pipit, *Anthus novaeseelandiae*. (16 cm. Grassland, open spaces. Common.) Also called Australian pipit and Groundlark. Its food consists of seeds and small insects taken on the ground. It runs, using its feet alternately, like the larks, not hopping like most other small perching birds. The chicks have down on the head and back when hatched, but quickly assume adult plumage patterns. *(K. & B. Richards)*

CUCKOO-SHRIKES AND TRILLERS CAMPEPHAGIDAE

Cuckoo-shrikes, it would seem, are not well named, unrelated as they are to both the cuckoo and the shrike, the latter bird not being seen in Australia. Admittedly the cuckoo-shrike does have some general resemblance to the cuckoo. There is something similar in the flight pattern and both birds are long in body and tail. But cuckoo-shrikes do not have barred tails, nor the parasitical nesting habit, the main trademark of cuckoos.

Ground cuckoo-shrikes are a little bigger than the others, with a slightly forked tail measuring 20 cm. It gets its vernacular name from its ground-feeding habits and from its fast movement when running, but is not a ground bird in the truer sense of the word, and will fly quickly enough into trees when disturbed, screeching as it does so.

Of the other cuckoo-shrikes, the one most frequently seen and commented upon is the interesting and attractive Black-faced cuckoo-shrike. These birds have a mystery movement of their own, which earns them the name "Shuffle-wing". Whenever they settle after flying, they carry on as though something is wrong with their feathered dress, shuffling and shaking themselves to re-arrange things. The performance appears to serve no purpose, other than being some form of display, but is an invariable procedure.

These birds have a distinctive flight, fast and undulating, with a few fast wingbeats being followed by a moment of gliding. The Black-faced cuckoo-shrike is a valuable pest destroyer and for this reason alone should be welcome in any locality. It has a very pleasing, rich song.

Trillers are smaller birds than cuckoo-shrikes, and in the two species seen in Australia there are noticeable differences between the sexes.

By far the more common is the White-winged triller. The plumage of the male bird in this species puts it into the prominent group of Australian black and white birds. However, it should not be confused with any of the others, size providing a clear distinction in most cases and it is heavier and more rotund than the Willie wagtail and Restless flycatcher. Perhaps the bird it most likely could be confused with, is the male Hooded robin.

In the south, they are strict migrants, arriving at the start of spring and leaving in late summer or early autumn. Not all of these birds come south, perhaps seasonal conditions being a factor in determining a stay in the north.

Ground cuckoo-shrike, *Pteropodocys maxima*. (36 cm. Open timber, savannah woodland. Fairly common.) They are found in inland rather than in coastal areas. Usually nest low, a patchy nest on a tree fork, with 2 or 3 eggs, though often 2 females will lay in the one nest. Has a pigeon-like head-movement when walking. *(M. Bonnin)*

Top:
Black-faced cuckoo-shrike, *Coracina novaehollandiae*. (33 cm. Open timber, savannah woodland. Common.) The nest is small, plate-shaped, made of small sticks and bark, bound with spider web, in a tree fork up to 10 metres high. It lays 3 olive-green eggs, with brown or russet markings. It is only a partial migrant, many birds remaining in the south for the winter. *(C. Webster)*

Centre:
Little cuckoo-shrike, *Coracina papuensis*. (28 cm. Open timber, mangrove areas. Common in some areas, mainly in north.) The male has a small pale distinguishing patch above the eye. Observers frequently comment on variations in basic plumage patterns of cuckoo-shrikes in different parts of the continent. It has a shrill call, often uttered when flying. *(T. & P. Gardner)*

Bottom:
Barred cuckoo-shrike, *Coracina lineata*. (28 cm. Rain forests. Uncommon and in limited zone.) It feeds on native figs and other fruits of the tropical forests. It is known as a destroyer of insects and tree pests. It nests high in big trees. Its calls are reported to be a pleasant muttering when feeding and a more melancholy murmuring. *(E. Whitbourn)*

179

Top right:

White-winged triller, *Lalage sueurii*. (18 cm. Open timber. Fairly common.) Also called Caterpillar-eater. This fine performer has a melodious song. The nest is very small, with an outside diameter of only 6 cm and a depth of about 3 cm. There are 2 or 3 greenish eggs, with brown or rufous markings. *(L. Pedler)*

Bottom right:

Pied triller, *Lalage leucomela* (male). (19 cm. Tropical and coastal forests, mangrove areas. Common in limited zone.) Also called Varied triller. There are noticeable differences between the sexes. It is quieter and less energetic than the White-winged triller, but has its own trilling song, used from time to time. It nests near to the ground. *(N. Chaffer)*

Below:

Cicadabird, *Coracina tenuirostris* (female). (25 cm. Timbered areas, mangroves. Uncommon.) Those who have heard and pin-pointed the call of this bird, feel that it is aptly named. Its diet includes cicadas, so probably the call is made as a lure. It is a rarely-sighted, shy bird, keeping to the tops of trees. Also called Jardine triller and Jardine caterpillar-eater. *(F. Lewitzka)*

BULBULS PYCNONOTIDAE

The bulbul, in Australia, is pretty much a "city slicker". He is, or has been, sighted in Sydney, Melbourne, and Adelaide, with numbers far greater in Sydney than elsewhere.

There was a reported release of bulbuls in Sydney in the 1880s, although they did not establish themselves there at once. They are unlikely to travel far across country, and the subsequent sightings in other, well-removed cities would be additional releases or, just as likely, escapees.

Releasing of birds has not always been in the best interests of the community or the environment, and often has been done to suit somebody's whim or convenience. Frequently exotic birds seen are "free" because they managed to get away from cage or aviary, and in many cases such freedom is short-lived, as the birds are ill-equipped to cope with natural hazards and introduced predators.

The red bristles or whiskers after which the single species of bulbuls seen in Australia is named, are really inconspicuous, the red eye patch, the black crest, and the red undertail being much more noticeable. Other features in what is mainly a plain-coloured bird, are the white cheeks and throat and the shiny black bill.

The birds give an impression of friendliness and of liking to know what is going on about them, and their chatter suggests a line of conversation that they would be willing to share. Other people, who tend their gardens carefully or have well-loaded fruit trees, put these birds in the pest category.

In spite of the bird's facility for attracting attention, its nest is usually well hidden in a dense bush, up to three metres high. The nest is cup-shaped, made of bark, small sticks, and garden refuse, with paper sometimes used as a firming base.

As well as its chattering, the bird has a cheerful whistling song. Overseas it is a prominent songbird and the common name came from an interpretation of the call. It is common in many countries, mainly in the tropics. The first species here were said to have come from China.

A second species, the Red-vented bulbul, has been seen on rare occasions in Melbourne, with a number of years between sightings. This bird lacks the crest and the red and white face markings of the Red-whiskered bulbul, and has a pale edging to its upper plumage pattern and a white tail tip.

Red-whiskered bulbul, *Pycnonotus jocosus*. (20 cm. Parks, suburban gardens. Common in Sydney only.) An introduced species that breeds during the spring and summer months, usually laying 3 eggs, with rust-coloured or brown spots. It often occupies a bird bath in a suburban garden or park. It is an active bird, frequently catching insects on the wing. *(N. Chaffer)*

THRUSHES TURDIDAE

An unusual mixture of some very popular introduced species and some lesser-known native birds make up this family.

The Ground thrush, also called the Australian ground thrush, is fairly common in those places where the dense and damp bushland that it likes is still untouched, but it will soon disappear once forest clearing commences. An attractive bird, it has a resemblance to the introduced Song thrush.

The Scrub-robins appear to have been rare always, although their shyness and their natural camouflage would have made study difficult for the early ornithologists as they do for observers today. The Southern scrub-robin has a range in the mallee type country in the south and south-west, while the northern bird is seen in very limited zones in the top north.

On the other hand, the introduced birds of the family provide opportunities second to none for close study and observation. The Blackbirds have moved right in and taken over people's yards and gardens, especially in Victoria and Tasmania, with indications of doing like-wise in Adelaide and in southern New South Wales. Usually they are well received and assume almost the status of pets about a place.

It does not need close observation to discover where the Blackbirds have built their nest. They choose any suitable low, fairly thick bush, usually accessible enough to permit opportunity to see and to count the eggs, and later to watch the progress of the young.

They are magnificent songbirds, starting their music in the morning and programming a longer, repeat evening session. The male bird is especially attractive in his pure black plumage, with bright yellow beak.

There is no question that the Blackbird is well suited to southern Australian conditions. It is said that the life expectancy of the bird in Australia is much longer than it is in its home country. A feature of the Blackbird here is that although it likes suburban and town areas, it does not attempt to settle in the bush.

The other introduced species in the family, the Song thrush, also makes itself known and liked around Melbourne gardens. In mid-winter, especially in the first weeks of July, it will occupy a high point in a leafless tree and sing lustily into the morning for long periods.

Ground thrush, *Zoothera dauma*. (25 cm. Dense, damp forests. Fairly common in limited range.) Also called Mountain thrush. The northern birds are sometimes listed as a separate species and called Atherton ground thrush. The generally darker plumage and scalloped, not spotted, breast of the Ground thrush are distinguishing features. (*T. Pescott*)

Above:
Song thrush, *Turdus philomelos*. (23 cm. Suburban gardens. Common in Melbourne only, rare to uncommon elsewhere.) An introduced species. The sexes are alike. The spotted breast is a main identifying feature. Well liked, and not so common as to be regarded as a pest. In fact it accounts for many pests itself, breaking open snails on garden rocks and concrete paths, leaving pieces of shell as evidence. *(T. Pescott)*

Top left:
Southern scrub-robin, *Drymodes brunneopygia*. (20 cm. Mallee and mulga scrublands. Uncommon.) Although shy and elusive, it is said to answer imitations of its call, a several-syllabled whistle. Long-legged, it prefers running to flying. It goes to much trouble over its nest building, including the erection of a miniature protective "fence" made of twiglets, but lays only 1 egg. *(G. Chapman)*

Centre left:
Northern scrub-robin, *Drymodes superciliaris*. (20 cm. Tropical forest margins. Uncommon.) Although in some ways resembling its cousin from the south, it lives in much denser country, goes to a little less trouble over its nest, and lays 2 eggs. It finds its food in the litter of the forest floor: insects, minute animal life, and bush snails. *(G. Chapman)*

Bottom left:
Blackbird, *Turdus merula*. (25 cm. Town and suburban areas in south. Very common.) An introduced species. The young and the females are so different from the black male bird that they may be mistaken as a different species. The nests are of grass or vegetation, bound with mud. There are usually 4 eggs, green-blue, with rufous-brown spots. *(H. Wright)*

BABBLERS TIMALIIDAE

The name "babbler", as often with bird family titles, embraces a multitude of other names.

Birds of the first group are called Rail babblers, with five species listed. These include the two logrunners, which are rain forest birds, the species having many similarities but occupying distinct territories.

These are solidly-built birds, with especially strong legs and feet, which are used for constant scratching on the forest floor in search of food. The birds have a practice, when scratching, of supporting themselves on their tails, which wears away the feather webbing at the "tail end", leaving the shafts of the feathers revealed and giving them the alternative name of spinetails.

The other species in this first group are the Quail-thrushes, so called because they possess some physical points and behaviour mannerisms of both quails and thrushes.

The True babblers or Scimitar babblers make up a second group, and are noisy, noticeable, and distinctive birds, which, with the dovetailing of their zones, cover the entire continent. The Grey-crowned babbler must take the award for the possession of the longest list of alternative names.

These birds are famous for their community efforts. They live and move in groups of varying number, sometimes up to twelve (hence the name Apostlebirds or Twelve apostles), and their team work, if observed closely, is astounding. Each bird has a specialised line of work in nest building and in the feeding and care of the young. They move bouncingly over the ground or through the trees in a follow-the-leader routine. It is said that they use a nest for sleeping quarters and even at night the group stays intact.

The last group consists of two whipbirds and the Wedge-bill. Whipbirds are another species heard more often than seen. They are well named, the call being introductory notes, followed by the sudden exploding "crack" of the whip. Then the female usually adds concluding notes to the call.

In some places, whipbirds are the species most imitated by lyrebirds, and frequently people start the lyrebird calling by imitating the whipbird. Therefore it is interesting to note that whipbirds themselves are very capable mimics, with the lyrebird possibly getting some counter-imitations.

The Wedgebill, too, is heard more often than seen. Its call is a delightful, rich, bell-like sound, heard often on moonlight nights in the dry areas that are this bird's territory.

Bottom left:
Southern logrunner, *Orthonyx temminckii*. (20 cm. Rain forests. Common in limited area.) Though living in dense forest, these birds will give away their presence by the noise of their scratching and their loud, penetrating calls. The nest is like a smaller edition of that of the lyrebird, built of sticks and moss, covered with dead leaves. (*N. Chaffer*)

Bottom right:
Northern logrunner, *Orthonyx spaldingi*. (25 cm. Tropical rain forests. Common in limited area.) Also called Chow-chilla, after the sound of its call, and Auctioneerbird, after the repetitive volume of the same call. The *spaldingi* is after Edward Spalding, a Queensland bird collector. It usually congregates in small groups. (*L. Robinson*)

Top:
Spotted quailthrush, *Cinclosoma punctatum.* (28 cm. Open timber, heathlands, rocky areas. Uncommon.) Also called Groundbird and Babbling thrush. When flushed, they rise like quails, with the same whirring sound from their wings. It is a shy bird, with a mainly quiet, thin whistling call, with louder utterances in the mating season. *(W. Labbett)*

Centre:
Chestnut quailthrush, *Cinclosoma castanotum.* (20 cm. Open timber, heathlands, rock areas, dry mallee. Fairly common.) A sub-species, *Cinclosoma alisteri,* also called Nullarbor quailthrush, is sometimes listed as a separate species, and inhabits a section of the Nullarbor. The Chestnut quail-thrush has a general preference of areas covered by small gum trees of various kinds. *(W. Labbett)*

Bottom:
Cinnamon quailthrush, *Cinclosoma cinnamomeum.* (20 cm. Semi-desert, mulga country. Fairly common in limited range.) It blends well with the colours of the country which is its habitat. The cupped nest is made of available vegetation, and sheltered by low bushes or protruding roots. It hides in the hottest part of the day under roots or in discarded burrows, to escape both the heat and predators. *(E. McNamara)*

Top right:
Grey-crowned babbler, *Pomatostomus temporalis*. (25 cm. Savannah country, mixed scrub. Common.) Sadly, this multi-named, previously well-known species is not as common as it was. Suggested reasons are the destruction of habitat and, in some areas, indiscriminate shooting, friendliness and group gatherings making them an easy target. It has a repertoire of chattering calls as well as its "yahoo". *(T. & P. Gardner)*

Centre right:
Chestnut-crowned babbler, *Pomatostomus ruficeps*. (22 cm. Mallee and dry timber, saltbush area. Fairly common.) Also called Red-capped babbler and Chatterer. Similar to other babblers in behaviour and breeding patterns, including the community efforts. but it is shyer. It lays 4 or 5 light brown eggs with pencilled lines. *(P. Munchenberg)*

Bottom right:
White-browed babbler, *Pomatostomus superciliosus*. (20 cm. Dry savannah, arid country. Fairly common.) Generally it occupies that part of Australia not in the zone of the Grey-crowned babbler, although they may overlap in some areas. Emits loud and lively chattering and some cat-like calls. As with other babblers, the domed nests are well made and long lasting, often with an extra storey added. *(T. & P. Gardner)*

Below:
Hall babbler, *Pomatostomus halli*. (18 cm. Mulga, timber country in dry area. Uncommon.) This species was recently discovered (May 1963) by a British Museum party, near Langlo Crossing, Qld. It was named as a tribute to Harold Wesley Hall who did much to encourage bird and nature study in Australia and in other parts of the world. *(N. Hooper)*

186

Left:
Wedgebill, *Psophodes cristatus*. (20 cm. Mulga, arid areas, dry savannah. Fairly common.) Some authorities list two species, naming them Chirruping wedgebill and Chiming wedgebill *(Psophodes occidentalis)*. At night, in the arid and semi-desert regions, the bird calls continually, quietly at first, but gradually increasing in volume, so that campers or tourists have the impression that it is moving closer. *(R. Garstone)*

Below:
Western whipbird, *Psophodes nigrogularis*. (23 cm. Sandhills, mallee scrub. Fairly common in limited range.) Although it bears the same name as its cousin, it does not make the sharp whipcracking call. However, has its own range of loud and unusual calls, and a game for the imaginative is to decide what the bird is saying. *(From collection of E. Paton)*

Left:
Eastern whipbird, *Psophodes olivaceus*. (25 cm. Dense forest, fern gullies. Fairly common.) As well as its whip call and mimicry, it also indulges in a chattering in which both male and female join. It moves quickly on the ground, occasionally flying for short distances. It feeds among leaves and ground debris, usually silently. *(K. & B. Richards)*

187

FAIRY-WRENS, EMUWRENS, AND GRASSWRENS MALURIDAE

A feature of bird observation in Australia is that, wherever one may be, the area will have some local ornithological interest. The family of wrens provides an example of the fact that there is no part of Australia where the little birds with the characteristic long, cocked-up tails will not be in near-by residence. Blue wrens alone, cover the continent.

In watching for blue wrens, it must be remembered that not all of them show blue in their plumage all of the time. And although the male in all his blue glory is the most eye-catching member of the family, his wives and daughters, the Plain Janes or Jenny wrens, though less glamorously plumaged, have their own quiet appeal. Likewise his sons, when not in breeding regalia, will be almost as plain as the females.

In the winter months, before younger males assume their blue colouring, their only visible distinction from the females is a darker bill and a little dark blue in the tail.

A family or group of blue wrens, which could consist of several generations and number a score or more, during the winter months might have only one bird in blue plumage. A male blue wren does not retain his blue feathering permanently until he is about four years old.

Among blue wrens, the Superb blue wren is the most common and best known, being found in parks and gardens of the larger cities and their suburbs, as well as in bush haunts. There are some species of the genus showing almost no blue at all.

Another interesting group of the wren family in Australia are the very small emuwrens, so called because the erect tail feathers resemble the feather of an emu. There are three species listed, each occupying distinctive areas, but all of them uncommon, even in their own zones. They are furtive birds, scurrying under low bushes or grass clumps when disturbed, often permitting such a brief glimpse that they are mistaken for bush mice.

Finally there are the grasswrens, even rarer than the emuwrens. Grasswrens are birds of remote places, written and read about more often than seen. They share several features with the emuwren—they are small, shy, and furtive, and have the same preference for ground movement and disinclination to fly. Their study and observation presents a challenge, taken up occasionally by keen ornithologists, with time and opportunity to pursue this useful service.

Superb blue wren, *Malurus cyaneus*. (13 cm. Bushland, heathland, gardens. Common.) Also called Blue wren. The characteristic tail measures up to 6 cm. In a garden, these dainty and delightful miniatures will become quite friendly, welcoming any facilities provided, especially food to their liking, with cheese a noticeable preference. *(M. Seyfort)*

Top:
Black-backed wren, *Malurus melanotus*. (13 cm. Savannah country, temperate heathlands. Moderately common.) It has a liking for mallee and mulga growth. Its territory generally does not overlap that of the Superb blue wren. Similarities between the two species include the rich, trilling song and the careful building of a dome-shaped nest. It lays 3 or 4 spotted eggs. *(K. & B. Richards)*

Centre:
Turquoise wren, *Malurus callainus*. (13 cm. Dry heathlands, arid timber. Moderately common.) The male birds are shy and hide in the thicker undergrowth which is a feature of their habitat. The nest sites, too, are chosen to deter intruders or predators. It lays 3 or 4 whitish eggs with rufous markings. *(E. Paton)*

Bottom:
Banded wren, *Malurus splendens*. (13 cm. South-western timberlands with thick undergrowth. Moderately common.) Also called Splendid wren. The species seem to become shyer as they move westwards. However they lose nothing of their brilliance and beauty in the minor colour changes. Nests are typically dome-shaped, low down in a small bush. *(A. Wells)*

Top left:
Variegated wren, *Malurus lamberti*. (14–15 cm. Heathlands,
timber with thick undergrowth. Moderately common.)
The *lamberti* is after a former English naturalist and the
species is also called the Lambert wren. Its voice is higher
and thinner than other blue wrens. Nests are similarly built
and placed, eggs whitish and spotted red. *(A. Young)*

Top right:
Blue-breasted wren, *Malurus pulcherrimus*. (14–15 cm.
South and south-western timber with thick undergrowth.
Moderately common.) Many of the scientific names refer
to the loveliness of these birds. Here *pulcherrimus* means
"very pretty". These are shy birds, and the male, though
vocal and vigorous during mating time, is especially
elusive. *(A. Wells)*

Bottom right:
Purple-backed wren, *Malurus assimilis*. (14–15 cm. Timber
with thick undergrowth. Moderately common.) This bird
has the most extensive range of any Australian wren. It has
a preference for dry country, and for the spinifex, mulga,
saltbush, and bluebush found in this terrain. Like most of
the wrens, it is seen in pairs or family parties. *(L. Robinson)*

Right:
Lovely wren, *Malurus amabilis.* (14 cm. Tropical rain forest with thick undergrowth. Moderately common.) Both the scientific and the common name justifiably refer to its attractiveness. Its first habitat preference is towards the mangroves and low growth of tropical water margins, but it is also seen in near-by drier areas. *(J. Gould)*

Bottom left:
Red-winged wren, *Malurus elegans.* (15 cm. Swamps, heathlands with thick undergrowth. Uncommon.) Draining of swamps and destruction of habitat have resulted in declining numbers. Another shy bird of the west, not often seen or heard. It is a typical industrious and thorough nest builder, with the usual low, dome-shaped wren nest. *(R. I. Green)*

Bottom right:
Lavender-flanked wren, *Malurus dulcis.* (14 cm. Rocky areas with thick, low growth. Uncommon.) There are two distinct "settlements" of this species, one in Arnhem Land, N.T., the other in the Kimberleys, W.A., but the two groups never meet. The preference for rock outcrops is a characteristic feature. *(P. Trusler)*

Top right:
Black and white wren, *Malurus leucopterus.* (12 cm. Arid areas with low growth. Moderately common.) Believed to be found, in its true black and white, only on Barrow Island and Dirk Hartog Island, W.A., the latter island being its place of original discovery in 1818. In some of its area, the country is treeless, with saltbush the only vegetation. *(A. Wells)*

Centre right:
White-winged wren, *Malurus leuconotus.* (12 cm. Arid areas with low growth. Uncommon.) Also called White-backed wren. This species is often listed as a race of the Black and white wren. The male in this mainland species has blue instead of black colouring. It is very shy, and on the open, treeless plains, has the opportunity to sight approaching visitors and to go into hiding, making observation difficult. *(E. Bound)*

Bottom right:
Red-backed wren, *Malurus melanocephalus.* (12 cm. Low tropical and sub-tropical vegetation. Moderately common.) Although its preference is for wet areas, it is also found in dry places. Its main requirement is an abundance of thick grass. Also called Scarlet-backed wren and Black-headed wren. *(E. McNamara)*

Below:
Lilac-crowned wren, *Malurus coronatus.* (15 cm. Tropical wet areas, mangroves. Moderately common in limited zone.) The tail measures up to 7·5 cm. It likes the vegetation of its tropical area, including pandanus palms and cane grass. The fairly large nest is constructed of cane grass, and includes a side entrance. *(G. Chapman)*

Top left:
Southern emuwren, *Stipiturus malachurus* (female). (16–22 cm. Heathland, swamps, sandhills with low growth. Uncommon.) The length of the body is 6–9 cm, the tail measuring 10–13 cm. Sometimes their resemblance to bush mice is accentuated by their hopping movements. As well as in mainland areas, it is found on Kangaroo Island, Dirk Hartog Island, and Tas. *(A. Wells)*

Bottom left:
Rufous emuwren, *Stipiturus ruficeps* (top left-hand bird). (20 cm. Arid areas, sand-dunes. Uncommon.) Also called Rufous-crowned emuwren. These birds like the spinifex and porcupine grass of their arid zone and the insects found in this vegetation. Some of their high-pitched calls are beyond the hearing range of many people. [Other birds in this illustration are Southern emuwrens (centre left and top right) and race *hartogi* (bottom and centre right).] *(G. Mathews)*

Bottom right:
Mallee emuwren, *Stipiturus mallee*. (16–17 cm. Mallee scrub. Uncommon.) This elusive species is seen occasionally in Wyperfeld National Park, Vic. Its talent for moving unhurt through the prickly grasses of the mallee area is amazing. The call is a quieter version of that of the Superb blue wren. It builds a small, oval nest in the porcupine grass, where it lays 2 off-white eggs, with dull markings. *(W. Labbett)*

Top left:
Thick-billed grasswren, *Amytornis textilis*. (15–18 cm. Salt-bush plains. Uncommon.) They also frequent sandy-based areas of debris left behind by flood. Their breeding season is indefinite, depending on climatic conditions, the birds waiting for rain before mating. They lay 2 white or near-white eggs, spotted brown. *(G. Chapman)*

Top right:
Thin-billed grasswren, *Amytornis purnelli*. (15–18 cm. Arid areas in centre, with rocks. Uncommon.) Also called Dusky grasswren. The *purnelli* honours H. A. Purnell, an ornithologist of Geelong, Vic. This bird has a fondness for porcupine grass and spinifex. The rocks, essential to its habitat, could be the feature best distinguishing it from the Thick-billed grasswren. *(T. & P. Gardner)*

Centre:
Dorothy grasswren, *Amytornis dorotheae*. (15–18 cm. Arid, sandstone area. Rare.) The name honours Dorothy White, of Scone, N.S.W. Also called Red-winged grasswren. Its range is in a limited area in the N.T., where it is difficult to sight, choosing rock clusters for hiding places. *(G. Mathews)*

Bottom:
Striated grasswren, *Amytornis striatus*. (15–18 cm. Sand-dunes, with low growth. Uncommon.) Also called Striped grasswren. It nests in grass or under the shelter of spinifex in a domed, well-made nest of bark and dried grass. Grass-wrens share the emuwren's talent for scuttling safely through harsh mallee grasses. This bird's chances of survival could be heightened by its presence in some National Parks. *(W. Labbett)*

Above:
Eyrean grasswren, *Amytornis goyderi.* (14 cm. Grassed sandhills in vicinity of Lake Eyre. Rare.) The *goyderi* honours G. W. Goyder, an explorer in remote S.A. in the nineteenth century. Its original discovery was recorded in 1874, then the bird was not heard of again until 1961. The varying conditions caused by alternate drying and flooding of Lake Eyre could be a factor contributing to its rarity. (*J. Gould*)

Top:
White-throated grasswren, *Amytornis woodwardi*. (20 cm. Rocky, spinifex areas. Rare.) The *woodwardi* honours Bernard H. Woodward, a former director of the Perth Museum, W.A. Its rarity and behaviour match that of the Dorothy grasswren, and although there are no records of its breeding or nesting, it could be assumed that they would follow the lines of similarly-located species. *(G. Mathews)*

Centre:
Black grasswren, *Amytornis housei*. (20 cm. Rocky, spinifex area. Rare.) The *housei* honours Dr F. M. House, an ornithologist of W.A. It is confined to a very limited area in the Kimberleys of that State. This is another bird so rare that a recent sighting was the first recorded for over half a century. *(G. Mathews)*

Bottom:
Grey grasswren, *Amytornis barbatus*. (18 cm. Watercourse on plains. Rare.) Another grasswren with a small, limited field, the Bulloo watercourse in north-western N.S.W. and south-western Qld. Although apparently well established. its official recognition did not come until July 1967. It lays 2 eggs in a well-hidden nest. *(E. McNamara)*

WARBLERS SYLVIIDAE

This is a large family of small birds. Mainly they are inconspicuous, because of their size and, in most cases, their plain plumage.

Heading the family list is the Reed warbler, the popular Australian representative of a wide-ranging genus, there being a score or more of reed warblers throughout the world. This bird is well named, as reeds are its main habitat and retreat.

Others in the group of old-world warblers include the two species of cisticolas. A feature of the breeding programme of these birds is the magnificently-made nest. They are said to be related to the Tailorbird of Asia and the nests are masterpieces of architecture and natural needlework. Holes are made in leaves or vegetation with the beak, then the material is stitched together with a cobweb thread.

Next come the grassbirds, swamp dwellers, also called marshbirds. Then two species of songlark, both normally coming south in the spring from northern Australia, although the migratory pattern is not regular.

The fairy warblers, of which there are nine Australian species—one is specifically called the Fairy warbler—are birds of the tropical and sub-tropical wet areas, liking the rain forests, the mangrove clusters, and similar damp haunts of that zone. These birds live and feed in the tree foliages, fluttering and frisking about after insects.

The little Weebill is found over almost the entire continent. The thornbills, on the other hand, of which there are twelve species, generally occupy the drier, more southerly woodlands, where they replace the fairy warblers.

Whitefaces have white marking on the forehead only, and this is a good distinguishing feature. They are birds of the arid desert and semi-desert areas, they feed on the ground and nest where they can find a place, the Southern whiteface particularly building a rather sloppy nest in any hollow or crevice that can be found.

Scrubwrens are mainly ground feeders, some of them furtive and difficult to see, but all possessing typical loud and revealing voices. Although each species is generally confined to a limited zone, the type of habitat is variable, usually with dense undergrowth but including the low-growing heaths of coastal sand-dunes in the south-west to the taller, luxuriant rain forests of the north.

Reed warbler, *Acrocephalus australis*. (16–17 cm. Reed beds, mangroves, swamp growth. Common.) This bird renders a lovely song, often on moonlight nights, and is frequently heard in city gardens and park ponds. It is a migrant from the north, but possibly not to the extent often thought. Many stay south for the autumn and winter, although then their song is not heard. *(K. Stepnell)*

Top right:
Golden cisticola, *Cisticola exilis* (female). (10 cm. Dense grass in damp areas. Common.) Also called Tailorbird and Golden-headed cisticola. To make its amazing nest, about the size of a cricket ball, it uses leaves, grasses, thistledown, and spider web. In the breeding season, the male will be seen displaying in the air. He also makes the first moves towards nest building, inserting the initial stitches, then stepping aside for his mate to carry on. (*E. & N. Taylor*)

Centre right:
Streaked cisticola, *Cisticola juncidis*. (10 cm. Grassed edges of coastal flood plains. Moderately common in limited range.) Very similar to the Golden cisticola. Distinct populations of this species are seen in pockets in Qld and N.T. In its display flight in the breeding season, its "lik-lik" call rhythmically matches its flight pattern. (*P. Trusler*)

Bottom right:
Tawny grassbird, *Megalurus timoriensis*. (19 cm. Reed beds, thick grass. Uncommon.) A shy bird, its call is a harsh, staccato, repeated "chut", with a richer, more melodious display song. It builds a well-secluded nest of dried swamp grass, lays 3 or 4 eggs, pinkish, with purple markings. As its name indicates, the species extends to Timor, and to other northern islands. (*C. Webster*)

Below:
Little grassbird, *Megalurus gramineus*. (14 cm. Reed beds, grassed swamps. Moderately common.) Even shyer than the Tawny grassbird, its call (a melancholy 2- or 3-note whistle), the smaller size and the patterned head are distinguishing features. Usually seen in pairs, it lays up to 5 rufous-white eggs, heavily spotted in purple. (*A. Wells*)

Top.
Rufous songlark, *Cinclorhamphus mathewsi*. (15–18 cm. Open timber, grasslands. Common.) Ranges over Australia, except for Tas. Its lively and musical song is rendered both in flight and when still. It feeds off the ground on insects and seeds, and builds a cup-shaped nest, on the ground but well hidden, made of dry grass and lined with finer material. It lays 3 or 4 eggs, reddish and spotted. *(W. Taylor)*

Centre:
Brown songlark, *Cinclorhamphus cruralis* (male). (18–25 cm. Open timber, grasslands. Common.) Its range is similar to that of the Rufous songlark, except that it does not reach the most northerly sections. The male is larger than the female. It shows a preference for planted grasses in grazing areas. Its call has been likened to a wheelbarrow that needs oiling. A ground nester, it lays 3 or 4 pale eggs, speckled darker. *(T. & P. Gardner)*

Bottom:
Spinifexbird, *Eremiornis carteri*. (15 cm. Spinifex, porcupine grass, tropical shrubbery. Uncommon.) It flies and perches with drooping tail, as though unwell, but its liquid song is reassuring. On Barrow Island, off the W.A. coast, shares the terrain with the Black and white wren. There have been some imaginative interpretations of the words of its song. Although well established, it was not discovered until 1900. *(G. Chapman)*

Top:
Eastern bristlebird, *Dasyornis brachypterus*. (22 cm. Dense coastal and mountain heathlands. Rare.) Its limited zone is in coastal N.S.W. Also called Brown bristlebird. Cocks its long tail when feeding on the ground, where it finds insects and seeds. This bird has suffered very much from the influx of settlers and in earlier years was more common. (*J. Purnell*)

Right:
Western bristlebird, *Dasyornis longirostris*. (18 cm. Dense coastal and mountain heathlands. Rare.) Very similar to Eastern bristlebird, although smaller. Its restricted zone is east of Albany, W.A. Just as the Eastern bristlebird once lived where Sydney now stands, this bird had to make way for the city of Perth. (*J. Gould*)

Bottom:
Rufous bristlebird, *Dasyornis broadbenti*. (23–25 cm. Low coastal scrub. Rare.) Its limited zone is a coastal area in the extreme south-west of Vic., extending over the border to the Coorong in S.A. In the latter State it could gain some protection within the boundaries of a National Park. Previously seen in small areas in the extreme west of W.A. but evidently no recent sighting. (*K. Stepnell*)

Top right:
White-throated warbler, *Gerygone olivacea*. (11 cm. Open timber, tall river trees. Common.) An evocative, liquid song which has won it the names, in some places, of Native canary and Bush canary. A well-made, pear-shaped nest, with tail piece, usually built clinging to a light, leafy branch. Often, when these birds are moving about trees, the sun on the leaves will match their yellow fronts, making them difficult to pinpoint. *(E. & N. Taylor)*

Bottom right:
Black-throated warbler, *Gerygone palpebrosa* (female, top left; male, top right); Fairy warbler, *Gerygone flavida* (bottom). (Both: 10 cm. Rain forest, mangroves, tropical watercourses. Common in limited area.) Only the male Black-throated warbler has the black throat. The zones of both birds adjoin, and their habits are similar, including the building of their nest near a wasp nest. *(M. Kröyer-Pedersen)*

Top right:
Large-billed warbler, *Gerygone magnirostris.* (12 cm. Mangroves, tropical watercourses. Moderately common in limited area.) Another warbler which sings a lovely, liquid song, rather like the White-throated. Its nest, dome-shaped and with a hooded side entrance, normally hangs low over a watercourse, looking like flood debris. *(K. & B. Richards)*

Bottom left:
Green-backed warbler, *Gerygone chloronota.* (9 cm. Mangroves, tropical watercourses. Moderately common in limited area.) Similar in appearance to the Lemon-breasted flycatcher, which is found in the same area. It has a pleasing, down-the-scale call. 2 or 3 eggs are laid in the pear-shaped nest. Its tropical area of residence is from Yirrkala, east of Arnhem Land, N.T., to Derby, W.A. *(J. Gould)*

Bottom right:
Dusky warbler, *Gerygone tenebrosa.* (12 cm. Mangroves, tropical watercourses. Moderately common in limited area.) Its zone adjoins that of the Large-billed warbler, along the coastal area from Port Keats, near the N.T.–W.A. border, to Carnarvon, W.A. It sings a lullaby type of song, varying this with some noisier chatter. *(G. Mathews)*

Top:
Brown warbler, *Gerygone mouki.* (9 cm. Rain forests. Common.) Its 3-note song goes up the scale, as though the bird is asking a question. It has a liking for the lilly pilly tree, in which it often nests and from which it will fly out to catch insects, fanning its tail as it does so. The *mouki* is said to be an Aboriginal word. *(M. McNaughton)*

Centre:
Mangrove warbler, *Gerygone levigaster.* (10 cm. Mangroves, coastal and tropical rivers, watercourses. Common.) Also called Buff-breasted warbler and, because of its attractive song, Little angel. The well-made nests are frequently used by the parasitical cuckoos. Mangrove warblers found in the coastal areas of Qld and N.S.W., have more brown in the back and are placed in the race *cantator.* *(H. Frauca)*

Bottom left:
White-tailed warbler, *Gerygone fusca.* (10 cm. Semi-arid woodlands, urban areas. Common.) Also called Inland warbler and Western warbler. In the west, where it replaces the White-throated warbler of the east, it is prevalent around Perth and its lovely song ("the unfinished symphony") is heard to advantage in Kings Park in that city. It builds the usual well-made fairy warbler's nest. *(R. Garstone)*

203

Top right:
Weebill, *Smicornis brevirostris.* (8–9 cm. Light savannah, arid woodland. Common.) Believed to be Australia's smallest bird, not having the long tail of the smaller-bodied emuwren. In spite of its size, the Weebill succeeds in making itself heard, with a "wee willie winkie" call. It finds it easy to hide, an ordinary-sized leaf usually providing sufficient cover. *(I. McCann)*

Bottom left:
Little thornbill, *Acanthiza nana.* (9 cm. Temperate woodland, brigalow, mallee, urban areas. Common.) Also called Yellow thornbill. It will flutter around trees in search of insects and also feeds off the ground. The thin, pointed bill is ideal for catching insects. The species favours some native trees, especially eucalypts, wattles, and casuarinas. It also shows a preference for lemon trees. *(E. & N. Taylor)*

Bottom right:
Striated thornbill, *Acanthiza lineata.* (9 cm. Temperate woodland, some urban areas. Moderately common.) A very industrious little bird, a mother feeding young on the nest will keep up a constant supply of captured insects. It is equally energetic with its vocal efforts, and likes to come into gardens and occupied areas. It is not seen in Tas. *(K. Stepnell)*

Top left:
Brown thornbill, *Acanthiza pusilla*. (10 cm. Rain forest, river margins. Common.) This bird may be seen feeding in the lower branches of tall trees. It is an accomplished mimic, some observers saying that it is more inclined to use this talent when disturbed. It is found in varied areas, but avoids the far north. Its preference is for thick undergrowth. *(I. McCann)*

Centre left:
Tasmanian thornbill, *Acanthiza ewingi*. (10 cm. Forest areas. Common, but restricted to Tas. and near islands.) The *ewingi* honours T. J. Ewing, a Tasmanian naturalist and friend of John Gould. Its habits and voice are similar to the mainland Brown thornbill. It builds a neat nest, dome-shaped, and lays 3 white eggs, spotted purple. It is said to sing only in the breeding season. *(J. Napier)*

Bottom left:
Mountain thornbill, *Acanthiza katherina*. (10 cm. Rain forests. Rare.) Has a very limited range in north-eastern Qld. It is known to occupy the forest canopy, but because of the remoteness of the habitat and the rarity of the bird, reports have been scanty, with no record of voice or breeding and nesting habits. *(H. & J. Beste, Ardea)*

Bottom right:
Broad-tailed thornbill, *Acanthiza apicalis*. (10 cm. Undergrowth in varied timber areas. Common.) Very much like the Brown thornbill and often wrongly identified as the former bird. It has a pleasing voice and mimics other birds, including feared birds of prey and the disliked cuckoo. Over its extensive range, from district to district, there are minor plumage colour changes. *(E. Paton)*

Top left:
Slate-backed thornbill, *Acanthiza robustirostris*. (9 cm. Mulga, dry heathlands. Common.) Also called Robust thornbill and Thick-billed tit. It occupies the arid areas in W.A., from just north of Kalgoorlie, west to Shark Bay and east to central Australia. Its breeding programme is dependent on weather conditions. The nest is pear shaped and there are 3 eggs. *(P. Trusler)*

Bottom left:
Western thornbill, *Acanthiza inornata*. (10 cm. Forest areas. Common.) Likes the jarrah, karri, and marri big-tree forests of the west, where it flutters about the lower branches and undergrowth. It is a capable mimic of the Western rosella and Western fantail. It builds an oval nest, against the bole of a large tree or behind a piece of loose bark on the tree trunk. *(J. Gould)*

Bottom right:
Yellow-rumped thornbill, *Acanthiza chrysorrhoa*. (10 cm. Farm and urban areas. Very common.) Also called Tom tit. The yellow rump is a very distinctive feature when the bird is flying. The nest is domed, with a cup-shaped upper storey. It has been said the upper storey is there to mislead cuckoos or as a roosting place for the male bird, but neither theory has stood up to tests. *(J. Ferrero)*

Above:

Buff-rumped thornbill, *Acanthiza reguloides*. (9 cm. Open timber. Common.) Also called Bark tit. Materials collected for the dome-shaped nest include bark, leaves, grasses, spider web, horsehair from fences, and bits of rabbit fur from burrow surrounds. It prefers to build on a loose piece of bark hanging low on a tree trunk. (*M. McNaughton*)

Bottom left:

Chestnut-rumped thornbill, *Acanthiza uropygialis*. (9 cm. Open timber, mallee, and mulga areas. Common.) Often seen in the company of Yellow-rumped thornbills and whitefaces in mallee country. It builds its nest in loose bark on a tree trunk, in a fence post, or tree hollow. Mimics larger birds and it has been suggested it does this to scare off likely attackers. (*I. McCann*)

Bottom right:

Samphire thornbill, *Acanthiza iredalei*. (9 cm. Salt flats, samphire areas. Moderately common.) Also called Slender thornbill. A bird of the centre mirage country, where it is rather inconspicuous among the surrounds. Even its call is a quiet and unobtrusive repeated "tit-tit-tit". It nests in available low bush. (*D. Paton*)

207

Top left:
Banded whiteface, *Aphelocephala nigricincta.* (10 cm. Salt-bush and spinifex areas, dry savannah. Uncommon.) Its habits are similar to those of the Southern whiteface, but its song is more fluid. Observers have reported that this bird will build its nest, then wait for rain and suitable conditions before proceeding with its breeding programme. *(E. McNamara)*

Top right:
Chestnut-breasted whiteface, *Aphelocephala pectoralis.* (10 cm. Inland semi-desert, gibber plains. Uncommon.) Its range is the arid area from Port Augusta to Oodnadatta, S.A. Not often seen, but appears occasionally in twos or in small flocks, sometimes in the company of the Banded whiteface. Its call is quiet and feeble. *(G. Mathews)*

Bottom right:
Southern whiteface, *Aphelocephala leucopsis.* (10 cm. Open timber, dry grassland. Moderately common.) Also called Eastern whiteface. A confiding bird, with a pleasant, though wistful, call. It flies in short, direct bursts, keeping close to the ground, and has the habit of flicking its tail when feeding. Its diet consists of various seeds, with occasional insects. *(M. Seyfort)*

Top left:
Spotted scrubwren, *Sericornis maculatus*. (11 cm. Dense scrub patches, sandy heathland. Uncommon.) This is a shy bird, but sometimes can be summonsed with a high-pitched whistle. It builds a well-hidden nest in a dense bush, dome-shaped, with a side entrance, using bark, leaves, and grass, and lined with softer material such as feathers and fur. It lays 3 whitish, colourfully spotted eggs. *(D. Paton)*

Top right:
Brown scrubwren, *Sericornis humilis*. (14 cm. Dense forest undergrowth, urban areas. Common.) Its range is limited to Tas. and some Bass Strait islands. It is very similar in habit and behaviour to the smaller White-browed scrub-wren, moving quickly in and out of undergrowth, generally shy and hard to see. However it will "talk" angrily to would-be intruders. *(G. Chapman)*

Bottom left:
White-browed scrubwren, *Sericornis frontalis*. (11 cm. Dense scrub patches. Common.) This bird flies fast over grassed areas from one timber clump to the next. A very busy insect-catcher, it is bold and inquisitive. It becomes loudly agitated when a cuckoo is in the vicinity. It is often seen in the company of thornbills and blue wrens. *(K. & B. Richards)*

Top right:
Atherton scrubwren, *Sericornis keri*. (13 cm. Rain forest undergrowth. Rare.) This bird was named in 1920 and little information on it has come to hand. It closely resembles the Large-billed scrubwren. As its name suggests, its territory is the high Atherton Tableland. There is no record of its voice or breeding habits. *(K. & B. Richards)*

Centre right:
Large-billed scrubwren, *Sericornis magnirostris*. (13 cm. Dense forest undergrowth. Moderately common.) Another insect-catcher that hunts on the ground as well as in trees and undergrowth. If necessary will build itself a nest, the size and shape of a football, but it prefers to occupy a deserted nest of a Yellow-throated scrubwren. *(G. Chapman)*

Bottom:
Little scrubwren, *Sericornis beccarii*. (11 cm. Undergrowth of rain forest. Uncommon.) This occupies the limited area at the northern tip of Cape York. Research has been restricted and there are at present few reports. It feeds on insects found among the ground debris and in the lower foliage of the forest trees. *(D. Hollands)*

Left:
Yellow-throated scrubwren, *Sericornis lathami*. (14 cm. Rain forests. Moderately common.) This bird builds a large, well-made nest of assorted materials, hanging from the end of a tree branch, often over a river or standing water. It may be observed hopping on the forest floor, where it gathers food in the form of insects and seeds. (*C. Webster*)

Below:
Scrubtit, *Sericornis magnus*. (11 cm. Forest undergrowth. Fairly common.) It has a limited range in southern Tas. where it can be confused with the Brown scrubwren and Brown thornbill, with which it associates. The white face and the bar on the wing are identifying features, but otherwise distinction could be difficult, even the voices being similar. (*T. Waite*)

Above:
Fernwren, *Oreoscopus gutturalis*. (13 cm. Rain forest. Uncommon.) This bird has a very limited range in north-eastern Qld, and lives on the floor of this secluded forest. Its presence is revealed by its voice, as it is heard uttering a rapidly-repeated note, or something more musical, or even mimicry; or by its scratching on the jungle floor, as it works vigorously to uncover the insects and food it likes. *(G. Mathews)*

Top right:
Chestnut-rumped heathwren, *Sericornis pyrrhopygia*. (14 cm. Open timber, scrub, and heathland. Fairly common.) This little bird is famous for its beautiful singing, heard solo or in choirs of its kind. Then it will sing the songs of other birds as well, being a very gifted mimic. It nests on or near the ground. *(M. McNaughton)*

Bottom right:
Shy heathwren, *Sericornis cauta*. (12 cm. Open timber, semi-arid woodland. Moderately common.) The *cauta* means "cautious" or "shy". Also called Shy groundwren and Mallee heathwren. It is similar in habits to the Chestnut-rumped heathwren, with not quite the same vocal talents. Its territory is an extension of that of the former bird, ranging from central-western N.S.W. right across to the south-west coast. *(T. Hutchins)*

Above:
Redthroat, *Pyrrholaemus brunneus* (male, top left; female, bottom left); Striated fieldwren, *Calamanthus fuliginosus* (right). Redthroat: (12 cm. Semi-arid woodland, saltbush plains. Uncommon.) It moves smartly over the ground, catching insects, but usually will fly into a low bush to sing its musical song. In flight, the wings make a distinctive quick-beating sound. Striated fieldwren: (13 cm. Open timber, semi-arid heathlands, saltbush, and sand plains. Common.) This bird of varied habitat and climatic conditions will always seek dense ground cover. *(M. Kröyer-Pedersen)*

Right:
Speckled warbler, *Chthonicola sagittata.* (11 cm. Savannah, with sparse undergrowth. Moderately common.) It is mainly a ground feeder, and lives on insects and some seeds. Also called Speckled Jack, Blood tit, and Chocolate-bird, the last two names from the colour of its eggs. The Black-eared cuckoo lays an egg of similar chocolate colouring, and frequently chooses this bird as foster parent. *(N. Chaffer)*

Above:
Rock warbler, *Origma solitaria.* (14 cm. Rock gullies. Moderately common in limited range.) Its small range is the sandstone area in the vicinity of Hawkesbury, N.S.W. Also called Cavebird, Rock robin, and Cataractbird. The caves and rock holes of the area are a necessary habitat, as it nests and breeds in the semi-darkness of such places. The scientific name means "a solitary resident in a cave". *(M. McNaughton)*

Right:
Pilotbird, *Pycnoptilus floccosus.* (17 cm. Floors of dense forests, fern gullies, mountain areas. Uncommon.) This bird shadows the lyrebird and received its name from this practice. Its presence often assisted those seeking the lyre-bird (frequently with ulterior motive) as it "piloted" them to the bird they wanted. The lyrebird does much of its catering, stirring up the forest floor for the insects and grubs this bird likes. *(N. Chaffer)*

OLD WORLD FLYCATCHERS MUSCICAPIDAE

Here is a family with an all-star cast, among which are some of the most loved and most beautiful of Australian birds.

First on the list is the Brown flycatcher, who seems to be called Jacky Winter everywhere. He is also called Postsitter, because he is often seen occupying a favourite post as though it were his personal property.

Unlike most other members of the family, Jacky Winter is not colourful. In fact he is of plain plumage, not dissimilar to a number of other species of different families. A good identification is provided by the white feathers edging the tail and wings. The bird also has a habit of swinging its tail from side to side when it settles after flight.

Next in the family are the striking "robin redbreasts", which are not related to the famous European robins. There are three particularly noticeable members of the family, the Scarlet, the Flame, and the Red-capped robin, each with its own individual and appealing colour pattern. The Flame robin has the magnificent red front with a grey back. The Scarlet robin has not quite as much red, but has an attractive black top coat and a patch of white on the forehead. The Red-capped also is black on the back, but wears a red cap matching the breast.

The group of yellow robins like to steal the show. When you go into the bush, often they are the first birds you see. If you set up a bush camp at night, it's likely their song will be the first heard in the morning, because of all bush songsters, usually yellow robins are the first to start and the last to finish.

In appearance, they are most appealing, with yellow rump or underparts, varying in different localities from olive to golden yellow, and with beautiful bright button eyes. Their tameness in the forests is amazing. Yellow robins have been seen to settle on the shoulders of timber workers, and a naturalist reports that a yellow robin often sits on his boots while he eats his lunch.

Their friendliness, either tameness or boldness, makes them ideal birds to film, in the nest or going about their hunting. In fact they are birds most suited to any kind of observation or study. Their song is worthy of recording. The scientific name, *Eopsaltria*, means harpist or psalm singer of the dawn, a tribute to their continual song.

They reside in varied habitats, from rain forest and wet sclerophyll forest, to mallee country and sandy heathland.

Brown flycatcher, *Microeca leucophaea*. (12·5 cm. Open timber. Very common.) Its saucer-shaped nest is so small that the sitting bird completely hides it. They range widely over the country, with a fondness for gum trees, avoiding only dense forests. Jacky Winter does not form flocks and is seen either alone or in pairs. Although friendly to humans, will aggressively defend his territory against other intruding birds. *(M. Seyfort)*

Above:
Lemon-breasted flycatcher, *Microeca flavigaster*. (12 cm. Mangroves, tropical timber. Common.) Behaviour and habits are like those of the Brown flycatcher, building a similar small nest (about 4 cm) in the fork on a dead tree branch. This bird is also a cheerful singer or whistler. Like the Brown flycatcher, it catches insects on the wing, a talent not shared by many members of the family. *(J. Gould)*

Right:
Yellow flycatcher, *Microeca griseoceps*. (12 cm. Rain forest, tropical timber. Rare.) This bird occupies a very limited range at the northern tip of Cape York and, like several other species that inhabit that remote area, has had limited research, so that very little reliable information is available. Its range extends to New Guinea, but even there it is not common. *(G. Mathews)*

Left:

Flame robin, *Petroica phoenicia*. (13 cm. Mountain forests, open timber, cultivated fields, town edges. Common.) Probably the most prolific of the "red" robin species, and is seen around Canberra, Melbourne, and Hobart. It builds a neat, cup-shaped nest, in a wide range of sites, including trees, overhanging banks, eaves, and in sheds or unoccupied buildings. *(K. & B. Richards)*

Bottom left:

Scarlet robin, *Petroica multicolor*. (13 cm. Dry forest, open timber, cultivated fields, town outskirts. Common.) In spite of the family name, this bird rarely catches flying insects. In the "redbreast" species, there are marked differences between the sexes, the females all being much more quietly coloured, yet possessing their own attractiveness and making a pleasing contrast when seen with their brighter mates. *(M. Seyfort)*

Bottom centre:

Red-capped robin, *Petroica goodenovii*. (12 cm. Inland, semi-arid heathland. Common.) The *goodenovii* honours Samuel Goodenough, a scientist from England. It is noticeable that when this species travels to the southerly areas in winter, the females are in the first flocks to arrive, sometimes a fortnight or so before the males. *(T. Pescott)*

Bottom right:

Rose robin, *Petroica rosea*. (10 cm. Coastal and mountain timber areas, open timber. Moderately common.) Unlike most other red or pink robins, this bird catches many insects in the air, darting out of a tree perch with fanned tail. It builds a small, cup-shaped nest, usually high in a tree, and lays 2 or 3 usually blue-grey eggs. *(M. Seyfort)*

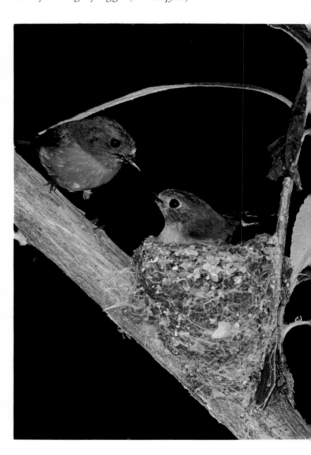

Top right:
Hooded robin, *Petroica cucullata*. (15 cm. Open timber, savannah. Moderately common.) The male's attractive pied plumage means he could be confused with some other families, though (as illustrated) usually he is with the distinctive female. They like mallee growth, native pine, and wattle trees. If surprised near its nest, it performs the "broken-wing" act efficiently to lure away the intruder. *(K. Stepnell)*

Bottom left:
Dusky robin, *Petroica vittata*. (16 cm. Open timber. Moderately common.) This species is found only in Tas. and Bass Strait islands, where it appreciates many of the marks of civilisation, occupying areas where timber felling and milling has been undertaken and, frequently, cleared areas and farms. The sexes are alike. *(R. H. Green)*

Bottom right:
Pink robin, *Petroica rodinogaster*. (13 cm. Gullies and lower areas of mountain forests. Moderately common.) This species feeds on the wing and on the ground. It is usually seen in pairs, with sexes easily distinguishable. It will move into more open country in the winter months. It has a distinctive "tick tick" call and a quieter song, and builds a cup-shaped nest, larger than that of the Rose robin. *(G. Chapman)*

Top left:
Mangrove robin, *Peneoenanthe pulverulenta.* (16 cm. Mangrove areas, tropical coastlines. Uncommon.) This bird shares some physical features of the Hooded robin. It feeds both on the ground and in the air, taking off from perches in the low tropical growth. It has an individual tune of several notes, and a sharper whistle, and nests in the mangroves. The sexes are alike. *(J. Gould)*

Top right:
Grey-headed robin, *Heteromyias cinereifrons.* (17 cm. Rain forest margins. Uncommon and in limited zone.) The small area it occupies is in the north-east of Queensland. The *cinereifrons* means "ashen forehead" and this species is also called Ashy-fronted robin. It has a high-note call, followed by some lower notes, and is mostly seen flying low at roadsides. *(N. Chaffer)*

Centre left:
White-browed robin, *Poecilodryas superciliosa.* (14 cm. Tropical forest. Fairly common.) This is another bird of north-eastern Queensland, but with a wider range than the Grey-headed robin. Feeds on the trunks of large trees and on the ground. It has the habits of cocking its tail and drooping its wing. It has a strong whistle and a quieter but harsher series of single-syllable utterances. *(A. Whittenbury)*

Bottom left:
Buff-sided robin, *Poecilodryas cerviniventris.* (14 cm. Mangroves, tropical river growth. Fairly common.) Its range roughly meets up with that of the White-browed robin, with which it shares many features and customs. The westerly extreme of its territory is approximately Derby, W.A. It builds a well-architectured, cup-shaped nest and lays 2 pale green eggs. *(M. Kröyer-Pedersen)*

219

Above:
Southern yellow robin, *Eopsaltria australis*. (15 cm. Forest and wooded areas, gardens. Moderately common.) The nests are cup-shaped, well made from bark stripped from trees or dry bark from the ground, and leaves. This bird lays 2 or 3 apple-green eggs with rufous markings. When the young hatch, the nest and surrounds are kept very clean. *(A. Olney)*

Right:
Western yellow robin, *Eopsaltria griseogularis*. (15 cm. Forest, wooded areas, gardens. Moderately common.) Yellow robins are also called Yellowbobs in some localities. This species occurs on the Eyre Peninsula, then from Eucla across to the west coast. Its general behaviour and habits are very similar to its eastern cousin. *(T. Modra)*

Below:
White-breasted robin, *Eopsaltria georgiana*. (15 cm. Forest, wooded areas, coastal scrub, gardens. Moderately common.) This is the only member of the genus without the yellow plumage. It likes the big trees of the jarrah and karri forests, especially with occasional clearer patches. Also it will frequent domestic gardens with timber country near by. It is friendly, and very similar to the Yellow robins. *(M. Bonnin)*

Above:
Pale-yellow robin, *Eopsaltria capito*. (15 cm. Rain forest, tropical and sub-tropical jungle. Moderately common.) This species frequents and nests in the lawyer vine. Like other yellow robins, it will cling sideways to a tree trunk. Also like the others, the sexes are similar. It has most of the common habits of the genus, but its main call is said to be quieter. *(A. Wells)*

Right:
White-faced robin, *Eopsaltria leucops*. (14 cm. Rain forest, jungle. Uncommon.) This is the yellow robin representative in Cape York Peninsula. Reports say that its voice is a bar or so of pleasing music, and a harsher alarm signal. Like the Pale-yellow robin, it likes to nest in the lawyer vine. The black crown above the white face would be noticeable. *(G. Mathews)*

221

FANTAIL FLYCATCHERS RHIPIDURIDAE

A great Australian naturalist, the late P. Crosbie Morrison, when asked to name his favourite bird, replied: "Give me the willies!"

Doubtless many others feel the same about the Willie wagtail. This magnificent little character, always dressed for dinner in his immaculate white shirt front, black tie, and black coat and tails, has friends everywhere. He is a great roadside personality and can be seen from a car in just about every part of the continent. It seems that traffic stirs up insects for him and he will dart expertly among fast-moving cars.

Friendly and adaptable, he likes human company. Usually his nest is in a well-chosen, secluded position, but sometimes it will be placed more conspicuously. His movements are most distinctive, as he swings his tail sideways back and forth, flitting and darting about unceasingly. He will tackle any bigger bird which infringes on his territory and will hop and chirp cheekily about a reclining cat, spoiling its daytime nap. A wise cat soon learns not to try to do anything about it.

The Rufous fantail is one of Australia's most beautiful birds. It is the despair of photographers, because it will not "sit still" and pose for them, but is forever on the move, hopping and flying about, opening and closing its tail to show the magnificent rufous feather colouring. It catches much of its food on the wing. Its breeding season is late—November to February—and it is seen at its best in cool, shady places in mid-summer.

This bird builds an interesting nest, shaped like a wine glass without a base, the stem just tapering away. It is believed that the peculiar shape is adopted as a camouflage, the eye being inclined to follow the line of the tapering tailpiece so that the nest merges into the surrounds. Experienced observers, watching the bird working on its nest, then taking their eyes away to follow it in flight, say that they have great difficulty in trying to relocate the nest, and often do not see it again until the bird returns.

The Grey fantail resembles the above two species in air and ground movement. It likes thick forest areas, where it breeds and nests, but it will leave the woods in the winter and show up in urban parks and gardens. It is just as hard to photograph or to study through binoculars as the other family members. It builds the same type of wine glass nest as the Rufous fantail.

The last member of the group, the Northern fantail, lives in the northern tropical timber areas and in the heat is not as active as his southern cousins. He is more inclined to perching and takes much of his food on the ground.

Grey fantail, *Rhipidura fuliginosa*. (15 cm. Forests, urban areas. Common.) Also called Cranky fan. It ranges over the entire continent, its high-pitched, not unpleasing, twitter is heard in many places. The breeding season is from September to December. This species is most sensitive about its nest site and eggs, and will desert the nest entirely if it is touched by intruders. (*K. & B. Richards*)

Top left:
Northern fantail, *Rhipidura rufiventris*. (16 cm. Dry tropical forests. Common in limited area.) This species does not indulge in such energetic tail fanning as the southern family members. The song is quite musical. The breeding season extends from July to February, when it builds a similar type of nest to that of the Grey and Rufous fantails. *(J. Gould)*

Bottom left:
Rufous fantail, *Rhipidura rufifrons*. (15 cm. Dense forest, open timber, and urban areas. Fairly common.) This bird comes out of the denser forest areas in the autumn, after its late breeding season. In the distinctively shaped nest, it lays 2 or 3 eggs, pale brown and speckled. The Rufous fantail, like the Willie wagtail, is rarely seen at any great height, preferring to flit around lower tree branches or near the ground. *(M. Seyfort)*

Bottom right:
Willie wagtail, *Rhipidura leucophrys*. (20 cm. Open timber, town areas, parks and gardens. Very common.) This is the biggest bird of the family. The Willie wagtail is one of the famous bold black and white brigade, often seen in the same vicinity as magpies and mudlarks. It will sometimes raise 2 or 3 broods in a season. *(G. Taylor)*

MONARCH FLYCATCHERS MONARCHIDAE

Generally the members of this family are birds of the tropics and sub-tropics. They do not, as the name might suggest, catch all of their insect diet on the wing. Many feed on the ground for at least some of the time and two species, the Pied flycatcher and the Frill-necked flycatcher, climb up the trunks of trees in search of prey, like treecreepers.

One species of the family, the Restless flycatcher, is frequently confused with the Willie wagtail. The "restless" in its name is most apt, for as well as the black and white colour pattern, it shares with the Willie wagtail the habit of being ever on the move. However, there are several points of distinction between the two species. This bird has a white throat, compared with the black throat of the Willie. It does not cock its tail or fan it out like the Willie does. It also has a habit of hovering in one spot near to the ground, then, on sighting an insect, darting to pick it up. The Restless flycatcher is also often called the Scissors grinder, a name derived from one of its calls.

Another bird of some prominence in this family is the Leaden flycatcher, also called Frogbird, because one of its calls is croaking and frog-like, a characteristic shared with some other birds of the family. In September it arrives in the south of the continent, where it breeds and spends the spring and summer months, leaving for the north at the beginning of the autumn. While in the south, it seeks a dry forest habitat, whereas in the north its preference is for tropical coastal forest and mangrove swamps. Often it is seen high in trees, where it will catch insects while flying or take them from the tree foliage.

Both cock and hen birds in this species have crests, which they raise at certain times, often, it is believed, when agitated or aroused. They also have a practice of quivering the tail.

One other interesting species is the Shining flycatcher. A point about this bird is the different, but striking, colouring seen in both sexes. Both birds are brightly coloured, but with an entirely different colour pattern. The male has an over-all colouration of shining blue-black, while the female is just as prettily attired in red or chestnut dress and tail, with a black head and white front.

The birds of this family have flat beaks, with five rather stiff whiskers or bristles on each side of the mouth, which are used to scoop in insects when catching them on the wing.

Leaden flycatcher, *Myiagra rubecula*. (15 cm. Tropical, sub-tropical forest, mangroves, temperate woodlands. Moderately common.) Its main call, heard more frequently than its frog-like croak, is a loud and clear whistle. The nests are made of new bark, bound with cobweb, and well lined. Usually 3 eggs, pale blue, with dark brown and grey spots. *(G. Chapman)*

Above:
Broad-billed flycatcher, *Myiagra ruficollis*. (15 cm. Tropical woodlands, mangroves. Uncommon.) The sexes are alike, and very closely resemble the females of Leaden and Satin flycatchers. They are usually seen in pairs, and build a cup-shaped nest of bark, bound with spider web and the outside decorated with lichen. They quiver or shiver their tail, like the Leaden and Satin flycatchers. *(J. Gould)*

Top left:
Satin flycatcher, *Myiagra cyanoleuca* (female). (15 cm. Tropical and temperate forest, mountain timber. Common in limited zone.) Although it ranges along the entire east coast, it is seen mainly in Tas. Noticeably similar to the Leaden flycatcher, with which it is often confused. These are very attractive birds, especially when catching insects. *(K. Stepnell)*

Centre left:
Shining flycatcher, *Myiagra alecto* (male). (16 cm. Mangroves, tea-tree swamps, water margins. Fairly common.) This species is seen only in Qld and northern N.T. and W.A. Many of these tropical birds, not seen at all in the south, are now being promoted as tourist attractions and this species well justifies efforts to sight it in its home territory. *(N. Chaffer)*

Bottom left:
Restless flycatcher, *Myiagra inquieta* (male). (20 cm. Open timber. Fairly common.) This bird will come close to dwellings in its quest for insects. As well as its scissor-grinding sound, made when hunting insects, it has a more musical whistling, similar to that of the Leaden flycatcher. The nest, sometimes built in a high place, is cup shaped and bound with cobweb. *(W. Taylor)*

Pearly-winged flycatcher, *Monarcha melanopsis*. (18 cm. Rain forest, tropical timber. Uncommon.) Also called Black-faced flycatcher. Feeds at "half-tree height" in the forest, comparatively slow in movement, taking insects from foliage, but rarely in flight. The cup-shaped nest is made of green moss and bark, placed in a tree-fork, at varying heights. *(H. Frauca)*

Top left:
Spectacled flycatcher, *Monarcha trivirgata*. (15 cm. Rain forest, tropical and sub-tropical timber, mangrove areas, woodland. Fairly common.) The sexes are alike. It visits the south to breed, arriving late in September, leaving in early autumn. Its food is mainly flying insects. It builds a cup-shaped nest, bound with cobweb, and with outside decorations. *(L. Robinson)*

Centre left:
Black-winged flycatcher, *Monarcha frater*. (18 cm. Rain forest, tropical timber. Rare.) Also called Pearly flycatcher. Very similar in appearance, voice, and habit to the Pearly-winged flycatcher. Its zone is mainly limited to the tip of Cape York and very few observations on the species have been recorded. *(G. Chapman)*

Bottom left:
White-eared flycatcher, *Monarcha leucotis*. (14 cm. Rain forest, mangrove areas. Moderately common.) An active, fast-moving bird, seen frisking about the leaves of tall forest trees, catching insects on the wing. It has a distinctive call of three syllables, with a high middle note, also a harsh alarm call and a more musical whistle. *(J. Gould)*

227

WHISTLERS PACHYCEPHALIDAE

The name "whistler" perhaps underestimates the outstanding vocal talents of the birds of this family, for, although one species sounds a call which very much resembles a man whistling his dog, their songs are rich, musical, and generally unlike those heard from other birds.

There are three main groups within the family.

First, are the whistlers themselves. The name of the genus is *Pachycephala*, which means "thick head", and in some places the birds are referred to as thickheads. There are approximately thirty species spread about the world, many in tropical islands, and nine of these are listed as Australian representatives. Of these, two only, the Rufous and Golden whistlers, are well known. Four species are confined to the more remote areas of jungle and mangroves, while the other three are inclined to stay hidden in dense timber, not caring to show themselves to mankind.

The birds are similar in size and in most physical characteristics, other than plumage colour, where there is a vast variation from bright colouring to plain patterns. They all possess the strange and apparently unexplained habit of slightly turning their heads sideways from time to time.

The second group covers the thrushes, sometimes called shrike-thrushes, as it was thought that the birds had features of both the named families. Apart from some minor similarities in the bill, these birds carry no real resemblance or relationship to the overseas shrikes, and the name "thrush" is used here alone.

The group list is headed by the very popular Grey thrush. Although not brightly coloured—it is grey, with a touch of brown on the back—the bird is pleasing to the eye. It is friendly, tame, and trusting, frequenting backyards and camps, always ready to receive a tossed titbit.

The third main group are the shriketits, and here again there is only superficial resemblance to the shrikes and tits of overseas countries. The three species—Eastern, Northern, and Western shriketit—occupy three separate and well-removed areas. All are similar in appearance, the Eastern species having the biggest range and the greatest numbers. The bright yellow breast and the black crested head make them striking birds.

Also included in this family is the interesting and ventriloquial Crested bellbird, which has a wide range over the more arid sections of the continent.

Rufous whistler, *Pachycephala rufiventris*. (16 cm. General forest areas. Common.) Except for Tas. its range is the whole of Australia. It appears in the south in springtime, when its well-known call is heard in many places. It will call through the summer, even during the hottest day. The whip-crack sound in its song has been interpreted as "Ee-chong". (I. McCann)

Above:
Mangrove golden whistler, *Pachycephala melanura.* (15 cm. Mangroves, coastal jungle. Uncommon.) Also called Black-tailed whistler. In appearance, habits, and voice it resembles the Golden whistler, but is smaller. All species build a nest that is cup shaped, of fibre, bark, and local vegetation. Eggs are usually cream or fawn, sometimes green, with a darker area at the larger end. *(J. Gould)*

229

Top left:
Golden whistler, *Pachycephala pectoralis* (male). (16 cm. Forest, open timber. Common.) The sexes are altogether different in this species. It is the most widespread of the whistlers. It has been called Thunderbird because of the way it reacts to any sudden, loud noise, such as a burst of thunder. The voice is often imitated by lyrebirds. It spends much time, unseen, high in the tree tops. *(H. Wright)*

Bottom left:
Olive whistler, *Pachycephala olivacea.* (19 cm. Dense forest. Fairly common.) It likes the beech forest in northern N.S.W., the tall timbers of Tas. and the thick, fern-gullied bush of Vic. It has a range of delightful tunes, often given matching words by the imaginative. Its songs in the northern areas are even more melodious. *(M. Kröyer-Pedersen)*

Bottom right:
White-bellied whistler, *Pachycephala lanioides.* (19 cm. Mangroves, tropical water margins. Uncommon.) Also called White-breasted whistler. This is one of the whistlers restricted to the jungle of the north and north-west coastline. It is said to stand upright like a bittern when disturbed in its mangrove haunts. Its beautiful song has been successfully recorded. *(J. Gould)*

Top left:
Red-lored whistler, *Pachycephala rufogularis*. (20 cm. Mallee. Fairly common, but in a limited area.) The lore is the section of the bird's head between the eye and the upper bill. The bird occupies a small area in the mallee of north-western Vic. and across the border into S.A. John Gould, in his day, found some near Adelaide. This bird is another beautiful songster. *(G. Chapman)*

Top right:
Gilbert whistler, *Pachycephala inornata*. (19 cm. Open timber, mallee, mulga country. Fairly common.) It will sing its wistful, sweet songs while engaged in hopping about on the ground searching for insects and grubs. This bird has a call resembling a man whistling his dog, while other calls are ventriloquial. *(W. Labbett)*

Bottom left:
Brown whistler, *Pachycephala simplex*. (16 cm. Mangroves, rain forest, jungle. Common in limited zone.) It is found along the N.T. coastal areas from Port Keats to the Roper River. Travellers report that this bird sings a melodious and quite distinctive song. Male whistlers are "helpful about the house", taking a turn in sitting on the eggs and ably assisting in feeding the young. *(J. Gould)*

Bottom right:
Grey whistler, *Pachycephala griseiceps*. (14 cm. Rain forest. Fairly common in limited range.) Another bird possessing fine song phrases. Unlike other birds, who might shriek or squawk when alarmed, whistlers will utter a most melodious sound. This species catches insects on the outskirts of tall forest trees or among jungle vines. *(G. Mathews)*

Top left:
Grey thrush, *Colluricincla harmonica*. (23 cm. Open timber, urban areas. Common.) The "button eyes" add to the bird's attraction and are suggestive of its friendliness. It feeds mainly on the ground, the diet including caterpillar pests, which many other birds shun, as well as seeds of unpopular weeds. Sometimes 2 broods are reared in a season which could extend from late July to December. *(M. Seyfort)*

Centre left:
Brown thrush, *Colluricincla brunnea* (immature). (23 cm. Open timber, heathlands, watercourses. Fairly common.) It is very similar to the Grey thrush and in some books is not listed as a separate species. The cup-shaped nest, of bark and leaves, will be in a rock crevice, a tree or post hollow, or even in a vacated nest of some other species. *(G. Chapman)*

Bottom left:
Western thrush, *Colluricincla rufiventris*. (23 cm. Open timber. Common.) Very similar to the Grey thrush, though perhaps its song is not quite as musical. It occupies an area which dovetails with that of the Grey and Brown thrushes, so that between the 3 species, the entire continent is covered. Its breeding season is shorter, September to November, but it will sometimes breed in the autumn. *(R. Garstone)*

Bottom right:
Rufous thrush, *Colluricincla megarhyncha*. (18 cm. Rain forest, mangrove areas. Common.) It sings a long song, as well as its lovely whistling notes, and is a capable mimic. It also occasionally issues a sound resembling a sneeze. It feeds on insects in the low growth of the tropical swamps or takes prey from the ground. *(C. Webster)*

Top right:
Stripe-breasted thrush, *Colluricincla boweri.* (20 cm. Mountain rain forests. Fairly common.) Also called Bower thrush, but not to be confused with bowerbirds. The alternative name, and the *boweri,* honour Thomas Henry Bowyer-Boyer, a British naturalist of the last century. It frequents the ranges of north-eastern Qld. *(A. Whittenbury)*

Bottom left:
Little thrush, *Colluricincla parvula.* (18 cm. Mangrove, coastal jungle. Fairly common.) This species inhabits the northern coastline and Arnhem Land, which takes in much barely-accessible territory, with consequent sparse reports on the bird's behaviour, breeding patterns, and voice. There are records of it building cup-shaped nests in hollows in low trees, containing 2 eggs, dull white with coloured spots. *(J. Gould)*

Bottom right:
Sandstone thrush, *Colluricincla woodwardi.* (22 cm. Cliffs, fallen boulders in tropical sandstone ranges. Uncommon.) Also called Brown-breasted thrush. The *woodwardi* is after B. H. Woodward, a former director of the Perth Museum, W.A. This beautiful songster adds to the quality of its renditions by singing in the crevices and sandstone valleys, where echoes enhance the tone and volume of the song. *(G. Mathews)*

233

Top left:

Northern shriketit, *Falcunculus whitei*. (15 cm. Open timber, dry tropical forest. Uncommon and in isolated pockets.) The *Falcunculus* means "little falcon". It has been suggested frequently that a good name for the genus would be "barktits", as these birds take bark from tree trunks in a quest for grubs and insects. *(P. Trusler)*

Bottom left:

Western shriketit, *Falcunculus leucogaster*. (16 cm. Timber forests. Fairly common.) The slight differences in size between the three species of the genus will be noticed. The nests are cup shaped, very well made of strips of bark, bound with cobweb and lined with grass. 2 or 3 eggs are laid, white, with dark blotchings. *(J. Gould)*

Top right:

Eastern shriketit, *Falcunculus frontatus*. (18 cm. Open timber, temperate woodland. Fairly common.) These striking birds are quite distinctive. They will respond to an imitation of their call and reveal their nest, usually placed high in a tree, woven into a fork or to a light branch. Sometimes the surrounding leaves are snipped off the tree. *(I. McCann)*

Bottom right:

Crested bellbird, *Oreoica gutturalis*. (20 cm. Open timber, arid woodland. Common.) An unhurried ground feeder of insects and caterpillars. A peculiar characteristic is the taking of caterpillars into the nest, where they are put into "cold storage" among the eggs, the caterpillar being paralysed by some unique method employed by the bird. *(G. Chapman)*

CHATS EPHTHIANURIDAE

Chats are birds which generously provide good opportunities for their identification, and for general bird study and observation. They are common in fairly extensive areas; they are ground-frequenting birds with a habitat usually devoid of high trees into which they could escape; and they nest close to the ground, so that this part of their behaviour can be glimpsed.

They are appealing, colourful birds, and it is this colouration that raises the first point of interest. There are five species listed and in four of these the sexes are different, in every case the male being the more colourful of the pair.

This is not unusual in the bird kingdom and there are two main reasons advanced as to why it should be so. The first is that this bright plumage is the male's courtship garb, with which he attracts, woos, and wins his mate. It is his first and main method of drawing attention to himself. The second reason is that the plain, more sombre-coloured female is less likely to be sighted by predators when going about her nesting duties.

The chats are an exception to this latter theory, for quite often the male chat takes a turn in the hatching duties. But it is significant that, in spite of his quite bright colouring, the back or top parts of his plumage which would be seen from above when he is sitting on the nest, are comparatively pale and more in line with the female's quieter shades of colour.

Another noticeable feature is the able manner in which chats perform the "broken-wing" display. This is performed by many species of birds. If you approach a nest containing eggs or young, the parent will suddenly appear to be the victim of a badly-damaged wing. The bird flutters away, wing dragging on the ground, as though in pain and difficulty. The impression is that if you gave chase the parent would be easily caught.

Of course, if you give chase, you do not catch the bird. He will let you get so close, but no closer, so that he is always just out of your reach.

But the interesting point, demonstrated by the chats, is that if the bird is not chased, he will flutter along for some distance, then discovering that the intruder is still near the nest, he will fly back, fit and well, then immediately go into the "broken-wing" act again.

This would indicate that the performance is not a reasoned act by the bird. If it were, he would also reason that the evidence of his flight would reveal that actually he is uninjured. So the "broken-wing" performance must be an instinctive ploy by the birds, triggered off by the presence of an intruder.

White-faced chat, *Ephthianura albifrons*. (10 cm. Coastal heaths, plains of stunted growth, saltbush, samphire. Common.) This bird has a long list of alternative names, including White-fronted chat, Tintack, Nunbird (apt because of its appearance), and Tang (an interpretation of its call). It is rarely seen in timbered country. When disturbed, it will fly up with a distinctive flight, settling very soon on the ground or a low bush. *(I. McCann)*

Top left:

Crimson chat, *Ephthianura tricolor*. (10 cm. Low covered plains, saltbush, samphire. Common.) Also called Tricoloured chat. The white, crimson, and brown markings make identification easy. Unlike the White-faced chat, it seems able to manage for long periods without water. Consumes flies, small insects, and larvae, found on the ground or in the low bushes which they frequent. *(D. Mann)*

Top right:

Orange chat, *Ephthianura aurifrons*. (10 cm. Arid, low covered plains, saltbush, samphire. Common.) This species ranges over most of Australia's dry areas, where it is seen in pairs or flocks. It sometimes visits town areas, where it is in colourful contrast to other birds. The nests of chats are neatly made, cup shaped and wide brimmed. Usually 3 eggs are laid, whitish, spotted with red markings. *(L. Robinson)*

Centre right:

Yellow chat, *Ephthianura crocea*. (10 cm. Saltbush, samphire, tropical watercourses. Uncommon.) It occupies disconnected pockets in the north. The call is slighter and perhaps more musical than that of the other chats. Usually seen in pairs where water may be lying. Reports say that, unlike the other species, it will feed in higher tree foliage. *(J. Gould)*

Bottom right:

Desert chat, *Ashbyia lovensis*. (12 cm. Gibber plains. Moderately common.) One of the few birds found on these plains, also called Gibber chat. The scientific names honour Edwin Ashby, its discoverer and a former South Australian ornithologist, and J. R. B. Love, an inland missionary to the Aborigines. In this land of little or no ground coverage, the bird shelters and nests in holes in the ground. It is distinctive in the chat family in that the sexes are alike. *(G. Chapman)*

SITTELLAS NEOSITTIDAE

The presence of sittellas, or as they are often called, tree-runners, in Australia means, among other things, that no one should feel deprived when looking in a bird index and noticing the absence of woodpeckers. Sittellas are a good substitute, as they fly in rowdy groups from one tree to another, using the bark of the trees as a feeding base.

Their method of feeding, on landing in a tree, is to stop, look, and listen. The listening, which follows when no insect is sighted, is done by the bird actually placing its small ear against the bark of the tree and listening intently for a sound of movement from an insect under the bark.

These birds are able to move in any direction in trees. They differ from the family of treecreepers here, which can move only upwards. Somehow sittellas seem to get away with ignoring the law of gravity as they twist about, turn upside down, and go above and below the boughs and branches, taking insects from the bark.

Sittellas build a remarkable nest, something to be admired as a piece of bird workmanship, yet difficult to locate, because the bird takes the precaution, a fairly rare one among birds, of camouflaging the nest.

These are usually placed high in a tree on the fork of a dead branch, and are shaped like a cup or a larger coffee mug. They are made of bark fibre and bark, cobwebs, thistledown, and occasionally other material. Their "shingles", made of bark, are attached to the outside of the nest, becoming both an attractive piece of architecture and at the same time the means of effective camouflage, making the nest appear just part of the tree.

An on-site report of the building of one of these nests revealed that several birds worked on the job, the team carrying only one female, and that she assumed the rank of foreman. The males carried material to the job and proceeded to put it into place, while the female went to fetch more material, which she gave them to work on.

As the job progressed, she would inspect the details, putting on finishing touches, rubbing her beak along outside surfaces, and attending to the cobweb binding. There would be work stretches of about an hour, then the birds spent half an hour or so catching themselves insects, and then back for another hour's work. The entire job takes about a fortnight.

Sittellas are usually seen in groups of up to a dozen or so, moving about restlessly and noisily. When they are in flight, a bright patch or "window" on the wing shows up. These patches are white on the birds in tropical areas and orange in the southern species.

Orange-winged sittella, *Neositta chrysoptera*. (12 cm. General timbered areas. Moderately common.) The *Neositta* actually means "new kind of woodpecker". Also called Nuthatcher. Its voice is a twittering note, which is more noticeable when a group calls in unison. The flight, usually just from one tree to another, is weak and undulating. (*W. Taylor*)

237

Right:
White-headed sittella, *Neositta leucocephala*. (12 cm. General timbered areas. Moderately common.) The White-headed resembles the Orange-winged sittella in behaviour, habit, and choice of habitat, with paperbark trees a first choice for nesting sites. In proportion to their overall size, these birds have large feet, the strong claws being necessary for their all-direction climbing on tree trunks and limbs. *(G. Chapman)*

Bottom left:
Striated sittella, *Neositta striata*. (12 cm. General timbered areas. Moderately common.) This species occupies a tropical zone in the north-east. Usually 3 eggs are laid in the well-made nests. The eggs vary in shade, generally white or off-white, with dark rufous or slate-coloured blotches. Immature birds of different species may be alike, but identification is helped by observing the adults, more easily distinguished in the flocks. *(J. Gould)*

Bottom centre:
Black-capped sittella, *Neositta pileata*. (12 cm. Timbered areas. Fairly common.) This bird prefers drier areas and is found in box trees and in the mallee country. The black mask of the hen is an important aid in distinguishing the sexes. The breeding season extends from August to January. *(J. Gould)*

Bottom right:
White-winged sittella, *Neositta leucoptera*. (12 cm. Timbered areas. Fairly common.) Although all sittellas build the same type of nest, local conditions will determine the choice of nesting tree. Some observers report that the eggs of this species are slightly smaller than those of others. The zone occupied is in the top north-west, which means that, like so many other bird families, sittellas have an around-Australia representation. *(J. Gould)*

TREECREEPERS CLIMACTERIDAE

The seven Australian species of treecreepers are in the genus *Climacteris*, a Greek word meaning "a staircase". It is an appropriate name, for these birds seem to spend their lives going up an imaginary spiral staircase.

Always upwards, never down, for unlike the sittellas, they are equipped for climbing this way only. A feature is the tail, longer than that of the sittellas, which they frequently use as a support in their spiralling.

They are seen climbing boughs and tree trunks in their never-ending quest for insects and larvae and bush grubs. The spiral movement pays off, because this way they cover a larger area as they go completely around a tree. Also their approach on any one side of the tree is thus sudden and unexpected, and the insects "do not see them coming" until it is too late for an escape. The area of a tree trunk covered, they will fly to the next tree, landing low, to begin again the spiralling quest.

Although it has been said that the tree-climbing families are some substitute in Australia for the woodpecker, they do not possess the strong, chisel-shaped bill of the overseas bird, and are not given to tearing strips of bark off the trees to recover insects from under it. Rather they are bark-surface feeders, pecking at what they see on the outside of the trunk or limb, with only limited ability for removing pieces of bark or for getting underneath it.

The nests of treecreepers are simply made, usually just some material lining a suitable small hole in tree, tree stump, log, or post. The provision of "artificial" nesting sites is an interesting side of bird study. For the treecreeper family, nothing elaborate is required. A small log with an opening at one end, placed on a fence post, is ideal.

It is inadvisable to place any nesting material in the hole. This is better left for the birds. They are fulfilling a natural function which, in the case of treecreepers, is often a fairly limited construction job anyway. All sorts of lining material are used in their nest building—grass, leaves, hair, fur, wool, feathers, animal droppings, bark, and charcoal.

A big advantage of having accessible nests in a vicinity is the opportunity they give to examine eggs. The eggs of treecreepers are beautiful in themselves, generally pink or pinkish-white, well spotted in red or purple, with likely variations in shades or colour tones. Some eggs tend to be nearly white, or even, sometimes with the White-throated treecreepers, pure white.

Brown treecreeper, *Climacteris picumnus.* (15 cm. Open forest, general woodlands. Common.) These birds are seen usually in pairs. This species frequently feeds on the ground, more so than other members of the family. Its call is a high-pitched "pee-pee" often repeated many times. Treecreepers like to find a small nook or hollow to roost in at nights. (*T. & P. Gardner*)

Top left:
Black treecreeper, *Climacteris melanota.* (15 cm. Open forest, partly cleared areas. Fairly common.) This bird is similar to the Brown treecreeper in habits and habitat. Unlike the sittellas, these birds will hunt for insects on dead trees and on fallen logs or branches. Its call is a single, penetrating note which it sounds when disturbed. *(J. Gould)*

Bottom left:
Black-tailed treecreeper, *Climacteris melanura.* (15 cm. Open forest, semi-arid woodlands. Moderately common.) The Black-tailed is found in two pockets, an area in the north and north-west of the continent, and a smaller zone near Broome, W.A. Observers in these areas report that this species does not press its tail against the tree trunk. It likes the trees bordering watercourses. *(J. Gould)*

Bottom right:
Red-browed treecreeper, *Climacteris erythrops.* (15 cm. Rain forest, dense timber. Moderately common.) Its call is quite distinctive and more varied than that of other species, and includes some fast chattering, high-pitched notes. It nests fairly high in the forest trees and lays 2 eggs. It is often seen in small groups. *(J. Gould)*

Top left:
White-browed treecreeper, *Climacteris affinis.* (14 cm. Mulga, arid woodland. Moderately common.) A bird of the semi-desert and arid inland, its zone dovetails with that of other species, so that the family is represented over most of the continent, excepting those parts, of course, where there are no trees on which to creep. It utters a loud, sharp call and some quieter, organ-like notes. *(N. Chaffer)*

Bottom left:
White-throated treecreeper, *Climacteris leucophaea.* (15 cm. Wet sclerophyll forest. Moderately common.) It sometimes will betray its presence by its shrill, piping call. Also warbles a pleasing, musical tune in the breeding season. Very active in the trees, it is rarely seen on the ground. The absence of prominent pale eyebrows will identify it from other tree-creepers in its zone. *(K. & B. Richards)*

Bottom right:
Rufous treecreeper, *Climacteris rufa.* (15 cm. Open forest, partly cleared areas, arid country. Moderately common.) This species takes over for a westerly extension of the zone of the Brown treecreeper, which it resembles in behaviour. Its breeding season is from September to December and it normally lays 3 eggs. The sexes are slightly different, generally the case with treecreepers. *(T. & P. Gardner)*

FLOWERPECKERS DICAEIDAE

Flowerpeckers are small birds, mainly brilliantly plumaged. The family is divided into two groups, the Mistletoebird and the pardalotes.

Kissing under the mistletoe might be the extent of an association with that growth for many people, but for the Mistletoebird it regulates his whole life, supplying him with food and determining the course of his travels and his place of residence.

It is really only the skin of mistletoe berries that the bird digests. Occasionally it eats berries from other sources, and also insects, which are a main food supply for the young at the start of their lives.

The Mistletoebird is probably more common than realised because, although colourful, it keeps mainly out of sight, frequenting dense foliage and flying high over treetops. Nor is its full song often heard by adults, some of its notes being out of the hearing range of many people. As mistletoe does not grow in Tasmania, that State is not in the bird's range.

The nest of the Mistletoebird reminds some people of a lady's purse, others of a baby's bootie. These nests are so fragile that often, because of wind or weather damage, they do not last through the breeding season. Built of soft material—wool, cobweb, down, and flower petals—they are equipped with a small slitted side entrance, and hang lightly from branches. The bird is obviously attracted by brown objects, just as the Satin bowerbird prefers blue. All the nest trimmings are of a brown colouring and often include the outer skin cases of some caterpillars, which are used to put final touches to the small and flimsy creation.

The group of pardalotes are themselves divided into two sections, the spotted and the striated or streaked pardalotes, each section covering four species. It is the top of the head or crown that is either spotted or striated within each group respectively.

Pardalotes occur only in Australia. They have plump bodies, short tails, and stout, blunt bills and often are the shortest bird found in a locality. Like the Mistletoebird, they spend their time in the higher parts of the trees, mainly out of sight. In gum trees, they are useful insect eaters.

Their nests frequently attract attention. The Spotted pardalote—the individual species—likes to nest in tunnels, which they will drill into the bank of a watercourse or a roadside cutting. However, if there is a ready-made tunnel about, they will be glad to occupy it and there are records of nests in a variety of strange places. Lengths of downpipe, a roadside newspaper holder, a stored sheepskin, a roll of discarded linoleum, a corrugated iron roof, are some of the places used by these birds.

Mistletoebird, *Dicaeum hirundinaceum*. (10 cm. General, trees with mistletoe. Fairly common.) The *hirundinaceum* means "swallow-like", and there is a resemblance between the two birds, although Mistletoebirds do not have the swallow's forked tail. It also resembles the red-breasted robins. Scientists report that, because of the diet of berries, the gizzard, that part of a bird's anatomy which grinds or "chews" its food, in the Mistletoebird has practically disappeared. *(H. Frauca)*

Top:
Spotted pardalote, *Pardalotus punctatus.* (9 cm. Eucalypt forest. Common.) Also called Diamondbird. An industrious bird, it sings and catches insects continually. Its song, a tinkling call, pleases some people, irritates others. At the end of the tunnel they drill or select for a nest site, there is always a well-made nest of bark and grass. (*I. McCann*)

Centre left:
Yellow-rumped pardalote, *Pardalotus xanthopygus.* (9 cm. Mallee country. Common.) Pardalotes can, when aroused, raise their head feathers to form a crest. Also as a means of bluff the various spotted species will stretch upright to display the yellow throat feathers. It nests under similar conditions to the Spotted pardalote and, like that bird, lays 4 white eggs. (*L. Robinson*)

Bottom left:
Fortyspotted pardalote, *Pardalotus quadragintus.* (9 cm. Eucalypt forest. Fairly common.) This bird is shyer than the other species and rarely comes down to the ground. It nests in tree hollows, in a grass, cup-shaped nest, laying 3 or 4 white eggs. It has a distinctive two-note call, the first note pitched higher. (*J. Napier*)

Top right:
Red-browed pardalote, *Pardalotus rubricatus*. (9 cm. Water-course trees, open timber. Common.) It has an extensive range of the northerly areas of the continent. This is another tunnel nester, usually drilling its hole in the banks of the watercourses it frequents. It has its own repertoire of songs and possesses some ventriloquial talent. *(J. Gould)*

Bottom left:
Red-tipped pardalote, *Pardalotus ornatus*. (10 cm. Forest areas. Fairly common.) Also called Eastern striated pardalote. It is very similar to the Yellow-tipped, the red instead of yellow wing spot being the distinguishing feature. The species is believed to have resulted from the Yellow-tipped crossing with the Striated pardalote. It has a three-noted, persistent call. *(M. McNaughton)*

Bottom right:
Yellow-tipped pardalote, *Pardalotus striatus*. (10 cm. Forest areas. Fairly common.) This is another of the striated pardalotes and is also called Striated diamondbird. Its call has been interpreted as "pick it up". Its favourite nesting spot is a high tree hollow, though occasionally it will tunnel in a watercourse bank. It lays 4 white eggs. *(R. Good)*

Right:

Black-headed pardalote, *Pardalotus melanocephalus*. (10 cm. Timber areas. Common.) This is a bird of the more northerly areas and its suburban retreats are around Brisbane. Also seen near Darwin and Broome. It is very similar to its near relative, the Striated pardalote. It nests mainly in tunnels in the banks of watercourses, laying 4 white eggs in a breeding season extending from June to December. *(H. Frauca)*

Below:

Striated pardalote, *Pardalotus substriatus*. (10 cm. Timber areas, especially arid inland, urban areas. Common.) This species is seen often near Perth, and also in the vicinity of Sydney, Melbourne, and Adelaide. It avoids dense forest, preferring open timber country. In the breeding season, they stay in this type of country, flocking to the urban districts in the winter. *(G. Taylor)*

SUNBIRDS NECTARINIIDAE

The Yellow-breasted sunbird is the sole Australian representative of the sunbird family.

In a number of cases we see this same situation—a single species representing a family that is widespread in other parts of the world. We have one stork (the Jabiru), one swan, one bustard, one roller (the Dollarbird), one bee-eater (the Rainbowbird), one drongo, and so forth. Until a short time ago, it was also believed that we had only one crane, the Brolga, until the similar Sarus crane was discovered in Queensland. All these representations mean that Australia has at least one species of almost all the more common groups of birds.

Not only is the sunbird family limited to one species. It is also restricted to a very small range, along the north-eastern coast of Queensland, from the tip of Cape York to about Gladstone. It has something of the hummingbird's hovering habit, but there is no relationship between the two. Sunbirds are, in fact, related to the flowerpeckers and share a number of similarities.

They are usually seen in pairs, among flowering trees and bushes, where they consume honey and catch insects. The birds have a song which, sung when they are active, resembles the whisper of the goldfinch.

Like the related Mistletoebird, the sunbird builds a very distinctive nest. It is a long, elaborate, hanging, oval-shaped nest, with a pendulous tail beneath the central nesting chamber. This has a hooded side entrance, which needs to be moved to gain access to the inside of the nest. Made of bark fibre, grasses, and dead leaves, all of the material is expertly bound together with spider web, and the inside portion lined with plant down. The nest is hung from a branch of a small bush or, if around a farm or homestead, is just as likely to be on a verandah or in an open-fronted shed.

In this nest the bird lays two or three eggs, green-grey, marked with red or brown blotches. The breeding season normally is from September to January, although it has been known to occur later, perhaps when influenced by climatic conditions.

The sunbird has a long, thin bill and tubular tongue, which is ideal for taking honey from blossoms. "Sunbird" is a most appropriate name. The bird sings in the sun at the hottest time of the day, as though revelling in the heat and the sun's glare.

Yellow-breasted sunbird, *Nectarinia jugularis* (male). (12 cm. Mangrove areas, tropical rain forest, cleared and settled localities. Common in limited zone.) The main base of the family is Africa. The adaptation of these birds to cleared areas and occupied parts suggests that they might extend their zone. Spiders provide a good proportion of the bird's diet. *(K. & B. Richards)*

SILVEREYES ZOSTEROPIDAE

Silvereyes must rank as one of the most common native birds seen around people's homes and gardens. They are delightful little grey-green characters, with the white ring of feathers around the eyes being their main distinguishing feature.

The one possible count against them would be their inclination to eat fruit, or rather to peck at it, often just one peck per piece of fruit, which sometimes tests the humour of home gardener and commercial orchardist. However people in both of these categories usually take preventive measures, and come to appreciate that the bird's value as an insect destroyer outweighs the cost of damage it could do in an orchard. The birds are probably tackling the fruit to quench a thirst rather than to satisfy hunger.

One series of observations has taken place from a sunroom, immediately outside of which was a crab-apple tree. It was learned that although they pecked at the crab-apples, and at other fruit later hung there for their pleasure, it was the aphids infesting the tree which really interested them. This was brought home when the birds still came to the tree after all the fruit was gone.

The nest is the shape and size of a tennis ball sliced in half. It is made of fine grass, leaves, or available vegetation, and bark, all bound together with cobweb. The breeding season is usually from September to January. A mating pair will rear up to three broods in a season.

There is still much to be learned about the migratory movements of silvereyes and at the moment some banding programmes are under way for furthering knowledge in this direction. One thing that has been learnt is that silvereyes move between Tasmania and Queensland. Migrating flocks travel at night, and sometimes on a still evening their voices may be heard as they pass overhead, keeping contact with each other in the darkness.

The biggest recorded migratory movement of these birds occurred a little over a century ago, when a flock was apparently carried by a storm to New Zealand. They landed and settled, and now are established residents.

Silvereyes seem to have affinity with both flowerpeckers and honeyeaters. They have thin, slightly curved and pointed bills, with brush-tipped tongues for recovering honey. The colouration varies around the continent, with all species having a greener plumage during the winter, compared with the breeding colours.

Eastern silvereye, *Zosterops lateralis*. (12 cm. Coastal heathlands, open timber, urban areas. Very common.) Also called Grey-breasted silvereye. It has a tuneful song, but often twitters a quiet, plaintive series of notes in an unchanging key, interpreted as "tsee, tsee, tsee". The flight is jerky and uneven, but strong and fast for so small a bird. (*K. & B. Richards*)

Top right:
Pale silvereye, *Zosterops chloris*. (10 cm. Tropical islands. Uncommon.) This species is restricted, in Australian territory, to several small islands off the northern tip of Cape York, with no confirmed records of mainland sightings. It seems to be closely related to other species and apparently shares many habits and behaviour patterns. *(G. Mathews)*

Bottom left:
Western silvereye, *Zosterops gouldi*. (12 cm. Coastal heathlands, open timber, urban areas. Common.) From Eucla west to the W.A. coast, it replaces the Eastern silvereye. In the west, visitors could be confused by the popular local name for these, "greenie", which is used in the east for the well-known White-plumed honeyeater. The *gouldi* honours John Gould. *(J. Gould)*

Bottom right:
Yellow silvereye, *Zosterops lutea*. (10 cm. Mangrove areas, tropical woodland. Common.) This smaller species lives along the north-western and northern coastline. It will nest and breed in mangroves, then move to more varied country after the breeding season. It is a very active insect catcher, and its pleasing songs include some mimicry. *(M. Kröyer-Pedersen)*

248

HONEYEATERS MELIPHAGIDAE

Honeyeaters comprise the largest bird family in Australia with about seventy species. All honeyeaters possess a slim body, long tail and, the most typical distinctive feature of all, a brush-like tongue for sucking honey from blossoms.

The beak varies from medium to long and has a downward curve. Within the family there are variations in size, plumage, and sound of song.

Honeyeaters are generally active birds, full of personality, usually aggressive, but often, so far as mankind is concerned, tame and friendly. More species are coming into gardens, in many cases encouraged by the planting of the right kind of native growth and sometimes by the provision of specially-prepared honey-based mixtures in hanging feeders at strategic points in a garden, as additions to the bird's natural menu.

Perhaps an extreme example of honeyeaters sharing man's domain is provided by the White-eared honeyeater. When seeking hair for a nest lining and being unable to find the once abundant horsehair, this bird will take human hair. Jack Hyett, prominent Victorian naturalist, tells of how one of these birds tugged hair strands from the heads, chests, and even eyebrows of a team of railway workers, who, fortunately, cooperated with the honeyeater and took an interest in its nesting routine.

The underlying factor in the life pattern of the honeyeater family is the close relationship between the birds and living trees. Honeyeaters depend for their existence on eucalypts and related species of bush growth, and as these are Australia's most common trees, the birds will spread around the continent wherever gum trees are growing. In addition, grevilleas, melaleucas, banksias, kangaroo paws, and the range of eucalypts, large and small, are available for planting in varieties to suit practically any locality.

The Helmeted honeyeater is Victoria's faunal emblem and one of the world's rarest birds. In the 1960s genuine fears were held for its survival. Once it had been found in a number of places in South Gippsland, Victoria, but land clearance and destruction of the bird's habitat wiped it out in these areas, and it was found that the species was confined to three creeks in the Yellingbo district.

Dedicated and capable birds observers began a campaign to save the species. The Victorian Government allocated a handsome sum to aid the bird's survival and working parties have since built a research centre, made regular counts and observation notes, planted suitable trees along creek courses, and generally maintained a watchful eye for the bird's interests and progress.

It is a new and continuing chapter in a story that began on an official level in 1867, when John Gould recorded a description of the bird in the supplement to his great work, *Birds of Australia*.

Green-backed honeyeater, *Glycichaera fallax*. (12 cm. Canopies in tall tropical woodlands. Uncommon.) This species occupies a very limited area near the top of Cape York, Qld. Because of this limited zone, and the bird's high feeding habits, very little information on it is to hand. It resembles a silvereye in shape and overall plumage colour. (*J. Gould*)

Top left:
Brush-throated honeyeater, *Lichmera cockerelli*. (14 cm. Tropical swamps. Fairly common.) Also called White-streaked honeyeater. The *cockerelli* honours J. T. Cockerell, who did valuable observation work in the tropical zone for John Gould. This is another bird found in a limited area at the northern tip of Cape York. Its singing, resembling that of the Brown honeyeater, is rich and varied. *(J. Gould)*

Top right:
Brown honeyeater, *Lichmera indistincta*. (12–15 cm. Mangroves, general forest areas, open timber, town areas. Common.) A noisy and busy bird, it is seen around a number of the cities, especially Perth, and in parts of Sydney and Brisbane, but is not found in south-eastern Australia. The nest is cup-shaped, made of bark and grasses, bound with cobweb. *(M. Seyfort)*

Centre left:
Dusky honeyeater, *Myzomela obscura*. (13–14 cm. Tropical swamps and forests. Fairly common.) The genus *Myzomela*, of over 20 species, has only 3 Australian representatives, which between them cover most of the northern and north-eastern coastal area. The nest is small and frail, suspended from the end of a tree branch. Usually 2 white eggs are laid, spotted pink or light red. *(J. Gould)*

Bottom left:
Red-headed honeyeater, *Myzomela erythrocephala*. (11 cm. Tropical swamps and forests. Fairly common.) The colourful red head makes it one of the exceptions among the generally quiet-coloured family members. This is another very active species, flitting briskly through trees and bushes. Its nesting habits are similar to those of the Dusky honeyeater. *(J. Gould)*

Top left:
Scarlet honeyeater, *Myzomela sanguinolenta.* (11 cm. Tropical and coastal swamps, temperate woodland. Fairly common.) Also called Bloodbird. The male is similar to the Red-headed honeyeater. Its range in the summer extends as far south as Mallacoota, Vic., the movements being largely controlled by the blossoming of its favourite trees. *(E. & N. Taylor)*

Top right:
Black honeyeater, *Certhionyx niger.* (12 cm. Heathland, arid woodland. Fairly common.) This is an active, but shy, bird, with an extensive range, but rather difficult to observe. It nests within 2 m of the ground in a small cradle-type nest. It lays 2 buff or coffee-coloured eggs, with darker brown colouring at one end. *(E. Bound)*

Bottom left:
Pied honeyeater, *Certhionyx variegatus.* (17 cm. Heathland, arid woodland. Fairly common.) These birds have a unique call and a distinctive display flight, in some aspects not unlike that of the larks. In many ways they resemble the Black honeyeater. Observers report that a nesting site is chosen, the nest made, and eggs laid, all within a matter of days, both birds in the mating pair teaming well. *(M. Bonnin)*

Top right:
Lewin honeyeater, *Meliphaga lewinii.* (18 cm. Rain and coastal forest. Common.) The genus *Meliphaga,* birds of which are often called typical honeyeaters, is a large group of common honeyeaters. *Meliphaga* simply means "eater of honey" and *lewinii* honours John William Lewin, artist and nature observer, who died in 1819. This bird is bold and inquisitive, co-operative to observers and photographers. *(K. & B. Richards)*

Bottom left:
Lesser Lewin honeyeater, *Meliphaga notata.* (16 cm. Rain forest. Common in limited zone.) Though smaller, this bird is very similar to the Lewin honeyeater. Its zone is in the northern part of Cape York, Qld. It eats fruits and berries as well as the usual nectar and insect diet. Its territory overlaps that of the Lewin, but this species prefers the lowland forests. *(N. Chaffer)*

Bottom right:
Graceful honeyeater, *Meliphaga gracilis.* (14 cm. Rain forest, open forest. Fairly common.) This bird is similar to both the Lewin and Lesser Lewin honeyeaters. Its zone is in Cape York. Frequents lantana bush areas, feeding on insects and nectar from the plant. It is also called Grey-breasted honeyeater. The suspended nest is usually covered with green moss. *(N. Chaffer)*

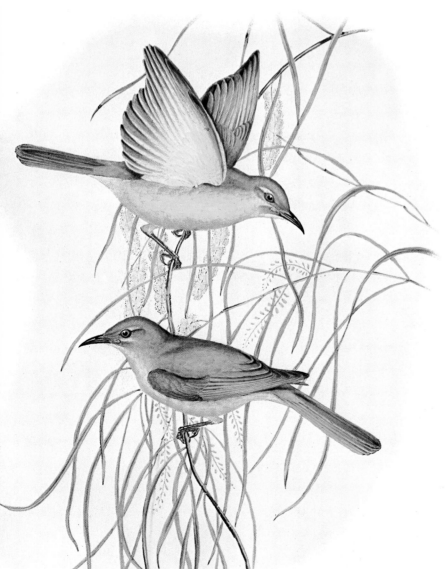

Above:

White-lined honeyeater, *Meliphaga albilineata.* (18 cm. Wooded sandstone gorges. Fairly common.) It occupies a limited area in Arnhem Land, N.T., possibly to Katherine. Also called White-striped honeyeater. It keeps to the dense bushland of these regions and observation has been restricted. Its voice has been noted as a loud, clear whistle. *(G. Mathews)*

Left:

Yellow honeyeater, *Meliphaga flava.* (17 cm. Rain forest, open forest, mangrove areas. Fairly common.) A plumpish, solidly-built honeyeater, very noisy, with a round of calls interpreted as "cheerweer-cheerweer". Its zone, as well as Cape York, extends some way along the north-east coast. It usually lays 2 eggs, white or whitish-pink, with red markings. *(J. Gould)*

Top left:
Singing honeyeater, *Meliphaga virescens.* (20 cm. Open timber, savannah. Very common.) This bird is found throughout most of Australia, except for rain forest areas and Tas. A belligerent and bossy bird, inclined to "take-over" the trees of its liking. Although it has a repertoire of trills and other sounds, it hardly does justice to its common name. *(G. Taylor)*

Bottom left:
Mangrove honeyeater, *Meliphaga fasciogularis.* (18 cm. Mangroves, coastal areas. Fairly common.) Also called Island honeyeater and Fasciated honeyeater. It is a much better "singer" than the Singing honeyeater. True to its name, it usually nests in a mangrove, and lays 2 eggs, pinkish or biscuit, darker at the larger end. Its breeding habits are similar to the Singing honeyeater. *(J. Gould)*

Bottom right:
White-plumed honeyeater, *Meliphaga penicillata.* (15 cm. Open timber, urban areas. Very common.) The popular Greenie of the eastern States, this bird is an active, bold, noisy, and pugnacious fellow. His distinctive "chick-o-wee" is a common garden call and he is the first to give an alarm when cats or other enemies show up. He will join with his fellows in a group to attack owls or other big birds of prey. *(W. Taylor)*

Top left:
Pale-yellow honeyeater, *Meliphaga flavescens*. (15 cm. Open forest. Common.) Also called Yellow-tinted honeyeater. A bird of the tropical eucalypt forests where it feeds on the blossoms and the insects of those trees. Its breeding programme is influenced by the fluctuation of the tropical wet season. It lays 2 salmon-pink eggs, spotted reddish brown. *(G. Chapman)*

Top right:
Varied honeyeater, *Meliphaga versicolor*. (20 cm. Mangroves, urban areas. Fairly common.) It is seen in the garden trees of Cairns, Qld, and also on some coastal islands. The name could justifiably be applied to its very wide range of songs and calls, many of which have led to imaginative interpretation. Seaweed and coastal grasses are common nesting materials. *(J. Gould)*

Bottom right:
Fuscous honeyeater, *Meliphaga fusca*. (15 cm. Light forest, open timber. Fairly common.) It has been described as a plainer edition of the well-known White-plumed honeyeater. This species is seen in gum trees in pairs or small groups, and has a distinctive call of several syllables. It builds a tidy, cup-shaped nest, bound with the common cobweb or down, which may be very near the ground or as high as 12 m. *(I. McCann)*

Top left:
Yellow-throated honeyeater, *Meliphaga flavicollis.* (20 cm. Open timber, urban areas. Common.) This honeyeater replaces some of the mainland species in Tas. Like the White-eared, it is bold in taking nest lining material such as wool from clothing and floor rugs. A feature of this species is that it is not distressed or concerned by snow, winter rain, or other harsh weather conditions. *(W. Murach)*

Top right:
White-eared honeyeater, *Meliphaga leucotis.* (21 cm. Open timber, heathland, arid scrub, mallee. Fairly common.) This is a bird of varied habitats. As well as honey, it consumes large numbers of insects and is sometimes seen on tree trunks and limbs moving like a treecreeper. It is a bold bird, with a loud voice, the main call being a slow "chop, chop, chop" *(W. Taylor)*

Bottom right:
Yellow-tufted honeyeater, *Meliphaga melanops.* (18 cm. Open forest with denser undergrowth. Fairly common.) This species is similar to the Helmeted honeyeater, though smaller. Its performance of the "broken-wing" act is said to be outstanding among honeyeaters. The diet includes fruit, which sometimes makes the bird unpopular with orchardists. *(C. Webster)*

Left:

White-gaped honeyeater, *Meliphaga unicolor.* (18 cm. Mangrove areas, tropical heathland. Common.) This is a belligerent, active, loud-mouthed honeyeater, with a tendency to cock its tail. As well as the usual insects and honey, it eats tropical fruits and berries. The nest is cup shaped, made of paperbark strips and grasses, bound with cobweb, and there are usually 2 pale pink eggs, marked with darker shades. *(J. Gould)*

Below:

Helmeted honeyeater, *Meliphaga cassidix.* (21 cm. Limited to creek margin growth near Melbourne, Vic. Rare.) The helmet can be raised into a small crest. It is a belligerent bird, defending its territory against other species and attacking predators. Its range of calls, like that of the Yellow-tufted honeyeater, includes a trilling note and a harsh chopping sound. *(L. Robinson)*

Top left:
Mottled honeyeater, *Meliphaga macleayana.* (18 cm. Rain forests. Fairly common.) Also called Macleay's honeyeater and Yellow-streaked honeyeater. The scientific and the alternative common name honour Sir William Macleay, a N.S.W. scientist of the nineteenth century. It occupies a limited zone on the Qld north-east coast, and will search diligently for wild fruits and berries as additions to its usual insect and honey diet. *(K. & B. Richards)*

Top right:
Mountain honeyeater, *Meliphaga frenata.* (19 cm. Rain forests. Common.) Also called Bridled honeyeater. It occupies mountain rain forests in a small north Qld area. This bird lays 2 white eggs in the neatly-lined nest, untidy on the outside. Its calls are interpreted as "we are", and "wachita", as well as a growling note. *(K. & B. Richards)*

Bottom left:
Tawny-breasted honeyeater, *Meliphaga flaviventer.* (20 cm. Mangrove areas, tropical forests. Fairly common in limited zone.) This is one of several honeyeaters from the northern-most tip of Cape York. Also called Buff-breasted honey-eater. It energetically feeds on nectarious plants, berries, and insects. The heavy, down-curved bill measures 2·5 cm. *(J. Gould)*

Top left:
Brown-headed honeyeater, *Melithreptus brevirostris.* (13 cm.
Open forest, arid woodland, urban areas. Fairly common.)
This is the first of the group of white-naped honeyeaters.
The genus name, *Melithreptus,* means "nourished by
honey". *Brevirostris* means "short-billed". A handsome,
unobtrusive bird with a loud though not tuneful song.
(G. Taylor)

Top right:
White-naped honeyeater, *Melithreptus lunatus.* (14 cm. Open
forest, parklands. Common.) *Lunatus* means "moon-shaped"
and refers to the white crescent head marking. It is of
energetic and acrobatic habits as it goes about taking honey
from blossoms. There are some migratory movements,
exact details of which are not yet known. *(M. McNaughton)*

Bottom right:
White-throated honeyeater, *Melithreptus albogularis.* (14 cm.
Open forest. Common.) This bird can be very easily
confused with the White-naped honeyeater. Its territory
ranges from the north-east, across the top of the continent
to Broome, W.A. Like those of the White-naped, its nests
are generally high, about 15 m or more, with 2 or 3 eggs.
(M. McNaughton)

Top left:
Black-headed honeyeater, *Melithreptus affinis.* (13 cm. Open forest, urban areas. Common.) Like the Strong-billed, this bird is often tamed in gardens and is also a Tas. honeyeater. It resembles the Strong-billed in many respects, though not a bark stripper. This species also eats fruit from orchards. *(F. Dowling)*

Centre left:
Strong-billed honeyeater, *Melithreptus validirostris.* (15 cm. Open forest. Common.) Also called Barkbird, because of its habit of climbing about trees and removing bark in its quest for insects, which form a large part of its diet. This species is confined to Tas. and is related to the mainland Black-chinned honeyeater. *(T. Waite)*

Bottom left:
Black-chinned honeyeater, *Melithreptus gularis.* (14 cm. Open forest, open timber. Uncommon.) This bird is likely to be encountered in the drier inland, but not in mallee country. It is a prolific songster of various lively notes. Usually found in parties, its mating season is variable between July and February. *(J. Gould)*

Bottom right:
Golden-backed honeyeater, *Melithreptus laetior.* (14 cm. Open forest, timbered watercourse margins. Uncommon.) Very similar to the Black-chinned honeyeater, which it replaces in tropical areas. It has a range of loud and jovial calls and is found in small community groups. Research on its breeding and nesting has been limited. *(J. Gould)*

Facing page:
Blue-faced honeyeater, *Entomyzon cyanotis.* (25–30 cm. Open forest. Common.) This bird often "borrows" the nests of other birds, including those of babblers, mudlarks, and friarbirds. When it builds a nest of its own, the result is usually slovenly and short lasting. Its call is a harsh squawk, which some find annoying. *(W. Taylor)*

Top left:
Little friarbird, *Philemon citreogularis.* (25–28 cm. Open forest, open timber. Fairly common.) The bare head patch is a distinguishing feature of friarbirds. There are six species found in Australia, mainly in the north and north-east. "Little" is a misnomer, especially for a member of the honeyeater family. Its call is loud and monotonous. *(E. Bound)*

Top right:
Sandstone friarbird, *Philemon buceroides.* (35 cm. Sandstone areas. Rare.) The very limited territory of this bird is a section of Arnhem Land, N.T. It is believed to be seen in groups of 2 or 3 and catches insects in flight, but more research is needed on this member of the family. *(P. Trusler)*

Bottom right:
Helmeted friarbird, *Philemon novaeguineae.* (35 cm. Tropical rain forest and woodland. Common.) Also called New Guinea friarbird. Its call has been interpreted in several places as "poor devil, poor devil". As well as insects and honey, it partakes of native fruits. Up to 4 eggs are laid. This bird is noisily aggressive towards smaller birds. *(L. Robinson)*

264

Top left:
Noisy friarbird, *Philemon corniculatus.* (31–36 cm. Forest, open timber. Common.) Also widely called Leatherhead. Its presence in an area is often determined by the flowering of the gums. Aptly named, it is very rowdy, in the usual friarbird manner. One of its calls is often interpreted as "four o'clock". The nest is large and cup-shaped, 3 eggs are laid, and both parents assist in incubation. *(G. Chapman)*

Top right:
Silver-crowned friarbird, *Philemon argenticeps.* (27 cm. Open tropical forest, mangrove areas. Common.) Although smaller, it is very similar to the Helmeted friarbird in both appearance and behaviour, but lays only 2 eggs. Its song phrases are unmusical. The breeding season is August to February. *(J. Gould)*

Bottom right:
Melville Island friarbird, *Philemon gordoni.* (30 cm. Mangrove areas. Uncommon.) This bird's range is limited to Melville Island and some coastline of N.T., but very limited observation of it has been made. There have been a few recorded sightings in gardens of residents in those areas. Little is known of its nest or eggs. *(G. Mathews)*

Top left:
White-fronted honeyeater, *Phylidonyris albifrons*. (18 cm. Arid woodland, heathland, mixed scrub. Common.) An elusive bird of the dry country, it is certainly heard more often than seen. Its nests are found in the mulga and mallee bushes in the late spring. These are about 6 cm deep, cup shaped, made of greyish bark, grass, spider web, and cocoons, and lined with wool, feathers, and down from flower heads. *(G. Taylor)*

Top right:
White-cheeked honeyeater, *Phylidonyris nigra*. (18 cm. Open timber, heathlands, native growth. Uncommon.) An acrobatic bird, it climbs about grevillea or banksia bushes. The birds usually stay in a flock and in a particular locality throughout the seasons. It makes a characteristic approach of diving to its nest with wings closed, then gliding to perch at the nest site. *(A. Wells)*

Centre right:
Crescent honeyeater, *Phylidonyris pyrrhoptera*. (15 cm. Coastal and mountain forests. Common in Tas., uncommon elsewhere.) Also called Tasmanian honeyeater. Distinguishing features are the yellow wing and tail patches and a call often interpreted as "Egypt, Egypt". Of a belligerent disposition, it chases away other birds with sounds of bill clicking and harsh calls. *(E. Bound)*

Bottom right:
White-bearded honeyeater, *Phylidonyris novaehollandiae*. (18 cm. Open timber, heathlands, native bushes. Common.) A bird with several alternative names, most common of which is New Holland honeyeater. Also called White-eyed and Yellow-winged honeyeater. It frequents banksia groves, feeding on nectar from the blossom and using the velvety down of the cone for a nest lining. *(E. Bound)*

Facing page:
Tawny-crowned honeyeater, *Phylidonyris melanops*. (17 cm. Heathland, mallee. Uncommon.) Shy and elusive, its presence is evident because of its musical talent. One of its characteristics is suddenly ascending from a perch, then singing on its descent. It will not be found among larger trees unless these are blossoming freely. *(A. Wells)*

Top:
Bar-breasted honeyeater, *Ramsayornis fasciatus*. (12 cm. Paperbark swamps, tropical river margins. Fairly common.) The two rather drab species of this genus are tropical birds, building a nest unique in the family—bulky, dome shaped, with a side entrance. Not an active bird, it collects insects and honey from the melaleuca in a more leisurely manner than other species. *(G. Chapman)*

Centre:
Brown-backed honeyeater, *Ramsayornis modestus*. (11 cm. Paperbark swamps, mangroves. Fairly common.) Like the Bar-breasted, it is self-effacing and unenergetic. This species has been known to take over the nest of a sunbird, which is also a domed structure. Their movements are controlled by the flowering of the blossoms on which they feed. *(N. Chaffer)*

Bottom left:
Striped honeyeater, *Plectorhyncha lanceolata*. (22 cm. Open timber. Moderately common.) Its food, as well as the usual honey and insects, is fruit from cultivated orchards, which makes it unpopular in some places. Its voice is a loud whistle; its flight is short, fast, and erratic. The nest is often in a casuarina tree and frequently lined with emu feathers. *(W. Taylor)*

Top right:
Rufous-banded honeyeater, *Conopophila albogularis.* (12 cm. Mangroves. Common.) Also called Red-breasted honey-eater. Active and with pleasant voice, it flits among the swamp bushes, catching the insects which form a large portion of its diet. The genus name *Conopophila* refers to a liking for gnats. The small, cup-shaped nest hangs from the end of a light branch, often over water. *(J. Gould)*

Centre right:
Red-throated honeyeater, *Conopophila rufogularis.* (12 cm. Tropical woodlands. Common.) This bird catches insects in flight, especially over rivers and creeks. It has also a liking for fruit. It is never far from water, in which it likes to bathe. The nest is made of soft material, with stiffer grass stems to hold the shape. *(G. Chapman)*

Bottom right:
Painted honeyeater, *Conopophila picta.* (15 cm. Open forest, timber with mistletoe growth. Uncommon.) This unusual species lives mainly on mistletoe berries. It spends a good deal of time removing the mistletoe jelly from its plumage. This same jelly, together with spider web, appears to be used as an adhesive for its flimsy nest, in casuarinas or yellow box. *(I. McCann)*

Bottom left:
Grey honeyeater, *Conopophila whitei.* (11 cm. Arid wood-land, mulga scrub. Rare.) This species resembles a silvereye in plumage as well as in behaviour, and is often seen with thornbills and warblers. It could be confused with the White-tailed warbler. As well as other items of diet, it is known to eat mistletoe berries. *(G. Chapman)*

Top:
Regent honeyeater, *Xanthomyza phrygia.* (22 cm. Forest, open timber. Fairly common.) Also called Flying coachman. It is rowdy and belligerent, fighting its own kind as well as birds of other species, but it is an attractive visitor to garden or near-by bush. It has been successfully encouraged by the planting of Yellow gum. *(J. Gould)*

Bottom:
Banded honeyeater, *Cissomela pectoralis.* (12 cm. Tropical woodlands. Fairly common.) It has a liking for blossoming melaleucas. An aggressive bird, it is sometimes seen in very large flocks. It builds a cup-shaped, suspended nest, often so poorly lined that the 2 beige-coloured eggs can be seen from below it. *(G. Chapman)*

Top:
Eastern spinebill, *Acanthorhynchus tenuirostris.* (15 cm. Rain forest, open timber, heathlands, urban areas. Common.) A restless, beautiful honeyeater, frequently encouraged into suburban gardens. Recent banding studies have revealed that individuals live as long as 7 years. It has a fast, erratic flight, the wings making a distinctive clipping sound. *(I. McCann)*

Centre:
Western spinebill, *Acanthorhynchus superciliosus.* (14 cm. Open timber, heathland, banksia, and tea-tree country. Common.) The distinctive bill measures 2·5 cm. This is a close relative of the Eastern spinebill, replacing it in the south-west in a fairly small zone. Its aerial activities include hovering like a humming-bird, also used by its eastern cousin. *(A. Wells)*

Bottom:
Bell miner, *Manorina melanophrys.* (18 cm. Dry sclerophyll forest. Common.) This bird, also called Bellbird, is one of four species of miners found in Australia. It is thought that the common name comes from some resemblance to the unrelated Indian myna, the name having been mis-spelt earlier. This species is very audibly prominent because of its tinkling, bell-like call. *(F. Lewitzka)*

271

Top:
White-rumped miner, *Manorina flavigula*. (25 cm. Dry woodland. Common.) Also called Yellow-throated miner. It replaces the Noisy miner in drier and mallee country. This bird feeds on blossoming trees and fruit, and catches insects on the ground. It becomes tame and friendly, and is frequently seen around home or farmyard. *(B. Lovell)*

Centre:
Noisy miner, *Manorina melanocephala*. (25 cm. Temperate woodland, urban areas. Common.) Also called Soldierbird. Bold and noisy, often seen in suburban gardens where it will chase and harry dogs, cats, and other birds, as well as humans. It is frequently observed in groups, when the harrying tactics are undertaken by the flock. *(T. & P. Gardner)*

Bottom:
Black-eared miner, *Manorina melanotis*. (25 cm. Dry woodland. Fairly common in limited local area.) The restricted area is the mallee type country where the borders of Vic., S.A., and N.S.W. converge. It is very similar to the White-rumped miner to which it is closely related. The egg clutch varies from 3 to 5. *(J. Purnell)*

Top right:
Little wattlebird, *Anthochaera chrysoptera*. (28 cm. Banksia clusters, open forest, urban areas. Fairly common.) John Gould reported that the Aborigines said the sound made by this bird reminded them of someone being sick. But it is a bird with personality, bold and pugnacious, and in a garden can become friendly. This relationship may be encouraged by feeding the birds cheese. *(B. Lovell)*

Centre right:
Spiny-cheeked honeyeater, *Anthochaera rufogularis*. (25 cm. Arid woodland, light forest, open timber. Common.) This bird has a pleasing song, which is often abruptly cut off, seemingly in mid-sentence. It builds a cup-shaped nest of grass and rootlets, bound with cobweb, lined with fur or down, and hanging from mistletoe or a forked tree branch, often high off the ground. *(E. Bound)*

Bottom right:
Yellow wattlebird, *Anthochaera paradoxa*. (38 cm. Open forest, suburban gardens. Common.) Its home ground is Tas. and some Bass Strait islands. The tail measures up to 25 cm. Observers report that these birds, on clustering densely in the flowering gums in autumn months, seem to become intoxicated with the nectar, and leave themselves vulnerable. *(T. Waite)*

Bottom left:
Red wattlebird, *Anthochaera carunculata*. (35 cm. Open forest, suburban gardens. Common.) In spite of comments on the voices of wattlebirds, many find the familiar notes endearing, especially the "quock, quock" of this bird. It likes native shrubberies, especially banksias and bottle-brushes. The red wattles are a distinctive feature. *(F. Park)*

FINCHES ESTRILDIDAE

The Australian finches often are referred to as grass finches, because they live mainly on grass seeds and, as a general rule, grass dominates their choice of habitat.

Their mating displays are of interest. As an initial move, the male puts on an act of singing and parading, possibly not directed towards an individual female but for all the girls to see. The actual selection of the mate is made by the female, as is also the selection of the nesting site.

The selection of the nesting site is important. The birds themselves (because of their plumage) and the nests (because of their size and shape) are noticeable to predators, and often the safety of the nest will depend on its situation.

Many nests are built in tangled and prickly scrub growth, inaccessible to predators. Some are placed in a tree surrounded by water, out of the reach of non-swimming marauders. Others are built among the sticks of the big nests of eagles. Finches are too small to interest the eagles as prey, and other would-be predators are scared of the eagles. Yet another device is to build the nest beside the nesting place of wasps or hornets, as likely predators would keep well clear of these stinging aggressors. The nests are well constructed, domed or globe shaped, with a side entrance.

Under good conditions, six or more eggs are laid. Incubation takes two weeks and usually the chicks can move out in another three weeks, so there is a quick turnover. In a season, two or three broods might be hatched. An interesting feature of the young finch in the nest is the bright pattern around the inside of the mouth of each juvenile bird. These are known as "Nature's candles", and have some luminous quality so they can direct the parent birds to the mouths of the infants, a useful aid in the semi-darkness of the nest.

Finches live mainly on half-ripened or ripe grass seeds, picked up from the ground or extracted from the grass stalk. During the breeding season they also catch a number of insects to aid their diet. As with all birds who exist on a dry diet, finches need a readily-available water supply. In very dry country, the presence of the birds means that there is water near and they are capable of leading thirsty travellers to it. However, the Zebra finch, a bird hardened to heat, could possibly lead one into trouble, as it can tolerate drinking water with a fairly high proportion of salt and of little use to a parched man.

Red-browed finch. *Aegintha temporalis.* (12 cm. Mangroves, open timber, parks and gardens. Common.) Also called Waxbill and Redhead. These are tame and friendly finches, often being fed in parks or backyards, taking a large variety of food. They have a wide range, generally following the eastern and south-eastern coastline, and are also found on Kangaroo Island. *(K. & B. Richards)*

Top right:
Painted finch, *Emblema picta.* (10 cm. Spinifex. Uncommon.)
Its preference is for rock formations covered with spinifex
grass. The tapering bill is well suited for picking up seeds
from between the grass tussocks. Although its usual habitats
are in the arid and isolated areas, it has been seen in gardens
in Alice Springs. *(F. Lewitzka)*

Centre right:
Beautiful firetail, *Emblema bella.* (12 cm. Open timber,
savannah. Uncommon.) This is the only Australian finch
found in Tas. It is similar to the Red-eared firetail in many
ways, but prefers a low nesting site and will feed on the
ground. Like the former bird, it has been greatly affected
by settlement and by introduced predators, especially cats.
(R. Good)

Bottom right:
Diamond firetail, *Emblema guttata.* (11 cm. Savannah,
mallee. Fairly common.) Although, like other firetails,
it has suffered because of land settlement, it appears more
capable of changing the location of its habitat. Sometimes
it is seen in home gardens. If flushed from the ground, it
rises with a whirr of the wings, like quail. *(W. Taylor)*

Bottom left:
Red-eared firetail, *Emblema oculata* (immature). (12 cm.
Damp, cleared grass areas in forests. Uncommon.) This
species does not respond to land settlement and the numbers
are declining. Although it is a low-flying bird, it is seldom
seen on the ground, preferring to find a dropped stick or
low shrub twig to perch on when feeding. It builds its
nest higher up than any other Australian finch. *(G. Chapman)*

Top:
Crimson finch, *Neochmia phaeton.* (14 cm. Tropical swamp
areas. Fairly common.) Also called Blood finch. This finch
is well adapted to man and his movements. In fact it follows
settlement and is found at stations and farm homesteads,
most likely because of the provision of water there. A
peculiarity of the species is that it does not fly great distances
at a time, preferring to move in short stages from bush to
bush. *(F. Lewitzka)*

Centre:
Star finch, *Neochmia ruficauda.* (12 cm. Tropical heathland,
tall grass areas. Fairly common.) These birds will appear
in huge flocks, flying fast and making simultaneous twists
and turns, like starlings. A peculiarity in their display
behaviour is that the female will flit around the male with
a long piece of grass in her beak, believed to be an encourage-
ment to courtship. Later, when actually courting, the male
is seen carrying grass. *(F. Lewitzka)*

Bottom:
Zebra finch, *Poephila guttata.* (9 cm. All areas except wet
sclerophyll forest. Very common.) The most common of
all Australian finches, adapting well to man's encroachment
and being able to vary its habitat considerably. It appreciates
the easier access to water brought about by settlement and
is sometimes seen in parks and gardens. *(F. Lewitzka)*

Top right:

Doublebar finch, *Poephila bichenovii*. (11 cm. Tall grass areas, scrublands with water, urban areas. Common.) *Bichenovii* is after J. E. Bicheno, a former prominent naturalist. Also called Bicheno's finch, Owl-faced finch. It is never seen more than 3 km away from drinking water. This is another finch that seems to prefer the nearness of men's dwellings to its former bush habitats. *(W. Taylor)*

Centre right:

Masked finch, *Poephila personata*. (11 cm. Tropical open timber, grasslands. Common.) They are seen in the street trees of Katherine and Darwin, N.T., and observers in that area report they are not uncommon roadside birds on the highways. They feed mainly on the ground. A number of finch species, including this one, drink water by continued sucking, instead of the usual sip method. *(F. Lewitzka)*

Bottom left:

Black-throated finch, *Poephila cincta*. (10 cm. Open timber with dense grass and available water. Fairly common.) Also called Parson finch. There are variations in colour patterns from district to district, the bird's range extending from the top north-east to central N.S.W. Males often carry a piece of grass when courting. This species will lay up to 9 eggs in a clutch. *(F. Lewitzka)*

Bottom right:

Long-tailed finch, *Poephila acuticauda*. (15 cm. Tropical open timber with near water. Fairly common.) Its range is in the top section of the continent. It builds an elaborate, well-made nest of dried material, lined with down and feathers, in the high sections of tall gum trees. Many finches have the habit of placing small pieces of charcoal in the nest, believed to be as a disinfectant. *(G. Chapman)*

Top and centre left:
Gouldian finch, *Chloebia gouldiae*. (14 cm. Tropical open timber with water nearby, mangroves. Uncommon). There are 3 recorded head colours. The common black and red are illustrated at top left. The rare yellow is shown in the pair at centre left. This beautiful bird, confined to the far northern areas and much exploited by bird catchers, was named Gouldian finch by John Gould himself. He wrote: "I . . . dedicate this lovely bird to the memory of my late wife, who for many years laboriously assisted me with her pencil." *(F. Lewitzka)*

Bottom left:
Blue-faced finch, *Erythrura trichroa*. (12 cm. Tropical rain forest and coastal hills. Rare.) Because of its rarity, very few observations have been made and records are meagre. It is said to be fairly common on some of the northern islands, and sometimes has been referred to as "sparrow of the islands". *(G. Mathews)*

Bottom right:
Plum-headed finch, *Aidemosyne modesta*. (11 cm. Heathland near watercourses or standing water. Rare.) Also called Cherry finch. Observers report that this species comes to drink every hour. The birds will perch on a grass stem to drink and will cling to a stem to feed on its seeds. They are known to be exceptionally tame and perhaps are easy prey to cats and other predators. *(J. Gould)*

WEAVERS PLOCEIDAE

Like the rabbit, the sparrow was deliberately brought to Australia and let loose to multiply. And like the rabbit, there is no doubt that the bird has developed into a major pest, with many counts against it. Unlike the rabbit, it has no value as a food item and anyone would be hard put to find much to be said in the bird's favour as an Australian resident.

Sparrows were introduced, it is said, to help the market gardeners combat the caterpillar pest. It did not take the gardeners long to realise that, although caterpillars were still flourishing, they had another pest on their hands.

Perhaps this should be said for the early colonists, that the sparrow played such a big part in their former lives that the little bird was missed in Australia, and it was brought over to fill the gap. Because the sparrow, more so than any other bird, infiltrates into people's lives, in fact often into their houses, as they are expert at finding nesting sites in roof apertures, under eaves, or beside a chimney. So the people could not imagine a country without sparrows.

A country without a sparrow? Yes, not only can it be imagined, but it can be pleasantly experienced, because in the populated south-west of Western Australia, the sparrow has not colonised. To the credit of authorities in the west, the bird has never come to stay in those parts. Today, if one shows up at a wharf or transport depot or anywhere at all, it is immediately set upon and destroyed.

Sparrows will drive away native birds and there are examples of their wrecking the nests of blue wrens in a garden. Perhaps they are seen at their worst around a farm homestead. They play havoc with an orchard, pecking at and destroying soft fruit. Likewise in a vegetable garden, they can do much damage in a short time. They will line up on the margin of a feeding poultry flock, when grain is scattered on the ground, appearing in large numbers and consuming a costly share of the grain. In fact they are a scourge of poultrykeepers, getting into fowl sheds where feeding appliances are placed in front of the fowls, eating away the profit margins, so that the poultryman is put to the additional expense of having to install fine-mesh netting on hen houses where a wider mesh should do.

The presence of the sparrow is mainly limited to towns and dwellings, and they are not regarded as having made a great influx into the bush, at least not as yet. They are seen frequently on country roadsides. At places, well into the bush, where feeding programmes are set up for parrots and honeyeaters, the sparrows appear.

Tree sparrow, *Passer montanus* (top). (15 cm. Towns, farms. Fairly common.); House sparrow, *Passer domesticus* (bottom, male and female). (15 cm. Urban areas, farms. Very common.) The Tree sparrow is often seen with the House sparrow, but could go unnoticed unless close observation is made. Sexes are alike in the Tree sparrow, and it does not have the same boldness or adaptability as the House sparrow. The black bib of the male House sparrow disappears in autumn, giving way to grey, but it shows again in the spring. (*J. Gould*)

OLD WORLD FINCHES FRINGILLIDAE

There are two species of old world finches resident in Australia. By far the more common of the two is the Goldfinch. The first Goldfinches brought to Australia arrived roughly at the same time as the sparrows. They came as cage birds, and it would seem that the species became established by some escapees.

However, the presence of the Goldfinch is not resented here. It is regarded as the most beautiful of introduced birds and is a constant source of delight in the usually populated areas where it is seen. It is noticeable because of its colourful garb, the flashes of yellow as it takes to the wing, and its very pleasing and well-known twittering, tinkling song. A seed eater, it does no harm to the environment, but it is probably a weed destroyer.

It nests near to man's dwellings, in fruit trees (orchardists do not resent its presence), in garden shrubs, and in pine trees. For their nests, they have been seen taking cobwebs from clothes lines and crevices.

Their song is particularly noticeable in the autumn, when they are heard singing in the grass clusters or on the telephone wires in the street. This bird likes thistle seeds and is often seen on roadsides or in paddocks where these plants grow. It also frequents boxthorn bushes and is said to have a fondness for cape weed (dandelion).

The nest is neat, cup shaped, and made of grasses, cobweb, and strong fibre, with a lining of down or soft material. This is usually well hidden in tree foliage. It lays four or five eggs, pale blue or whitish, spotted brown.

The Goldfinch is well known in many parts of the world. It figures in a legend which says that the little bird witnessed the crucifixion of Christ. It became very agitated, trying to pull the nails from the cross and the thorns from the head crown, without success, and was left with a blot of blood on its face. That is why, says the legend, the Goldfinch to this day has a red patch on its face and why these birds are so often found near thorn bushes.

The other species in this family, the Greenfinch, is also an introduced bird, but somewhat plainer and of a more limited range. Its main zones are in and around Adelaide, in Victoria generally, and in central New South Wales. It is a retiring bird and this, with its quieter plumage, tends to make it inconspicuous.

Top right:
Goldfinch, *Carduelis carduelis.* (12 cm. Parks and gardens, cultivated paddocks, urban areas, roadside. Common.) It is found mainly in south-eastern Australia, with a few pockets in the south-west. In winter it is seen in flocks of varying size, sometimes as many as 100. *(K. & B. Richards)*

Bottom right:
Greenfinch, *Chloris chloris.* (15 cm. Open timber, parks and gardens. Uncommon.) The sexes are slightly different, the female being a little duller. Even its calls are less conspicuous than that of the Goldfinch. It will occasionally twitter in flight, but its main call is a sharp "wee-we", sounded while perching. *(K. & B. Richards)*

STARLINGS STURNIDAE

Among the three species of the starling family in Australia, only one, the Shining starling of north Queensland, is a native Australian bird. This, as the name suggests, is a bird with a shining, metallic-like plumage. An interesting feature is its nesting habit. The birds move in huge flocks and will build their nests very close together, hanging in tall jungle trees.

An observer reported counting nearly 200 nests in one tree. Sometimes the combined weight of the nests is too much for a tree branch, which breaks under the strain. Each bird will lay three or four eggs, off-white, with grey or brown markings. The birds feed mainly on wild tropical fruits, especially the nutmeg, and insects are also taken.

The history of the European starling in Australia runs parallel with that of the sparrows, and the birds have a good deal in common. Like the House sparrow, European starlings are often seen in suburban gardens and around homes. They will nest in roof crevices and are not, like most other birds, sensitive to nest interference or easily discouraged. They have been known, when a nest has been removed and the entrance hole blocked with concrete, to peck out the concrete while still wet and to start nest-building all over again. The eggs, usually from five to seven in a clutch, are coloured a beautiful blue.

Individual birds among them are remarkable mimics.

An observer has heard, right at a suburban back door, a perfect imitation of the "chut-chut-chutting" of a plover. Investigation showed a European starling perched on the spouting next door.

European starlings are seen in huge flocks on country roadsides. They are masters at formation flying, banking, twisting, and turning as one bird. Long lines of them will settle on telephone wires. On the credit side, these starlings do account for a number of insect pests.

The third family member is the Indian myna, another bird which seems to be ever increasing and which also frequents backyards and suburban streets. These birds "take-over" a location, dispersing other birds, including their own species.

They are very vocal, with loud and raucous voices. They sing some pleasant songs, but when voicing a protest, as when one of their young might have been picked up by man, they utter sharp and harsh notes.

Shining starling, *Aplonis metallica*. (25 cm. Rain forests. Common.) These birds are very capable aerialists and are sometimes called Whirlwindbird. They migrate to New Guinea to winter, leaving Australia in May and returning in August. Not all birds make the trip, some remaining in Australia. *Metallica* means "like metal", a reference to its shining plumage. (*R. Garstone*)

Left:
European starling, *Sturnus vulgaris*. (20 cm. Towns, occupied areas, infiltrating into bushland. Very common.) An introduced species. Also called English starling. Among its many enemies are orchardists, for a flock, feeding greedily, can quickly strip a cherry tree. They also play havoc in dried-fruit areas. Like the sparrow, it has been successfully kept out of W.A. *(W. Moreland)*

Below:
Indian myna, *Acridotheres tristis*. (24 cm. Towns, occupied areas. Very common.) An introduced species. The sexes are alike. These have been described as Dickensian characters, full of their own importance and an acute sense of curiosity. Their nest is crude and untidy, made of grass and often paper, and the bird lays 4 or 5 blue eggs. *(K. & B. Richards)*

ORIOLES ORIOLIDAE

The family of orioles, birds of the forest and mountain slopes, is represented in Australia by four species, two orioles and two figbirds. The name "oriole" means golden, and both Australian species have some golden or yellow colouration.

One member of the family, the Olive-backed oriole, is a very capable mimic. Mimicry seems prevalent among Australian birds—an expert ornithologist has listed more than fifty species which imitate the calls of other birds—but recently an oriole gave an outstanding performance. A tape recording enthusiast was confident that he had listed and recorded a number of bird calls, until suddenly he realised he had the voice of just one bird on his tape—an oriole.

The written records of the mimicry talents of the Olive-backed oriole go back many years and there are some early accounts of remarkable imitations by the bird, placing it high on the list of mimics, perhaps not so very far behind the lyrebird.

As yet there are no records of the second species, the Yellow oriole, indulging in mimicry, although its voice is known to have a wide range and possibly its name may yet be added to the list of mimics.

The call of the Olive-backed oriole has often been interpreted as "ore-ree-ole", and anyone could be excused for thinking this is another instance of a bird being named after its call.

Both orioles and figbirds have fairly long, down-curved bills. They live mainly on soft fruits and berries of native trees, as well as insects. In the two species of orioles, the sexes are fairly similar, whereas in figbirds there are marked differences, with the males being the more brightly coloured.

The flight is undulating and not unlike that of bowerbirds. The birds are often seen in small flocks, which may comprise both orioles and figbirds.

Olive-backed oriole, *Oriolus sagittatus*. (25–28 cm. Forests, mountain slopes. Moderately common.) *Sagittatus* means "marked with arrows". The nest is basket shaped, made of soft bark and leaves, and lined with grass. It is placed at varying heights from near the ground to the top of a high tree. This bird's range is northern and eastern Australia. (E. Bound)

Top:
Yellow oriole, *Oriolus flavocinctus.* (25–28 cm. Rain forest, mangrove areas. Uncommon.) It could be confused with the Olive-backed oriole in the few places where the two species overlap. It favours native fig trees, near water. It has a pleasantly-toned call, which can grow monotonous, and a harsher, sneeze-like sound. (*G. Chapman*)

Centre:
Southern figbird, *Sphecotheres vieilloti.* (28 cm. Wet forests, especially areas of native fig trees, orchards. Moderately common.) *Vieilloti* honours L. J. P. Vieillot, a celebrated French bird observer. It has a range along the east coast and the items it occasionally includes in its diet are indicated by the alternative names Mulberrybird and Bananabird. It is a very active and noisy bird. (*H. Frauca*)

Bottom:
Yellow figbird, *Sphecotheres flaviventris.* (28 cm. Tropical forest. Moderately common.) It is similar to the Southern figbird in appearance, and in voice and habits. It builds a flat nest, often choosing the same tree as other species, especially the Helmeted friarbird. It lays 3 greenish eggs, with marks that convey an impression of being under the shell. (*S. Long*)

DRONGOS DICRURIDAE

The one species of drongo found in Australia is common in areas of the north and north-west. Further south, its numbers decline and it is not well known. In Victoria it is, at best, an occasional visitor.

In fact, for many people the bird was unknown until recently. The name has come into fairly common usage, but not to identify a species of bird. It was a favourite term of drill instructors in the armed services during the early days of the second World War, when they were seeking colourful words to impress incoming recruits. A soldier who dropped his rifle on the drill square was a drongo of the first order.

To call a man a "galah" is not to compliment him, and the term is much used, in work lunchroom, in bar-counter discussions, and among sporting onlookers. It seems that to liken anyone to a member of a particular bird species would indicate that the person referred to is lacking in all requirements, and is, in fact, bird-brained.

Of course, all of this is rather unfair to the birds. There is nothing about the drongo to make it comparable with someone who doesn't know his drill.

Drongos are bold little birds, stoutly defending their nests and territories, tackling big birds of prey and successfully driving them from the vicinity. Often they perch in a high tree on a forest margin, alert for flying insects, and will whip out to capture their prey in the air.

Drongos resemble starlings, possessing a shining black plumage. The most noticeable distinguishing feature is the long tail, shaped like a fishtail. This is frequently displayed by the bird, as it has a habit of drooping the tail as it perches in wait for insect prey. This tail measures 15 cm and has led to the bird being called Fishtail in some places.

As well as their migratory visits to the south, the birds also cross to New Guinea, but all of their movement patterns are not clear.

They nest in tall trees, in the denser foliage, but in slender branches well away from the trunk. The nest is saucer shaped and open, made of tendrils of creepers and fibre. There are usually from three to five eggs laid, coloured pinkish-white to pale grey, with chestnut markings.

The wings are long and pointed, ideal for the insect-catching flight and, for the same purpose, the bird is equipped with a strong bill and surrounding bristles.

Spangled drongo, *Dicrurus bracteatus*. (28–30 cm. Rain and coastal forests, mangroves. Common in local areas.) The *bracteatus* refers to the bird's shining metallic appearance. The voice is described as a harsh cackle or a chattering, with an occasional shrill whistle. Drongos are also listed as mimics. *(L. Robinson)*

MUDNEST BUILDERS GRALLINIDAE

It is the building of mud nests which unites these three species into a family, although the White-winged chough and the Apostlebird do have many similarities, and in some places the chough is alternatively known as the Apostlebird.

The little Mudlark certainly ranks as one of Australia's best-known birds. Black and white, it is the bantam magpie, with a lot of the bigger bird's character and fearlessness. It is known by several names, all of which are well used in different localities. These are Magpie lark, Peewit, Peewee, and Murray magpie.

They are very common roadside birds, sometimes being seen in flocks, but usually in pairs. The male mudlark is distinguishable by its black face markings.

Mudlarks are seen, and heard, around many suburban localities, as they sit on street power lines, proclaiming their presence. Often they can be observed over a period as they go about the whole procedure of nest building, and hatching and feeding the young. They will nest, often in a gum tree, in any locality in which mud for the little bowl-shaped construction may be found.

The name "Peewee" comes from the sound of the call. The song is often sung together by the pair, in a duet or antiphonal singing. They have a characteristic of raising their wings as they make their call.

The White-winged chough is, when on the ground, an all-black bird which might be mistaken for a crow or currawong. But in flight, or when preening, a large white wing-patch is displayed. It is a good identifying feature.

Out of the breeding season, these birds move around in a group of anything up to a score, the company usually consisting of parent birds and the young hatched in the previous season. It is said that if something should happen to the senior male member of the group, he is not replaced, but instead the group breaks up.

In their bowl-shaped mud nest, more than one female might lay eggs, up to five each in number, but no more than four young will be reared from the entire clutch.

Some observers say that the Apostlebird is the most intelligent of Australian birds. It feeds mainly on the ground and moves about with a peculiar strutting gait. If disturbed, the group of them will fly into the lower branches of a near-by tree, protesting loudly. When feeding, they will steady their food by standing on it.

Mudlark, *Grallina cyanoleuca*. (25–28 cm. Open timber, towns. Very common.) It has an unusual flight pattern of its own. When taking to the air, often rises vertically for a metre or two. Around a home, it becomes very friendly and can be tamed and fed by hand. It is of high value to agriculture as it consumes a snail which is a host of the liver fluke, so harmful to sheep. (*J. Ferrero*)

Above:
White-winged chough, *Corcorax melanorhamphos*. (45 cm. Woodlands, roadside trees. Common.) Like the Apostlebird, it will fly to a low point in a tree if disturbed, complaining loudly. Each bird will move about the tree, fanning its tail. The hardened mud nests are often used from season to season. Its range of calls includes a mournful whistle, and some hissing and grating calls of alarm. *(I. McCann)*

Right:
Apostlebird, *Struthidea cinerea*. (33 cm. Open timber. Fairly common.) On the road, they will often permit a close approach by car. In times of drought, the absence of mud for nest building can upset the breeding programme, but sometimes emu droppings are utilised to patch an old nest. The voice includes a noisy, repetitive chattering and some strident sounds of complaint. *(B. Lovell)*

WOODSWALLOWS ARTAMIDAE

The family of woodswallows, unrelated to ordinary swallows, is represented by six species in Australia.

The White-breasted, which heads the list, is known for its habit of utilising the abandoned nests of mud-nest builders, especially that of the Mudlark, but also of Apostlebirds and White-winged choughs. A peculiarity of this species is that they will perch tightly together along a tree branch, so close that the birds in the middle cannot move. When a bird darts out of the line after an insect, it loses its place, the others quickly moving up to close the gap.

Both the Masked and the White-browed woodswallows will migrate to a nesting locality, often arriving and staying together. Within a few days they will begin to build their small, bowl-shaped nests of grass and fibre strips. Usually there are two broods in a season, after which the birds will depart as suddenly as they came. There is no delaying when it is time to move and late nesters will desert nest and young if the latter are not advanced enough to join the travelling party. During the migratory flights, the birds prefer to cross areas of open timber, for they need to settle frequently to rest and to feed.

The White-browed is the most attractive and colourful of the woodswallows and is the only family member to have a chestnut breast. It consumes a variety of insects, being a particularly valuable destroyer of grasshoppers.

The Black-faced is easily distinguishable from other woodswallows, the brown body being a clear identifying feature as well as the black face. When settling, it has a habit of spreading its tail or wagging it sideways. It is a resident or stationary species, usually found in pairs or in small groups. It might move away looking for food in the winter, but pairs are known to return to the same locality to nest for a number of years. It is the most common and widely distributed of all the woodswallows. It lives entirely on insects, most of which are taken in flight, often as it swoops from a perch high in a tree or on telephone wires.

The Dusky woodswallow migrates to the south, arriving in early spring and leaving again in winter. It catches insects on the wing or in trees and also consumes some nectar. It has a pleasing, chirping call, often heard as the birds pass overhead. It is an excellent aerialist, capable of both long and high flight.

The Little woodswallow has a northern range, occupying much of the area not inhabited by the Dusky. It often breeds in rocky country and its call includes mimicry of other birds.

White-breasted woodswallow, *Artamus leucorhynchus*. (17 cm. Forest, open timber, mangrove areas. Fairly common.) This species normally is seen not far from water. It is very common in some northern Qld towns. Its eggs are milk-coffee in colour, with chestnut markings. A feature of woodswallows is that they have a brush tongue, like honeyeaters and lorikeets. *(J. Hannant)*

Top left:
Dusky woodswallow, *Artamus cyanopterus*. (18 cm. Forests, open timber. Fairly common.) These have a peculiar custom of roosting in clusters, like a swarm of bees. They will settle on the protected side of a hanging tree branch, with the bird on the bottom of the pile clinging to the tree, while those above apparently grip the wings or shoulders of the birds below them. *(M. Seyfort)*

Centre left:
Masked woodswallow, *Artamus personatus*. (18 cm. Open timber. Fairly common.) Both sexes assist in feeding the young. An observer reports that the female parent will stretch out her wings, protecting the chicks from the sun while the male parent feeds them. Like other woodswallows, it has a very graceful flight, soaring and circling high in the air in its quest for insects. *(B. Lovell)*

Bottom left:
Black-faced woodswallow, *Artamus cinereus*. (18 cm. Open timber, heathlands, acacia belts. Common.) It is a bird often seen on roadsides, seeming to like fences, telephone wires, and other signs of civilisation. It likes low stumps for nesting and open trees through which it can dart after insects. In the drier centre, this species is sometimes seen well away from water. *(A. Wells)*

Bottom right:
Little woodswallow, *Artamus minor*. (12 cm. Forests, open timber. Fairly common.) This smallest of the woodswallows has general habits similar to the others. Its nest is roughly made and it lays 3 eggs, off-white, with brown markings. There are 4 species of woodswallow found in other parts of the world, but the family is most richly represented in Australia. *(G. Chapman)*

Above:
White-browed woodswallow, *Artamus superciliosus* (male). (18 cm. Open timber. Fairly common.) Its migratory movements are irregular. At some places the birds will return annually, while in others they are seen only spasmodically. This is a noisy, active, and noticeable bird, whether flying low, so that its colouring is obvious, or up high, in clever aerial activity. *(M. Seyfort)*

BUTCHERBIRDS, MAGPIES, AND CURRAWONGS CRACTICIDAE

The members of this family are probably the most typically Australian of all birds. They are medium to large, all aggressive, bold, and full of personality, and all magnificent songsters. Their colouring varies from black, to black and white, and grey. Most of them are common and, fortunately, in many cases they have adapted to the settlement of man both in towns and on the land.

The butcherbirds are so named because of their method of "hanging up" their meat. Often they will tightly wedge their dead prey, or other items of food, into tree forks, an occupation not reserved for the bush, but sometimes seen in suburban gardens. The bird's butchering methods are assisted by the equipment of a strong, sharp hook at the tip of a large, bluish bill.

The magpies were named after the English magpie, a bird to which they bear no relationship. Originally the name was arrived at through a shortening of the name "Maggie", given to the bird as a gesture of friendliness, and "pie" from its pied plumage. The name was given to the Australian birds very soon after settlement and has become firmly established.

Magpies, seen on roadsides, in fields, and wherever people dwell with some trees about, have stout and strong bills, bluish with a black tip, but not so noticeably hooked as that of the butcherbirds.

Currawongs were previously called bell magpies, and the birds also have several other names in some areas. Currawongs are often found around a homestead or settled area, where they quickly become "boss birds", lording it over other species. They are often seen on roadsides, where they might at first be mistaken for crows, but closer observation will reveal the white tail tip and wing pattern. They have stout and strong bills, bluish, with a black tip, but like the magpie's, not noticeably hooked.

It is impossible to do justice to the calls of all these birds. Fortunately they record well and a tape of the Black-throated butcherbird is fine evidence of the magnificent musical richness of his song. For many people, the songs of butcherbirds and magpies are the finest sounds in the world.

John Gould found it difficult to put into words his appreciation of the carol of the magpies, and the sounds impossible to describe. He expressed regret that "his readers could not listen to the birds in their native wilds". Today it is still interesting to notice how new residents and visitors to Australia immediately become aware of the songs of the birds in this family, and grow to love them.

Black-throated butcherbird, *Cracticus nigrogularis*. (33 cm. Open timber, woodland. Common.) Also called Pied butcherbird. The melodious song is often heard at night. The nest is flat, with a shallow bowled area in the centre. Usually there are 4 eggs, pale coloured and spotted. The birds will defend their nest vigorously against any intruders. *(K. & B. Richards)*

Top left:
Grey butcherbird, *Cracticus torquatus*. (32 cm. Open timber, woodland, urban areas. Common.) The beautiful song is heard in many outer suburban areas. It sings in the autumn and often on the hottest days in summer. As well as the practice of placing dead prey in the forks of trees, it sometimes hangs the prey on thorns or sharp twigs. *(G. Churchett)*

Bottom left:
Black-backed butcherbird, *Cracticus mentalis*. (25 cm. Tropical woodlands. Fairly common.) Though slightly smaller, is very like the Grey butcherbird, including song similarities. Occupies a limited zone in Cape York, north of the Palmer River, where it also could be confused with the Black-throated butcherbird. The range of diet includes small reptiles, small birds, rodents, caterpillars, grubs, and insects. *(E. Whitbourn)*

Bottom right:
Black butcherbird, *Cracticus quoyi*. (33 cm. Tropical rain forests, mangrove areas. Fairly common in limited area.) Some of the tropical pockets it occupies are not inhabited by other butcherbirds, so it fills the gap and means that much of the continent has a family representative. It has its own repertoire of calls, well up to the family standard. Its diet includes some kinds of shellfish. *(L. Robinson)*

Top left:
Black-backed magpie, *Gymnorhina tibicen*. (36–40 cm. Open timber, cultivated paddocks, urban areas. Very common.) In some places the Black-backed and White-backed magpies interbreed, with a resultant hybrid cross. Magpies are ground feeders, often digging for grubs and worms. Magpies are aggressive when breeding, often suddenly and savagely attacking innocent passers-by. *(A. Young)*

Top right:
Western magpie, *Gymnorhina dorsalis*. (36–40 cm. Open timber, cultivated paddocks, urban areas. Very common.) This is the magpie of the south-west area of W.A. Its habits are similar to those of other magpies, but a physical difference is that here the male has a white back while the female's back is black. The usual egg clutch is 4. Eggs are greyish, with streaks of brown. *(J. Dart)*

Bottom left:
White-backed magpie, *Gymnorhina hypoleuca*. (36–40 cm. Open timber, cultivated paddocks, urban areas. Very common.) Magpies haunt the highways and roads and sadly there is a high fatality rate, mostly of young birds. Parent birds have been seen bodily pushing against young ones in the air, directing their flight. They build a big nest, of sticks and twigs, and often with twisted wire and other oddments. *(T. Modra)*

Top:

Pied currawong, *Strepera graculina.* (45 cm. Open forests, roadside timber, town areas. Common.) Also called Black magpie, Bell magpie. Two forms, found in Tas. and Bass Strait islands, are sometimes listed as separate species and are called Black currawong and Black jay. *(A. Young)*

Bottom:

Grey currawong, *Strepera versicolor.* (50 cm. Open forest. Fairly common.) It has a more varied diet than other family members, with a preference for fruit and berries. In the air, its flight is direct and slow, usually not very high above the tree-tops. Sometimes it is seen in flocks of Pied currawongs, with whom it shares many habits. John Gould compared one of its calls with the sound of a blacksmith's hammer. *(R. Good)*

BOWERBIRDS PTILONORHYNCHIDAE

This is a famous family of remarkable birds, whose exploits amaze people more and more, as they become better known as one of the wonders of nature and as a popular tourist attraction.

There are nine species in the family. The first listed here, Stagemaker, is named for its practice of making a stage for its act. It is also called Tooth-billed bowerbird. It sets its stage by clearing an area in the jungle, a circle of about 3 m in diameter. With its saw-like bill, it proceeds to cut through a leaf stem, a process sometimes requiring prolonged effort, taking up to fifteen minutes. Eventually the leaf is parted from its stem and then it is placed on the stage. The bird repeats the performance until the stage is fairly well decorated with leaves. It provides its own musical accompaniment, singing from a suitable perch. The location of the perch is a consideration in the selection of the stage site.

Next in the family are two species known as catbirds, which do not build bowers of any kind, but are appealing because of their beautiful plumage.

The Golden bowerbird is what is known as a "maypole builder". It piles up twigs around two adjacent small trees or saplings, which are joined above by a fallen branch or a stick, crossing horizontally from one to the other, serving as a display or song perch. Sometimes the maypole bowers are up to 2 m high.

Best known of the bowerbirds are the "avenue builders", especially the Satin and Spotted bowerbirds. Their bower consists of a platform of sticks, usually with two parallel walls. The walls are erected by the birds thrusting long, thin sticks or twigs, or with some species, even grass, into the platform base, which holds them in position. Thousands of sticks will be used, the bower being added to progressively, so that after a number of years the walls may be 7 cm or 8 cm thick.

Then the bird decorates the entrance to his bower, carrying in a variety of items. The Satin bowerbird favours anything blue, and will take blue flowers from a near-by garden, pieces of blue grass, a blue bag from a laundry, or pieces of blue paper.

As well as that, and possibly the most remarkable feature of all, some species, including the Regent, Satin, and Spotted bowerbirds, will then "paint" the inner walls of their bowers. Paint is mixed by items like charcoal or vegetable matter being chewed up and moistened with saliva. For a paint brush, the birds use a wad of vegetable matter which they hold in the beak.

It is said that the bower-building operation is allied to courtship and mating. The female often visits the bower, if only to watch what is happening, as mating does not take place until late in the year. All of this action leaves the male with no time for home duties. The female alone has to build the nest, incubate the eggs, and attend to the young.

Stagemaker, *Scenopoeetes dentirostris*. (23 cm. Tropical rain forest. Common in limited zone.) Its zone, likely to be sought out by tourists, is in north-east Qld. It gives away the position of its stage by its loud and noticeable singing. It nests in thick jungle foliage, well off the ground, and lays 2 milk-coffee coloured eggs. *(K. & B. Richards)*

Right:
Spotted catbird, *Ailuroedus melanotis*. (23 cm. Rain forest. Uncommon.) Occupies a more northerly area than the larger Green catbird, which it resembles in many ways. The name "catbird" perhaps is not ideal, as cats are one of the main enemies of bowerbirds, especially in occupied areas, where it seems the males are too prone to reveal their presence. *(N. Chaffer)*

Below:
Green catbird, *Ailuroedus crassirostris*. (33 cm. Rain forest. Uncommon.) Its call is very like a cat's meowing. Sometimes seen with Regent and Satin bowerbirds. Its diet consists of native fruits, berries, seeds, and some insects. The nest is usually placed on top of a fern or similar low tree, or in a tangle of vines. It lays 2 or 3 creamy white eggs.
(G. Chapman)

Right:

Golden bowerbird, *Prionodura newtoniana*. (23–26 cm. High rain forest. Common in very limited area.) *Newtoniana* honours Professor Alfred Newton, formerly of Cambridge University. It is also called Newton's bowerbird. Although a small bird, the maypole bower it builds is the largest of this type. Its decorations are usually lichen and white flowers. (*L. Robinson*)

Centre:

Regent bowerbird, *Sericulus chrysocephalus*. (23–28 cm. Rain forest. Fairly common.) The male is smaller than the female. The nest, which the female works on while the male is busy bower-building, is bowl shaped, made of light sticks and twigs, usually placed in dense foliage in a tree or in vines. It is said that this species is more inclined to hide its bower than are other birds, and its bower is infrequently found. (*J. Wessels*)

Bottom:

Satin bowerbird, *Ptilonorhynchus violaceus*. (27–33 cm. Rain forest, coastal scrubs. Common.) Its zone extends inland to the Great Dividing Range. It makes itself un-popular with orchardists as it assembles in flocks in late summer and autumn, and attacks the soft fruits. The satiny blue shows up in sunlight, but in the forest shadows it appears black. (*J. & M. Bennie*)

Top left:
Great bowerbird, *Chlamydera nuchalis*. (30–33 cm. Rain forest, open tropical forest. Fairly common.) This bird ranges across the top of the continent. It is very similar to the smaller Spotted bowerbird, sharing many of that bird's practices. Its voice has been described as resembling clothes being torn. Most bowerbirds are mimics and this species is highly qualified in that art. *(L. Robinson)*

Top right:
Spotted bowerbird, *Chlamydera maculata*. (27–31 cm. Open timber, dry savannah. Common.) This bird uses grass stems for the walls of its bower, short pieces on the outside, with longer pieces, up to 45 cm and with heads attached, on the inside. The bower is more elaborate than that of the Satin bowerbird. *(E. Bound)*

Bottom right:
Fawn-breasted bowerbird, *Chlamydera cerviniventris*. (23 cm. Mangrove swamps, melaleuca clusters. Uncommon.) It occupies the limited zone at the tip of Cape York, and builds a large avenue bower, with a platform at each end, decorated with green berries and leaves. This species lays only 1 egg, creamy white, with hairlines of umber or olive brown. *(W. Peckover)*

BIRDS OF PARADISE PARADISAEIDAE

It is said that the four species of birds of paradise seen in Australia are among the least glamorous of the family of forty-three, but they are, nevertheless, striking and beautiful birds. They often impress one as being less like birds than like gaudy, exotic, tropical plants.

They are related to bowerbirds, and both of these families have a good deal in common with crows. Features are the solid and robust build, strong legs and feet, and the large bills, which, in some members of the family, are extra long and down-curved.

Occasionally these birds might clear a forest area and display on the ground, but generally it is their showy adornments that they put on display. They go through the most elaborate routines in the trees, twisting around and about bare branches, turning upside down, lifting and lowering their wings, and generally indulging in a round of odd movements and contortions.

Although much information on birds of paradise is of only recent discovery, there are records of a report on them dating back more than 400 years. This was made by Pigafetti, an Italian who accompanied Magellan on his voyage around the world. In the Moluccas, the expedition had been given two bird of paradise skins as a present for the King of Spain. Pigafetti said there was a legend that the birds came from Paradise and were called "bolon dinata", meaning "divine birds".

There are four species of the family represented in Australia. The Manucode, or Trumpetbird, is found only in the north-eastern tip of Cape York. It resembles the Spangled drongo and the Shining starling of the tropical zones, but the long tail, which measures 14 cm, is a distinctive feature.

The genus *Ptiloris* embraces three species of riflebirds. These are also birds of the north, only one species, the Paradise riflebird, coming further south than the Queensland–New South Wales border, its range extending as far as the Hunter River.

These are rain forest birds, equipped with short, rounded wings. It is said that when they are flying, their plumage makes a swishing sound like rustling silk. Unfortunately their beauty does not extend to the voice. Though there are variations among the calls of the species, generally they are described as loud, squawking, and raucous.

Manucode, *Phonygammus keraudrenii*. (30 cm. Rain forests. Uncommon.) This bird occupies tall native trees, eating the fruits, and is accompanied usually by other fruit-eating birds. Its calls have been compared with a trumpet and with an organ, comments more kindly than those applied to riflebirds. The nest is often placed close to that of a Black butcherbird. *(W. Peckover)*

Top:
Paradise riflebird, *Ptiloris paradiseus.* (28 cm. Rain forests. Uncommon.) The diet includes native fruits and berries, and insects taken with the long, curving bill from the bark on tree trunks. Like the bird itself, its eggs are beautiful and are cream-red with streaks of chestnut and grey.
(G. Broinowski)

Right:
Victoria riflebird, *Ptiloris victoriae* (top). (24 cm. Rain forests. Common.); Magnificent riflebird, *Ptiloris magnificus* (bottom). (30 cm. Rain forests. Uncommon.) The Victoria is similar to the Paradise in habits and looks, but smaller. It often feeds on the ground, turning over leaves, bark, and forest debris. The Magnificent is also called Prince Albert riflebird, and is similar to the Paradise but slightly larger.
(G. Broinowski)

CROWS AND RAVENS CORVIDAE

The name "crow" is in general use for all members of this family, although in many places the raven is the more common bird. Identification of the species, especially when the birds are in the air, is difficult, and the everyday use of "crow" is understandable and no doubt a practice come to stay.

They are very common birds, seen practically throughout the continent. In some of the more isolated but larger towns—an example is Kalgoorlie—crows frequent the town in numbers and become one of the main bird species. They are seen in all cities and towns, on council rubbish dumps and in parks and gardens. They are plentiful on the open plains and in semi-arid areas.

Crows and ravens are birds with an appeal of their own and bird observers frequently develop fond feelings for them. They are intelligent birds, typically Australian, their plumage matching that of the black swan and cockatoo, so much at home in many parts of the continent.

There are five species listed, four found only in Australia, and one extending to New Guinea and other islands.

Sometimes it is thought that various species have different eye colours, an opinion no doubt arising from the fact that the eyes change colour as the birds mature, older adults having white eyes.

The difference between a crow and raven can be seen on a bird in hand. In crows, the base of the feathers is pure white, with a marked line of division. With ravens, there is a gradual change from the black to a smoky grey.

These birds frequently have been given a bad name by graziers and land holders, mainly because of their presence in lambing paddocks and apparent evidence that they have been feeding on dead lambs.

It is interesting to record that information is now to hand revealing that they are not enemies of the farmer but, on the contrary, being carrion-eaters, they assist in wiping out large numbers of blowflies and bacteria.

This defence of crows and ravens is contained in a recent report issued by the Commonwealth Scientific and Industrial Research Organization. Officers of this body conducted a ten-year research into the question and have published a summary of their investigations.

Research officers counted, studied, and dissected thousands of birds. They were assisted by keen members of the Australian Bird-banding Scheme, who banded approximately 11,600 crows. More than 600 hours of watching failed to reveal one death from an attack by a crow.

Crow, *Corvus cecilae*. (50 cm. Open timber, farm areas, semi-arid plains. Common.) Also called Australian crow. *Cecilae* is after a relation of G. M. Mathews, prominent ornithologist. This bird ranges across the north and centre of the continent and usually is not seen in the extreme south. It makes a practice of shuffling its wings several times on landing after flight, whereas others of the family do so only once. (*W. Moreland*)

PHOTOGRAPHIC ACKNOWLEDGMENTS

Photographers and artists are listed in alphabetical order, and following each name are the page numbers on which their work is reproduced.

Allwright, B. 19, 20, 21, 23, 27, 28, 111
Ardea Photographics 126

Bennett, I. 40, 110
Bennie, J. & M. 298
Berekmeri, S. 12
Beste, H. & J. (Ardea) 205
Bonnin, M. 23, 60, 63, 99, 104, 107, 113, 118, 135, 150, 178, 220, 251
Bound, E. 50, 52, 68, 71, 86, 92, 118, 119, 124, 145, 192, 251, 264, 266, 273, 284, 299
Broinowski, G. 34, 163, 301
Burt, J. 8, 9, 10, 11, 13, 15, 16, 74

Carlson, K. (Ardea) 105
Carter, M. 22, 116, 117
Cayley, N. H. P. 88, 167
Chaffer, N. 31, 94, 95, 98, 102, 104, 180, 181, 184, 213, 214, 219, 225, 241, 252, 256, 268, 297
Chapman, G. 43, 48, 59, 61, 92, 96, 98, 103, 114, 116, 117, 118, 123, 124, 125, 141, 150, 151, 158, 165, 183, 192, 194, 199, 209, 210, 218, 224, 226, 231, 232, 234, 236, 238, 255, 257, 265, 268, 269, 270, 275, 277, 285, 290, 297, 303
Churchett, G. 58, 293
Clements, A. 38, 166

Dart, J. 294
Dinsle, W. 34
Dorin, R. 68
Dowling, F. 262

Frauca, H. 9, 10, 11, 12, 13, 14, 16, 40, 57, 61, 62, 63, 64, 76, 126, 134, 143, 152, 158, 161, 168, 176, 203, 226, 242, 245, 285
Ferrero, J. 48, 65, 83, 114, 134, 137, 165, 206, 287
Fletcher, R. 165

Gardner, T. & P. 49, 179, 186, 194, 199, 239, 241, 272
Garstone, R. 187, 203, 232, 282
Gibb, A. 112, 155
Gill, C. 67, 115
Good, R. 43, 65, 72, 85, 244, 275, 295
Gosbell, G. 56
Gould, J. 24, 25, 29, 32, 40, 44, 46, 47, 50, 55, 57, 60, 66, 71, 73, 79, 80, 83, 84, 85, 94, 97, 101, 111, 114, 133, 141, 146, 150, 151, 152, 154, 163, 171, 172, 173, 174, 175, 176, 191, 195, 200, 202, 206, 216, 219, 223, 225, 226, 227, 229, 230, 231, 233, 234, 236, 238, 240, 244, 248, 249, 250, 253, 254, 255, 259, 260, 262, 265, 269, 270, 278, 280
Green, R. H. 218
Green, R. I. 191

Hannant, J. 84, 289
Hollands, D. 210
Hooper, N. 186
Hutchins, T. 212

Jamieson, B. 25

Kendall, T. 86, 99, 100, 106, 109, 115
Kröyer-Pedersen, M. 127, 151, 201, 213, 219, 230, 248
Kulikowski, W. 23, 24

Labbett, W. 49, 185, 193, 194, 231
Laslett, E. 107
Lewitzka, F. 41, 47, 49, 51, 52, 53, 55, 57, 58, 60, 61, 64, 66, 70, 77, 78, 79, 80, 81, 84, 120, 121, 123, 124, 125, 128, 130, 131, 140, 145, 147, 153, 158, 166, 170, 171, 180, 271, 275, 276, 277, 278, 279
Lindgren, E. 95, 109, 160, 169
Long, S. 285
Lovell, B. 59, 95, 118, 122, 132, 139, 272, 273, 288, 290
Lowe, T. 89, 115

McCann, I. 20, 43, 75, 93, 123, 126, 146, 156, 172, 204, 205, 207, 228, 234, 235, 243, 255, 257, 269, 271, 288
McNamara, E. 67, 128, 185, 192, 196, 208
McNaughton, M. 203, 207, 212, 214, 244, 261
Mann, D. 108, 236
Mathews, G. 29, 31, 44, 45, 80, 94, 97, 102, 136, 162, 174, 193, 194, 196, 202, 208, 212, 216, 221, 227, 231, 233, 248, 253, 265, 278
Milburn, B. 54
Modra, T. 69, 90, 220, 294
Moreland, W. 135, 283, 302
Munchenberg, P. 122, 147, 186
Murach, W. 258

Napier, J. 205, 243

Olney, A. 80, 220
Orrell, J. 154
Oxer, J. 61

Park, F. 57, 65, 93, 273
Paton, D. & E. 99, 100, 101, 103, 104, 187, 189, 205, 207, 209
Peckover, W. 299, 300
Pedler, L. 157, 180, 303
Pescott, T. 26, 27, 30, 37, 72, 76, 82, 84, 85, 182, 183, 217
Purnell, J. 47, 200, 272

Richards, K. & B. 116, 177, 187, 189, 202, 209, 210, 217, 222, 241, 246, 247, 252, 260, 274, 281, 283, 292, 296
Robinson, L. 17, 18, 28, 39, 42, 55, 59, 74, 87, 92, 113, 119, 129, 130, 131, 132, 133, 135, 136, 137, 138, 139, 140, 142, 143, 144, 145, 146, 148, 167, 184, 190, 226, 236, 243, 257, 259, 264, 286, 293, 298, 299

Seyfort, M. 79, 91, 176, 188, 208, 215, 217, 223, 232, 250, 290, 291
Soper, M. 30, 32
Sourry, L. 86
Stepnell, K. 10, 14, 31, 33, 81, 134, 176, 197, 200, 204, 218, 225

Taylor, E. & N. 198, 201, 204, 251
Taylor, G. 131, 147, 161, 223, 245, 254, 257, 261, 266

INDEX

INDEX

INDEX

INDEX

INDEX

INDEX

INDEX

INDEX